First World War
and Army of Occupation
War Diary
France, Belgium and Germany

7 INDIAN (MEERUT) DIVISION
19 (Dehra Dun) Indian Infantry Brigade
Seaforth Highlanders
(Ross-shire Buffs, the Duke of Albany's)
1st Battalion.
9 August 1914 - 31 December 1915

WO95/3941/1

The Naval & Military Press Ltd
www.nmarchive.com
Published in association with The National Archives

Published by

The Naval & Military Press Ltd

Unit 10 Ridgewood Industrial Park,

Uckfield, East Sussex,

TN22 5QE England

Tel: +44 (0) 1825 749494

www.naval-military-press.com

www.nmarchive.com

This diary has been reprinted in facsimile from the original. Any imperfections are inevitably reproduced and the quality may fall short of modern type and cartographic standards.

© **Crown Copyright**
Images reproduced by permission of The National Archives, London, England, 2015.

Contents

Document type	Place/Title	Date From	Date To
Heading	WO95/3941/1 1 Battalion Seaforth Highlander		
Heading	Meerut Div 19 Dehradun Bde 1 Bn Seaforth Hdrs 1914 Aug-1915 Dec		
Miscellaneous	Memorandum		
Miscellaneous			
Miscellaneous	To O.C "A" "B" "C" & "D". Coy	13/11/1914	13/11/1914
Heading	19 Dehradun Bde Meerut Division Aug-Dec 1914 (Dec 1914 Missing) 1st Seaforth Hrs		
Diagram etc	Diagram		
War Diary	Agra	09/08/1914	04/09/1914
War Diary	Bombay	06/09/1914	06/09/1914
War Diary	Karachi	08/09/1914	21/09/1914
War Diary	At Sea	23/09/1914	01/10/1914
War Diary	Suez	02/10/1914	03/10/1914
War Diary	Port Said	04/10/1914	05/10/1914
War Diary	Off Port Said	06/10/1914	06/10/1914
War Diary	At Sea	10/10/1914	11/10/1914
War Diary	Marseilles	12/10/1914	17/10/1914
War Diary	In Train	18/10/1914	19/10/1914
War Diary	Orleans	20/10/1914	24/10/1914
Operation(al) Order(s)	Order Of The Day No 1	10/10/1914	10/10/1914
Heading	War Diary of 1st Seaforth Highlanders From 25.10-14 To 30-11-14 Volume I		
War Diary	Orleans	25/10/1914	26/10/1914
War Diary	In Train	27/10/1914	27/10/1914
War Diary	Merville	28/10/1914	28/10/1914
War Diary	Vieille Chapelle	29/10/1914	29/10/1914
War Diary	Neuve Chapelle	30/10/1914	12/11/1914
War Diary	Lacouture	13/11/1914	16/11/1914
War Diary	Le Hamel	17/11/1914	17/11/1914
War Diary	In The Trenches Festubert	18/11/1914	22/11/1914
War Diary	L'Epinette	23/11/1914	27/11/1914
War Diary	Le Touret	28/11/1914	30/11/1914
Heading	War Diary of 1st Seaforth Highlanders From 1st To 31st Jan 1915		
Heading	War Diary of 1st Seaforth Highlanders From 1st January 1915 To 31st January 1915		
War Diary	Aumerval	01/01/1915	04/01/1915
War Diary	Ferfay	04/01/1915	04/01/1915
War Diary	Aumerval	05/01/1915	19/01/1915
War Diary	Ecquedecques	19/01/1915	19/01/1915
War Diary	Ferfay	19/01/1915	19/01/1915
War Diary	Aumerval	20/01/1915	23/01/1915
War Diary	Calonne	24/01/1915	24/01/1915
War Diary	La Couture	25/01/1915	29/01/1915
War Diary	Trenches	30/01/1915	31/01/1915
Heading	War Diary 1st Seaforth Highlanders From 1st To 28 February 1915		
Heading	War Diary of 1st Seaforth Highlanders From 1st February 1915 To 28th February 1915		

War Diary	In Trenches Rue Du Bois	01/02/1915	01/02/1915
War Diary	Richebourg St Vaaste	02/02/1915	04/02/1915
War Diary	Lacouture	05/02/1915	08/02/1915
War Diary	Riez Du Vinage	08/02/1915	22/02/1915
War Diary	Lacouture	23/02/1915	23/02/1915
War Diary	Rue Du Bois	24/02/1915	28/02/1915
War Diary	In The Trenches	28/02/1915	28/02/1915
War Diary	The Distinguished Conduct Medal		
Heading	War Diary With Appendices Of Seaforth Highlanders From 1st To 31st March 1915		
Heading	War Diary With Appendices Of Seaforth Highlanders From 1st March 1915 To 31st March 1915		
War Diary	In The Trenches	01/03/1915	02/03/1915
War Diary	Lacouture	03/03/1915	10/03/1915
War Diary	Neuve Chapelle	10/03/1915	14/03/1915
War Diary	Veille Chapelle	14/03/1915	22/03/1915
War Diary	Paradis	22/03/1915	24/03/1915
War Diary	In The Trenches	25/03/1915	28/03/1915
War Diary	Tempy	28/03/1915	28/03/1915
War Diary	Croix Barbee	29/03/1915	29/03/1915
War Diary	In The Trenches	24/03/1915	28/03/1915
War Diary	Croix Barbee	30/03/1915	31/03/1915
War Diary	Veille Chapelle	01/04/1915	01/04/1915
Miscellaneous	Special Order To The 1st Army	09/03/1915	09/03/1915
Operation(al) Order(s)	Operation Order No 22 by Brigadier General C.W. Jacob Commanding Dehra Dun Brigade	09/03/1915	09/03/1915
Map	Map		
Miscellaneous	Head Quarters Dehra Dun Brigade	12/03/1915	12/03/1915
Miscellaneous	Special Order To The 1st Army	14/03/1915	14/03/1915
Miscellaneous	Indian Army Corps Routine Orders by Lieut General Sir James Willcocks K.C.B., K.C.S.I., K.C.M.G., D.S.O., Commanding	14/03/1915	14/03/1915
Miscellaneous	Translation From "lille War Gazette" 3rd March 1915		
Heading	War Diary With Appendices Of 1st Seaforth Highlanders From 1st To 30th April 1915		
Heading	War Diary With Appendices Of 1st Seaforth Highlanders From 1st April 1915 To 30th April 1915		
War Diary	Veille Chapelle	01/04/1915	01/04/1915
War Diary	L'Epinette	02/04/1915	12/04/1915
War Diary	In The Trenches	12/04/1915	29/04/1915
War Diary	Lacouture	30/04/1915	30/04/1915
Miscellaneous	Treatment Of British Prisoners In Germany	17/04/1915	17/04/1915
Miscellaneous	Head Quarters Dehra Dun Brigade	09/04/1915	09/04/1915
Miscellaneous	Head Quarters Dehra Dun Brigade	10/04/1915	10/04/1915
Miscellaneous			
Miscellaneous	Head Quarters Dehra Dun Brigade	16/04/1915	16/04/1915
Miscellaneous			
Heading	War Diaries With Appendices 1st Seaforth Highlanders From 1st To 31st May 1915		
Heading	War Diary With Appendices Of 1st Seaforth Highlanders From 1st May 1915 To 31st May 1915		
War Diary	Lacouture	01/05/1915	31/05/1915
Operation(al) Order(s)	Operation Order No 37 by Brigadier General C.W. Jacob Commanding Dehra Dun Brigade	05/05/1915	05/05/1915
Miscellaneous	Relief May 7th 1915 Dehra Dun And Garhwal Bdes		

Operation(al) Order(s)	Operation Order No. 31 by Brigadier General C.W. Jacob Commanding Dehra Dun Brigade	06/05/1915	06/05/1915
Operation(al) Order(s)	Operation Order No. 32 by Brigadier General C.W. Jacob Commanding Dehra Dun Brigade	07/05/1915	07/05/1915
Miscellaneous	Head Quarters Dehra Dun Brigade	25/05/1915	25/05/1915
Operation(al) Order(s)	Operation Order 36 by Brigadier General C.W. Jacob Commanding Dehra Dun Bde	31/05/1915	31/05/1915
Heading	War Diary With Appendices 1st Seaforth Highlanders From 1st To 30 June 1915		
Heading	War Diary With Appendices Of 1st Seaforth Highlanders From 1st June 1915 To 30th June 1915		
War Diary		01/06/1915	30/06/1915
Miscellaneous	Head Quarters Dehra Dun Brigade	08/06/1915	08/06/1915
Miscellaneous	The Hymn Of Hate	05/06/1915	05/06/1915
Operation(al) Order(s)	Operation Order No 38 by Brigadier General C.W. Jacob Commanding Dehra Dun Bde	16/06/1915	16/06/1915
Miscellaneous			
Map	Map		
Operation(al) Order(s)	Operation Order No 39 by Brigadier General C.W. Jacob C.B. Commanding Dehra Dun Bde	28/06/1915	28/06/1915
Heading	Meerut Division Seaforth Highlanders From 1st To 31st July 1915		
Heading	War Diary With Appendices Of Seaforth Highlanders From 1st July 1915 To 31st July 1915		
War Diary		01/07/1915	31/07/1915
Operation(al) Order(s)	Operation Order No 43 By Lieutenant Colonel G.T. Widdicombe C.B. Commanding Dehra Dun Bde	09/07/1915	09/07/1915
Miscellaneous			
Miscellaneous	Temporary Composition Of Dehra Dun And Jullunder Brigades		
Operation(al) Order(s)	Operation Order No 27 by Brigadier General E.P. Strickland C.M.G. D.S.O. Commanding Jullundur Brigade	13/07/1915	13/07/1915
Operation(al) Order(s)	Operation Order No 29 by Brigadier General E.P. Strickland C.M.G. D.S.O. Commanding Jullundur Brigade	30/06/1915	30/06/1915
Heading	Meerut Division 1st Bn Seaforth Highlanders From 1st To 31st August 1915		
Heading	War Diary of 1st Bn Seaforth Highlanders From 1st August 1915 To 31st August 1915		
War Diary		01/08/1915	31/08/1915
Operation(al) Order(s)	Operation Order No 46 by Brigadier General C.W. Jacob C.B. Commanding Dehra Dun Brigade	06/08/1915	06/08/1915
Miscellaneous	Movement Table		
Operation(al) Order(s)	Operation Order No 47 by Brigadier General C.W. Jacob C.B. Commanding Dehra Dun Brigade	11/08/1915	11/08/1915
Operation(al) Order(s)	Operation Order No 48 by Brigadier General C.W. Jacob C.B. Commanding Dehra Dun Brigade	19/08/1915	19/08/1915
Operation(al) Order(s)	Operation Order No 49 by Brigadier General C.W. Jacob C.B. Commanding Dehra Dun Brigade	23/08/1915	23/08/1915
Miscellaneous	Movement Table		
Heading	Meerut Division 1st Seaforth Highlanders From 1st To 30th Sept 1915		
Heading	War Diary With Appendices Of 1st Seaforth Highlanders From 1st September 1915 To 30th September 1915		

Type	Description	Start	End
War Diary		01/09/1915	30/09/1915
Operation(al) Order(s)	Operation Order No 52 by Brigadier General C.W. Jacob C.B. Commanding Dehra Dun Brigade	03/09/1915	03/09/1915
Miscellaneous	Movement Table		
Miscellaneous	O.C. Coys	08/09/1915	08/09/1915
Operation(al) Order(s)	Operation Order No 53 By Lieutenant Colonel G.T. Widdicombe C.B. Commanding Dehra Dun Brigade	11/09/1915	11/09/1915
Miscellaneous	Movement Table	12/09/1915	12/09/1915
Operation(al) Order(s)	Operation Order 54 by Lieut Colonel W.J. St. J. Harvey Commanding Dehra Dun Brigade.	16/09/1915	16/09/1915
Miscellaneous	Movement Table	18/09/1915	18/09/1915
Miscellaneous	Instructions For Battalion Of Dehra Dun Brigade On Th Day Of Month	21/09/1915	21/09/1915
Operation(al) Order(s)	Operation Order 55 by Lieut Colonel W.J. St. J. Harvey Commanding Dehra Dun Bde.	22/09/1915	22/09/1915
Operation(al) Order(s)	Operation Order No 56 by Brigadier General W.J. St. J. Harvey Commanding Dehra Dun Brigade.	22/09/1915	22/09/1915
Miscellaneous			
Operation(al) Order(s)	Operation Order No 57 by Brigadier General W.J. St. J. Harvey Commanding Dehra Dun Brigade.	23/09/1915	23/09/1915
Miscellaneous	Movement Table		
Map	Map		
Diagram etc	Diagram		
Miscellaneous	Orders	21/09/1915	21/09/1915
Operation(al) Order(s)	Operation Order No 58 by Brigadier General W.J. St. J. Harvey Commanding Dehra Dun Brigade.	24/09/1915	24/09/1915
Miscellaneous	Report On Operations	27/09/1915	27/09/1915
Operation(al) Order(s)	Operation Order 59 by Brig Genl. W.J. St. J. Harvey Comdg Dehra Dun Bde.	25/09/1915	25/09/1915
Miscellaneous	Not To Be Carried Forward Beyond Our Front Parapet Under Any Circumstances		
Miscellaneous		25/09/1915	25/09/1915
Map	Map		
War Diary	Meerut Division Seaforth Highlanders From 1st To 31st October 1915		
Heading	War Diary With Appendices Of Seaforth Highlanders From 1st October 1915 To 31st October 1915		
War Diary		01/10/1915	31/10/1915
Operation(al) Order(s)	Operation Order No. 60 by Brigadier General W.J. St. J. Harvey Commanding Dehra Dun Brigade.	01/10/1915	01/10/1915
Miscellaneous			
Miscellaneous	March Table	02/10/1915	02/10/1915
Miscellaneous	Relief Table	02/10/1915	02/10/1915
Operation(al) Order(s)	Operation Order No 65 by Br General W.G. Walker V.C. C.b. Commanding Sirhind Brigade	01/10/1915	01/10/1915
Operation(al) Order(s)	Operation Order No 61 by Brigadier General W.J. St. J. Harvey Commanding Dehra Dun Brigade.	05/10/1915	05/10/1915
Operation(al) Order(s)	Operation Order No 92 by Brigadier General C.G. Blackader D.S.O. Commanding Garhwal Brigade	09/10/1915	09/10/1915
Miscellaneous	March Table To Accompany Garhwal		
Miscellaneous		12/10/1915	12/10/1915
Operation(al) Order(s)	Dehra Dun Brigade Operation Order No 62	18/10/1915	18/10/1915
Diagram etc	Diagram		
Miscellaneous	Movement Table		
Operation(al) Order(s)	Operation Order No 94 by Brigadier General C.G. Blackader D.S.O. Commanding Garhwal Brigade	18/10/1915	18/10/1915

Miscellaneous	March Table		
Operation(al) Order(s)	Dehra Dun Brigade Operation Order No 63	20/10/1915	20/10/1915
Operation(al) Order(s)	Dehra Dun Brigade Operation Order No 64	23/10/1915	23/10/1915
Miscellaneous	Movement Table	24/10/1915	24/10/1915
Miscellaneous	Headquarters Dehra Dun Brigade	27/10/1915	27/10/1915
Miscellaneous	Headquarters Dehra Dun Brigade		
Heading	Meerut Division 1st Seaforth Highlanders From 1st To 30 November 1915		
Heading	War Diary of The Officer Commanding,1st Seaforth Highlanders From November 1st 1915 To November 30th 1915 Volume XV		
War Diary		01/11/1915	30/11/1915
Operation(al) Order(s)	Dehra Dun Brigade Operation Order No 65	01/11/1915	01/11/1915
Miscellaneous	Posts To Be Taken Over Form Garhwal Brigade		
Miscellaneous	Movement Table	02/11/1915	02/11/1915
Operation(al) Order(s)	Dehra Dun Brigade Operation Order No 66	12/11/1915	12/11/1915
Miscellaneous	March Table		
Operation(al) Order(s)	Dehra Dun Brigade Operation Order No 67	17/11/1915	17/11/1915
Miscellaneous	March Table		
Heading	War Diary 1st Battn Seaforth Highlanders 7th (Meerut) Indian Division December 1915		
Heading	War Diary of The Officer Commanding, 1/Seaforth Highlanders From December 1st 1915 To December 31st 1915 Volume XVI		
War Diary		01/12/1915	31/12/1915

WO95/3941/1

1 Battalion Seaforth Highlanders

MEERUT DIV

19 DEHRA DUN BDE

1 BN SEAFORTH HDRS

1914 AUG — 1915 DEC

TO MESPOT

BOX 3941

MEMORANDUM.

CONFIDENTIAL

From: O.C.
1 Seaforth H[rs]

To: A.G.
BASE

Station: MARSEILLES Date: 16/10/14

Herewith War Diary for
Bn under my command
to date.

C Hom Capt.
for OC
1st Seaforth Hyrs

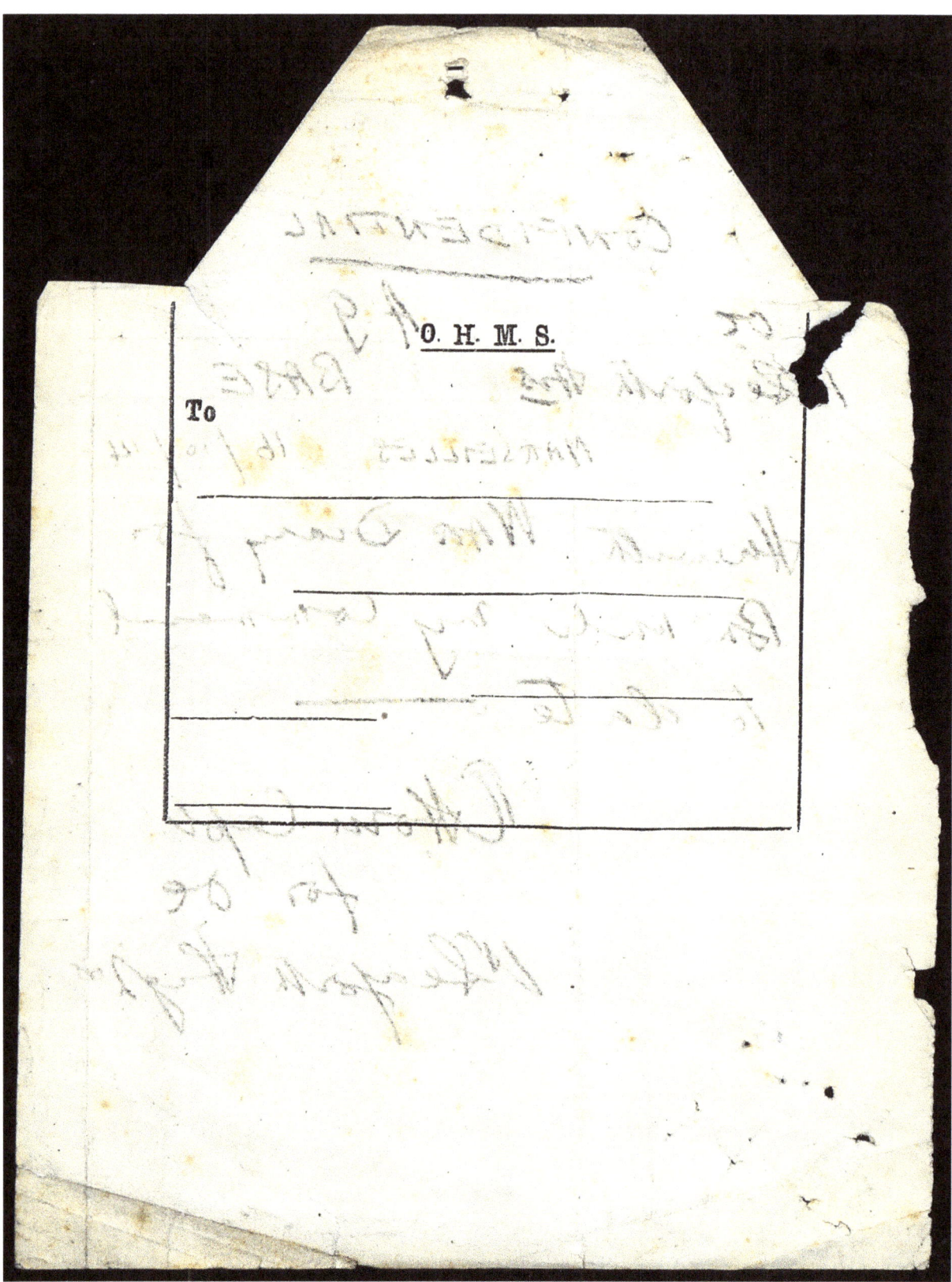

13/11/1914.

From Adjt. Sea Hrs.
To O.C. 'A. B. C. & D. Coy.

Please inform N.C.Os. & men, initial & pass:-

The following message recd last night.

I. A. Corps
10/11/1914

O.C. 1st Sea Hrs.

I was sure when your turn came that your fine Corps would take toll of the enemy & it has done so. I rely on you as in years past to add to your fine tradations & will relieve & give you a few days rest almost immediately I hope.

(sd) James Willcocks
Lieut General.

Appendix 'D'.

R Horn
Capt & Adjt
Seaforth Highrs

H DEHRA DUN BDE

Meerut Division Aug-Dec 1914
(Dec 1914 missing)
1st Seaforth Hrs.

Box 3941

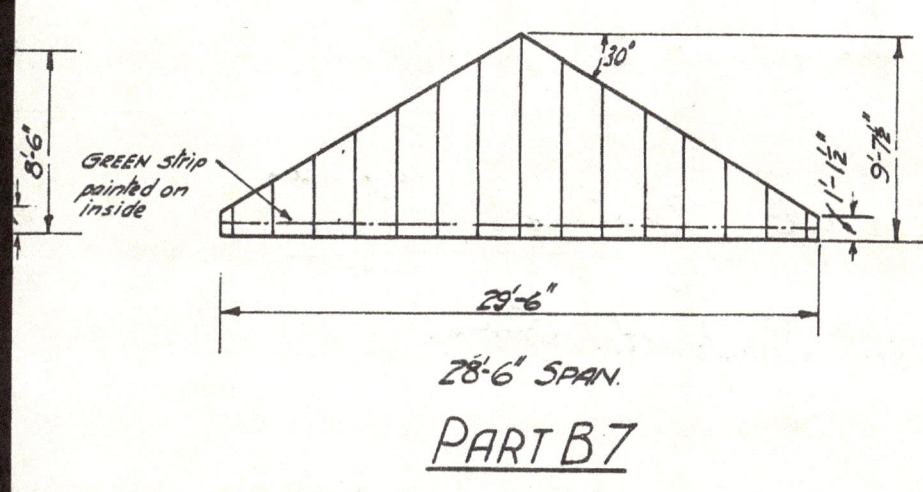

28'-6" SPAN.

PART B7

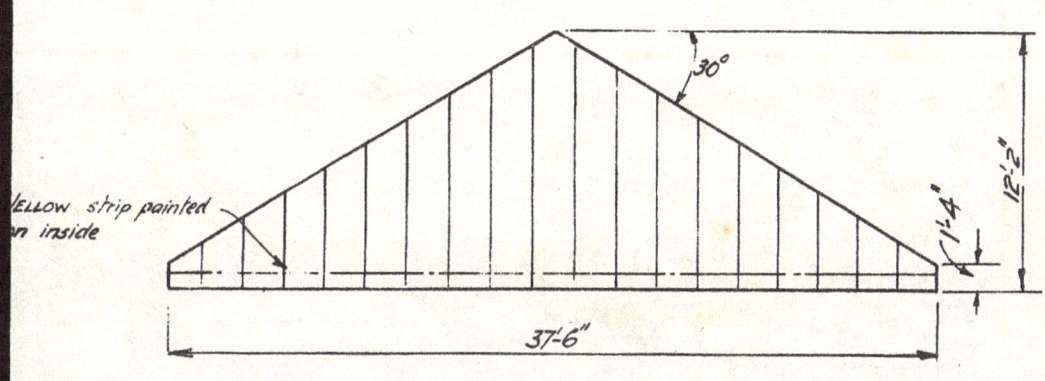

36'-6" SPAN

PART B8

SETS OF EXTERNAL GABLE SHEETING

WHEN FIXED

fixed they conform to the dimensions shown.
be clearly marked by means of a 6" coloured
indicated
× 24 gauge, & to be laid with single side laps.

AMENDED 19-10-38.

SHEETS.   DRAWING No. H. 356/37

Army Form C. 2118.

1st Seaforths

INTELLIGENCE SUMMARY.

(Erase heading not required.)

Instructions regarding War Diaries and Intelligence Summaries are contained in F. S. Regs., Part II, and the Staff Manual respectively. Title pages will be prepared in manuscript.

Hour, Date, Place.	Summary of Events and Information.	Remarks and references to Appendices.
8 AM 9th August — AGRA	Received orders to mobilise with 7th DEHRA DUN Bde of 7th MEERUT Divn.	Off. Capt. Tkpt
19th "	Mobilisation complete. Unit up to strength and ready to move	Off
5 PM 21st "	Ordered to concentrate on 23rd by rail to BOMBAY	Off
7 PM 22nd "	Ordered to "Stand fast" till further orders	Off
5 PM 29th "	Ordered to concentrate on 31st by rail to BOMBAY	Off
10.30 AM 31st "	Ordered to "Stand fast" till further orders	Off
7.30 PM 2nd Sept	Ordered to concentrate on 4th Sept by rail to BOMBAY	Off
8.30 AM 4th Sept.	Battalion strength 16 officers, 891 other ranks left by one troop train for BOMBAY	Off
6 AM 6th Sept. BOMBAY	Bn. arrived Alexandra docks & embarked (with other details) 2.30 pm on H.T. "DEVANHA". Strength 17 officers, 893 other ranks (33 additional other ranks left various dates on other ships as batmen & clerks)	Off
7 PM 8th Sept. KARACHI	Arrived Keamari docks. Battalion's details, horses & mules disembarked. Battalion's details remain on board	Off
11 AM 9th Sept	horses & mules with other details including	Off
8 AM 15th Sept	embarked horses & mules with other details including ½ Bn. Leicestershire Regt.	Off
6 AM 16th Sept	Steam out to mouth of harbour & anchor	Off
7 AM 21st Sept	Leave harbour join convoy of 11 transports with escort of H.M.S. HARDINGE & H.M.S. MINTO, H.M.S. DARTMOUTH	Off
	& H.M.S. HARDINGE. The whole sailing at 8 A.M. (Strength 884 other ranks & 17 officers)	Off

WAR DIARY
or
INTELLIGENCE SUMMARY

(Erase heading not required.)

Army Form C. 2118.

(2)

Hour, Date, Place.	Summary of Events and Information.	Remarks and references to Appendices.
1 PM 23rd Sepr At Sea	Our convoy (C Division/Mule by 11th B Divn) from BOMBAY. The latter escorted by HMS SWIFTSURE & FOX and RIMS DUFFERIN — The whole convoy of 42 ships proceed together —	R.H
10 PM 27th Sepr At Sea	The convoy passes ADEN at some distance. HMS BLACK PRINCE takes charge of convoy now reduced in numbers, attended by RIMS DUFFERIN —	R.H R.H
7 AM 28th Sepr. At Sea	Past PERIM —	
10 AM 1st Oct. At Sea	HT "DEVONHA" goes full speed ahead, leaving the convoy, as a number of transports have close ahead —	R.H R.H
6 PM 2nd October SUEZ	arrive — 2 men disembarked sick.	R.H
12 Midnight 3 Oct SUEZ	leave —	R.H
3 PM 4th Oct. PORT SAID	arrive Sgt Drever + 3 men disembarked sick.	R.H
3 PM 5th Oct. PORT SAID	leave 15 Officers (including Capstan) + 4 men rejoin Convoy	R.H
9 AM 6th Oct off PORT SAID	2 signallers transferred to French Battleship "BOUVET".	R.H

Army Form C. 2118.

WAR DIARY
or
INTELLIGENCE SUMMARY.
(Erase heading not required.)

(3)

Instructions regarding War Diaries and Intelligence Summaries are contained in F.S. Regs., Part II, and the Staff Manual respectively. Title pages will be prepared in manuscript.

Hour, Date, Place.	Summary of Events and Information.	Remarks and references to Appendices.
3 PM 6th October	Off Port Said – 1 Man reports from BOMBAY –	Pvt
5 PM 6th "	Vtt DENMAN Sank Just from Port Said with Convoy of 18, in Charge FRENCH battle ship JACQUI BERRY – T	Off
8 AM 10th Oct "AT SEA"	pass MALTA –	Pvt
11th Oct –do–	Pvt SARDINIA	Pvt
10 AM 12th Oct MARSEILLES	arrive + disembarked at once – spent night on the quay. 1/2 Bn on fatigues – Lieut A.C. MURRAY + 7 men to hospital – Bn. re-armed with new rifle (Mark III short L.E.) (Strength on landing 24 officers including Chaplain + 885 other ranks)	Pvt
8.20 AM 13th Oct –do–	Bn marched to Cabas (8 miles) at LA VALENTINE arriving about midday – pitched 160 lb Cir E 2 fighting men report from FRENCH	Pvt Pvt
14th Oct –do–	Rained all day – 2 fighting men from FRENCH battleship + 1 man from Dvl. Staff	Pvt
15th Oct –do–	Rained all day – orderly Room Clerk Jones A.G's office (Base) – 1 British + 2 French interpreters attached to the 1/4 Bn. Since the 13th October (Strength 23 Officers + 880 other ranks excluding interpreters) 16 P.O. to Join 2nd Bn. on promotion – 1 Man returns from hospital Br Lt Col VANDELEUR left on 13th Oct	Pvt Pvt

Gulab Singh & Sons, Calcutta—No. 22 Army C.—5-8-14—1,07,000.

WAR DIARY
INTELLIGENCE SUMMARY. (4.)
(Erase heading not required.)

Army Form C. 2118.

Hour, Date, Place. 1914	Summary of Events and Information.	Remarks and references to Appendices.
16th October MARSEILLES	Nown all day; camp a quagmire; orders received to leave by road on 17th.	
2 pm 17th October —do—	Bn (strength 21 officers + 854 other ranks with 3 interpreters, 1 British + 2 French, transp. Indian) marched from LA VALENTINE to D'ARENC Transport, 19 miles, reaching station at 5.25 pm, entraining camp at 6.30 pm – Lieut R H ALLANBY + 36 other ranks (B.H. hospital) left behind at Base Depot.	
	so first reinforcements –	
18th October In train —do—	Pass NARBONNE, CARCASSONNE, TOULOUSE, MONTAUBAN	
19th —do— —do—	Pass LIMOGES ST SULPICE LAURIÈRE ARGENTON + CAHORS. Bn.	
1 am 20th October ORLEANS	arriving ORLEANS 11.30 pm, where Bn. at once dis-entrained – 1 man dropped sick at ARGENTON – Bn. marched from Station to camp, one mile. Bn.	
	bottom 7a Rifle Oil. 17 rested till dawn in a gentle drizzle – promptly wet thro' as 6 am – rev to hospital – very cold –	
21st October —do—	6 more men to hospital – Division gradually assembling here. Bn Appx "A" attached order 8th Div No 1. Bn 15/10/14	
22nd —do— —do—	5 men to hospital –	
23rd —do— —do—	2 men to hospital – Draw 1st + 2nd line harbour complete – Bn. by Lt Gen Willcocks.	
	Bn. marched to rifle range + try new rifles – 10th Cavy Garhwal	
24 —do— —do—	Divisional Route March; Regimental Billeting party left 15 other. Army Corps. ORLEANS by rail.	

ORDER OF THE DAY, No. 1.

"A"

SOLDIERS OF THE INDIAN ARMY CORPS,

We have all read with pride the gracious message of His Majesty the King Emperor to his troops from India.

On the eve of going into the field to join our British comrades who have covered themselves with glory in this great war, it is our firm resolve to prove ourselves worthy of the honor which has been conferred on us as representatives of the Army of India.

In a few days we shall be fighting as has never been our good fortune to fight before and against enemies who have a long history.

But is their history as long as yours? You are the descendants of men who have been mighty rulers and great warriors for many centuries. You will never forget this! you will recall the glories of your race! Hindu and Mahomedan will be fighting side by side with British soldiers and our gallant French allies.

You will be helping to make history. You will be the first Indian soldiers of the King Emperor who will have the honor of showing in Europe that the sons of India have lost none of their ancient martial instincts and are worthy of the confidence reposed in them.

In battle you will remember that your religions enjoin on you that to give your life doing your duty is your highest reward.

The eyes of your co-religionists and your fellow countrymen are on you. From the Himalayan mountains, the banks of the Ganges and Indus, and the plains of Hindustan, they are eagerly waiting for the news of how their brethren conduct themselves when they may meet the foe.

From mosques and temples their prayers are ascending to the God of all and you will answer their hopes by the proofs of your valour.

You will fight for your King Emperor and your faith so that history will record the doings of India's sons and your children will proudly tell of the deeds of their fathers.

JAMES WILLCOCKS,
Lieut.-General,
Commdg. Indian Army Corps.

CAMP, 10th OCT., 1914.

War Diary
1st Seaforth Highlanders
From 25-10-14
To 20-11-14.
pp 5,6,16
Volume I

WAR DIARY
or
INTELLIGENCE SUMMARY.

(Erase heading not required.)

1st Leafeth HQ
Army Form C. 2118.
(5)

Hour, Date, Place.	Summary of Events and Information.	Remarks and references to Appendices.
25th October 1914 ORLEANS 6.45 AM 26th —do—	Bn. Church Parade — Orders received for Battalion to entrain. Bn. Strike Camp before daybreak; to entrain 6.45 am, leaving 8.45 am [Strength 22 officers including Chap. on 2 inspections, 844 Other ranks] (plus 1st & 2nd Line transport complete including 6 MG Drivers & 17 native followers). 5 men left in hospital at ORLEANS, remainder reported — Pass VERSAILLES, MANTES BARNTAL where the train was diverted to BEAUCOURT pass LONGPRÉ, DOULLENS, ST POL arriving at the railhead BETHUNE at 2.30 pm when fresh orders were received — train to HAZEBROUCK where further orders received — arrived MERVILLE 7 pm where Bn. at once disentrained — Bn. billeted by 10 pm.	Off
27th October "In train"		Off
28th October MERVILLE —do—	Remain in billets; remain dn S 19 2nd Inf. Bde; MEERUT DIVN headquarters; S. Ind army Corps HQ arriving Off.	
4.30 pm 28th —do—	Received orders to march forthwith to VIEILLE CHAPELLE (with the 2/2 Gurkhas in support of about 1 J 3 British Divn (about 8 miles SW of MERVILLE). Marched at 7.30 pm — billeted in VIEILLE CHAPPELLE by 10.30 pm.	Nil. Reference 5. St OMER & FRANCE Off.
29th —do—	recieved orders to support 7th Brigade 3rd Division held in VIEILLE CHAPPELLE BRITISH Division	Off.

Army Form C. 2118.

WAR DIARY
or
INTELLIGENCE SUMMARY. (6.)

(Erase heading not required.)

Instructions regarding War Diaries and Intelligence Summaries are contained in F.S. Regs., Part II, and the Staff Manual respectively. Title pages will be prepared in manuscript.

Hour, Date, Place.	Summary of Events and Information.	Remarks and references to Appendices.
11 AM 29th OCT. VIEILLE CHAPPELLE	Marched to RICHBOURG ST. VAASTE (3 miles) and put out of fight in billets. — About 4 pm heavily shelled from 100 east (8" HE Shell). Casualties FRENCH Interpreter Ogorra and I man killed, I man died of wounds — Revd. J.W. McKern Lieut W.A. Middleton, 2nd Lieut J.E. Lawrie wounded — Followers:— I killed, 2 wounded — Horses, 3 killed, I wounded, 2 missing. Mules — 2 killed, 12 wounded and missing — 2 Aº carts smashed up — Bn. scattered to avoid flesh and billets after dark. 1/2 mile W. of town — Bn. turned out for alarm at 8 — returned to billets and marched to relieve Troops in Le Touches at 12 midnight taking 157 echelon Transport —	Map St OMER No. 4 [Plt]
1.30 AM 30th OCT. NEUVE CHAPPELLE	Occupied trenches along Le ESTAIRES – LA BASSEE road from PONT LOGY to cross roads 110ºyds SSE. A front of 1400 yds altogether with all 4 companies in the firing line. Trenches merely the ditch running along the road side considerable firing on our front before dawn — were shelled and sniped all day. Some snipers being behind our line — No casualties —	[Plt]
31st October — do —	There were 3 infantry attacks on our right ("D"Co.) during the night which were not pressed home — Shelling all day — Collected four of our own men, wounded belonging Cº 9 & 7, Sikhs and West Kents who had been lying in road between Le Touches and Neuve Chapelle for several days – Improved trenches by night — Casualties 3 wounded (1 accidental) 2 remained with their companies.	[Plt]

Gulab Singh & Sons, Calcutta—No. 22 Army.C.—5-8-14—1,07,000.

WAR DIARY or INTELLIGENCE SUMMARY.

Army Form C. 2118.

(Erase heading not required.)

(7)

Hour, Date, Place.	Summary of Events and Information.	Remarks and references to Appendices.
1914		
1st November NEUVE CHAPELLE	Strengthened the trenches being shelled at Major S. Officers No 4 Piper; collected one dead and wounded 18 other caps between the 2 lines - Casualties 18 killed, 3 wounded (accidental) -	
2nd November -do-	Shelling and sniping as usual, occasional bursts of musketry at night, but apparently very few of enemy's infantry against us - Improving fire and support trenches when opportunity offers - 2nd questions on our left very heavy attacked by In Jan by Matins rifle fire - They shot very heavily - 2 wounded - Lieut Snow McKenzie accidentally shot - Revolver discharge away fell (while) in Casualties 2 wounded.	Rifts
3rd November -do-	Shelling continued as usual all day. Casualties 2 wounded -	Rifts
4th November -do-	Heavy shelling commenced at 8 p.m. all along our line especially on our right (D. Co.) - Shrapnel and high explosive mixed with occasional infantry attacks. These latter being apparently with the object of getting our men to stand up, when maxims and shrapnel opened at once and they had the range correct - "D" Co. reinforced by 3 platoons from our left and sent V.B Goorkha Rifles (on our right). Rgt Shell fire ceased at about at dusk - The wounded	

Army Form C. 2118.

WAR DIARY
or
INTELLIGENCE SUMMARY. (81)
(Erase heading not required.)

Hour, Date, Place. 1914	Summary of Events and Information.	Remarks and references to Appendices.
4th Nov. NEUVE CHAPELLE	(cont) - had to be carried over a mile to Regtl. aid post after dark; a difficulty matter with 8 stretchers - Casualties 2 Lieut W G FERRIER & 60 N.C.O.'s men wounded, 5 killed, 2 Died of wounds.	Map STOFFER No. 4. 2 Lieut W.G FERRIER Rtd
5th Nov.	The whole line shelled all day - Enemy entrenching and sapping up to within 400 yds. of our line in places with mortars - Very cold at night kept thick fog - Casualties 1 killed, 1 Sieic'y wounded & wounded.	1 Sieic'y wounded Rtd
6th Nov.	Not so much shelling as usual - Infantry attack on our right at 5.P.M. not pressed and few Man Infantry inside - Casualties 1 killed & wounded. Rtd	
7th Nov.	Heavy shelling along our line especially on our right ("D" Cy) enemy having its mortar reported to range of 600 yds. only - This shell made one hole 15 feet by four Colg' Baker and four men were buried in one trench two [of] the former being killed - Some 300 Infantry attack out right and one German got inside our trenches - Casualties in "D" & - The attack was repulsed - Causalties all due to either shell or fragres - Both. The latter are good shots and get into houses which	

WAR DIARY or INTELLIGENCE SUMMARY.

Army Form C. 2118.

C91

(Erase heading not required.)

Instructions regarding War Diaries and Intelligence Summaries are contained in F. S. Regs., Part II. and the Staff Manual respectively. Title pages will be prepared in manuscript.

Hour, Date, Place.	Summary of Events and Information.	Remarks and references to Appendices.
7th Nov. NEUVE CHAPELLE (cont.)	Enfilade our trenches at close range — then fight being close to the first inside the trenches. NEUVE CHAPELLE — Owing to casualties "D" Coy. was relieved tonight by "C" supported by "B" after dark — Casualties Captain P. S. WILSON + 17 first men killed, 2nd Lieut. I. M. McL. MACANDREW + 63 men wounded (of these 2 men died of wounds 2/Lt. MACANDREW + 14 men dangerously wounded. Their companies.)	Capt. BEAUCHAMP. DUFF and several of his men killed when moved (2nd Gurkhas) to their supporting trenches. 17th Ref Map St. OMER No 4
8th Nov. —do—	Shelling as normal — 20 infantry attack — Casualties 1 killed — 8 wounded (1 accidentally) — 2 officers died of wounds — Major C.P. DOIG admitted to hospital sick — Sgr. McDonald also killed on patrol duty.	
9th Nov. —do—	Shelling began at 7 & 5 pm all along the line, some TMs having to evacuate their dug outs temporarily. Casualties 15 wounded (2 accidentally) of these 5 remained with their companies — Lieut R.W. MURRAY Reported for duty.	
10th Nov. —do—	Shelling as normal — Casualties 3 killed, 5 wounded (1 accidentally)	

Gulab Singh & Sons, Calcutta—No. 22 Army C.—5-8-14—1,07,000.

Army Form C. 2118.

WAR DIARY
or
INTELLIGENCE SUMMARY. (10)

(Erase heading not required.)

Instructions regarding War Diaries and Intelligence Summaries are contained in F.S. Regs., Part II, and the Staff Manual respectively. Title pages will be prepared in manuscript.

Hour, Date, Place. 1914	Summary of Events and Information.	Remarks and references to Appendices.
12 MN 10/11 Nov NEUVE CHAPELLE	Battalion vacated trenches and retired some 150 yards while every available gun bombarded NEUVE CHAPELLE right up to our fire trenches. At 12.45' bombardment ceased. The Battalion reoccupied trenches without opposition —	[APP B (attached) letter from Lt Gen Sir James Willcocks]
11th Nov —do—	Very heavy shelling from HVE throughout — Several 8" shrapnel from field guns all day — Several 8" B Coy trenches knocked about and enfiladed temporarily — Very cold, high wind and rain — Casualties 4 killed 4 wounded (1 accidentally) — Lt. R.H. HUSSEY and 27 men rejoined from MARSEILLES — reinforcements from MARSEILLES —	Ref. Map ST. OMER No. 4 Ref. Ref.
12th Nov —do—	Very heavy shelling day to be all day — Several trenches having to be evacuated — The Battalion was relieved in fire trenches at 9pm by R. Scots and moved to LACOUTURE. Leaving 2 companies out in reserve for alarm. Casualties 3 killed 6 wounded Lieut R.H. ANDERSON rejoined from Depot 8PM.	Casualties up to 12th Nov in Chronie 45 killed 116(?) 191 wounded Off. 1 killed (5 officers) 1 missing 1 No — Ratt. killed includes died of wounds
2 AM 13th Nov LACOUTURE	Moved into billets —	

Army Form C. 2118.

La fulie tu

WAR DIARY
or
INTELLIGENCE SUMMARY.

(Erase heading not required.)

Instructions regarding War Diaries and Intelligence
Summaries are contained in F. S. Regs., Part II,
and the Staff Manual respectively. Title pages
will be prepared in manuscript.

Hour, Date, Place.	Summary of Events and Information.	Remarks and references to Appendices.
1914		
14th Nov LACOUTURE	Bn remained in billets — Casualties, Sick 10 —	R.H.
15th Nov — do —	— do —	R.H.
10 AM 16th Nov — do —	Battalion marched to LE HAMEL and billeted again (distance about 3 miles). Rain indifferent accommodation to return.	R.H.
10 AM 17th Nov. LE HAMEL	Received orders at 2.30 pm warning orders of BAREILLY BDE to march and FESTUBERT and march at 3 pm part of BAREILLY BDE extended from front. Shex 400 yards WEST of L of LA QUINQUE RUE to cross roads 600 yards South of ½ Bn under Major STEWART (C+D Coys) marched at 3pm under orders of GAREWALL BDE via LE TOURET and RUE DU BOIS and occupied trenches to the North and more or less in continuation of those occupied by the Rifle Regt Bn — A number of men for their Shock and Socks in the snow and suffered from cold during the night — A great deal of sniping continued until daylight. Casualties 4 Sick.	[Ref. Maps ST OMER No 4 MARTHES No 7]
18th Nov in the trenches FESTUBERT	A quiet day. The line was bombarded on and right and few shrapnel burst over us. Casualties 1 killed 2 Sick —	R.H.

Gulab Singh & Sons, Calcutta—No. 22 Army C.—5-8-14—1,07,000.

WAR DIARY
or
INTELLIGENCE SUMMARY.
(Erase heading not required.)

Army Form C. 2118.

(12.1)

Hour, Date, Place.	Summary of Events and Information.	Remarks and references to Appendices.
19 Nov. FESTUBERT	In the trenches. A quiet day. Snow in the afternoon and very cold. Casualties 3 sick.	(Ref. Map ST. OMER No.4 ARRAS No.7)
26 Nov. —do—	Hard frost. Some men sick with exposure (not frost bite). Each man carries a greatcoat and an indiarubber sheet on his back, and wears a British Warm Coat. Our blankets (1 per man and 35/16 K.115 remain mules in rear) on the Afrua—. A good deal of sniping day and night. The enemy sapping up to within 150 yards of our trenches in places—Casualties 13 sick — Captain R LAING and Lieut G M ALISON join 1st Bn. with 150 Med. Then (8 of these being our own build and wounded returned to duty).	Draft from 3rd Bn.
	Hand grenades — Coke issued in the trenches — Various forms of grenade tried with poor results — The rifle grenade being the only one which gave any results, and without a fixed rear it is impossible to hit anything (except a mass of men) with it except by accident — it has to be fired in the air at an angle of 45° degrees — Very cold night.	Left

Army Form C. 2118.

WAR DIARY
or
INTELLIGENCE SUMMARY.
(Erase heading not required.)

(131)

Hour, Date, Place. 1914	Summary of Events and Information.	Remarks and references to Appendices.
2.15 Nov. 1st In the trenches FESTUBERT	Situation unchanged. 6 ft Vats on our right very heavily bombed from about 100 yards range and forced to evacuate some of their trenches - Enemy still digging along our front - tunnel with a mortar toadstool the ammunition was badly put together and when the machine burst it blew on the 1309 direction - Finally the Turks they blew up whilst 1st R.E. officers were experimenting with it - Ammunition and mortar were made Turkish - 7 P.M. Casualties tamed 8 ricks -	Ref. Map ST. OMER No.4 ARRAS No.7
22nd Nov — do —	Situation unchanged. Still hand from with from lying — Casualties — — —	Including 3 sick
23rd Nov — do —	The Left Section of BAREILLY BDE. A returned HQ + ARB Co. are (Col. H.B. RITCHIE Seaforths Commanding the Section) relieved by 129th BALUCHIS and 59th R/115 of FEROZEPUR BDE — Relief carried out by 6 PM — 6th Coy. with the JULLUNDUR BDE also relieved by troops of JULLUNDUR BDE — HQ with A + B Cos moved to field at junction of RUE DE L'EPINETTE and RUE DU BOIS. C + D Coys billet at Crossroads North of RUE	
7 PM	des BERCEAUX —	

WAR DIARY

or

INTELLIGENCE SUMMARY.

(Erase heading not required.)

Army Form C. 2118.

Instructions regarding War Diaries and Intelligence Summaries are contained in F. S. Regs., Part II, and the Staff Manual respectively. Title pages will be prepared in manuscript.

Hour, Date, Place.	Summary of Events and Information.	Remarks and references to Appendices.
1914		
23 Nov. L'EPINETTE	Bn. remains in billets — W. & A Coys. companies Ordered to move to formation of RUE DE L'EPINETTE and RUE DE CAILLOUX to support counter attack by BAREILLY BDE whose trenches had been taken — C & D Coys. ordered to replace A.T.B. —	Ref. Maps. STOMER Sheet No 4 MORRIS Sheet No 7
4 P.M. –do–		
4.45 P.M. –do–	Arrival at position and remained out till 10 PM — The whole Bn. remained together in L'EPINETTE billets for the night — Casualties 4 wounded, 4 Sikh Ryt.	R.H.
24 Nov. –do–	"A" and "A.T.B." Coys. remain in billets — C & D landed Majrs M.B. A Stewart moved at 2 PM to ACHEBOURG St Vaaste where they billet again — The whole Bn. to moved factoryathy? from 16 JULLUNDUR BDE at 2 in Support of MANCHESTERS and 15th SIKHS, C & D in Support of 47th Sikhs and 59th Rifles — Casualties 1 wounded 4 Sick —	R.H.
25 Nov –do–	Bn. remain in billets as above — Strength of exchange of Interpreters. Chaplain, MSC Drivers, 19 officers and 736 other ranks — Note Strength y the Battalion the night before leaving Wellbrook? Barracks was 17 officers and 636 other ranks.	R.H.

Army Form C. 2118.

WAR DIARY
or
INTELLIGENCE SUMMARY.
(Erase heading not required.)

15

Hour, Date, Place. 1914	Summary of Events and Information.	Remarks and references to Appendices.
26th Nov. L'EPINETTE	Actual fighting strength of the Battalion after deducting shelter trenches 1st and 2nd line transport drivers and escort etc. 10 offrs 17 officers and 672 other ranks – Remain in billets – Casualties 9 sick –	Ref. Map Sheet No. 4 ST OMER No. 7 ARRAS
10 AM 27th Nov. —do—	The 1st/15th Battalion marched to billets in LE TOURET – Casualties 1 sick – Weather mild and wet with high wind – No snow or frost since the 24th – Casualties 2 sick –	R/H R/H
28th Nov LE TOURET	Church Parade after hymn Parade at 11 AM in the open, conducted by the Rev McNeill –	R/H
29th Nov —do—	Sir James Willcocks visited the Various Company billets at about 12 noon (only Indian Army Corps) Casualties 2 sick – Lt. Muirhead and 12 N.C.O.s and men proceed to Locon for instruction in "Bomb throwing" and return – 29th inst. At present there are 57 N.C.O.s men of the Battalion employed away from the Battalion as Batmen, Police, guards etc & there are also 66 who assist carry supplies to the trenches – 16 of these are Stretcher-bearers who carry stretchers & remain in the trenches –	R/H R/H
30th Nov —do—		R/H

Army Form C. 2118.

WAR DIARY
or
INTELLIGENCE SUMMARY.

(Erase heading not required.)

Hour, Date, Place.	Summary of Events and Information.	Remarks and references to Appendices.
30th Nov. LE TOURET 1914	50 remain with 16 & for the transport etc. in rear of the trenches, made up as follows:— Q.M. Sgt. i/c Regtl. Amn Reserve Escorts to 10 A.T. Carts 6 ammunition 2 entrenching tools 1 medical 1 signalling Escort to 12 Company Amn. Mules Escort etc. to 2 Water Carts (water boiling) Drivers to 2 — do — Driver 1 Cook's waggon Transport Sarjeant (a Sgt) Orderly Room clerks Quartermaster & 3 assistants Medical Officer, Assistant Surgeon & assistants (with FIRST AID POST) Machine Gun Drivers Cold Shifter Grooms (officers chargers) [NB Medical Officer has no horse & Transport Officer & Machine Gun Officer are absent wounded]	Ref: Nop [Gheer No 7 troops] 1 10 4 2 2 1 1 2 3 1 & 2 1 & 1 12 1 9 2 officers & 50 O.R.

War Diary of
1st Seaforth Highlanders

From 1st To 31st Jan 1915

WAR DIARY

of

1st Seaforth Highlanders.

From 1st January 1915 To 31st January 1915.

Army Form C. 2118.

WAR DIARY
or
INTELLIGENCE SUMMARY. (38)
Vol II

(Erase heading not required.)

Hour, Date, Place. 1915	Summary of Events and Information.	Remarks and references to Appendices.
1st Jan. AUMERVAL	The following is published in Battalion orders:— The Commanding Officer is very pleased to announce to the Battalion that he has been selected by the Brigadier and Divisional Commanders to express their high appreciation of the soldierly spirit and splendid behaviour of the Battalion in the Trenches at FESTUBERT between the 16th and 22nd December 1914 under very trying circumstances.— The 4th Battalion at FERFAY held Sports with teams of 6 to both Battalions.— A/Bugler 988 NCOs and men form a rifle of 1st and 2/2nd Anthony wounded and taken from 1st and 2/2nd Anthony wounded and from 1st 3rd Bn. section D and enlisted men from 1st 3rd Bn. section D also — Casualties 2 sick.— Revival duty —	(Ref. Map ARRAS Sheet No. 7)
2nd Jan. do	Casualties 12 sick.— These sick have all got a form of recruits in the feet due to the new speth in the Trenches.	Rgt Rgt
3rd Jan. do		
4th Jan. do	Casualties – Nil. The Battalion paraded at 12.30 PM and marched to FERFAY for inspection by Lieut Gen Sir James Willcocks. He expressed his admiration for the work of the Battalion during the Campaign	with the remainder of D/S the DEHRA DUN BDE

Army Form C. 2118.

WAR DIARY
Vol. VI
INTELLIGENCE SUMMARY.
(39.)

(Erase heading not required.)

Instructions regarding War Diaries and Intelligence Summaries are contained in F. S. Regs., Part II, and the Staff Manual respectively. Title pages will be prepared in manuscript.

Hour, Date, Place.	Summary of Events and Information.	Remarks and references to Appendices.
4th Jan. FERFAY.	Sir James Willcocks said that it was a very great pleasure to him to speak to the Battalion, that the Coot one he had already seen the Battalion, he agreed that he had then seen & agreed with them on seeing regret to serve with them again. But that he had never been in the field again. But that he had never thought that he would be with them in the great European war — the famed "Although there has been close to them with you the Bosis the trenches I have known your work closely. I have followed in J/Lakh you, Sepoys, day by day I have followed in J/Lakh you, Sepoys, have you in my command " onwards to that effect — He proceeded to say that he felt all the Battalion had deserved Mward, but all could not be singled out for special mention that is would be a unfair all thanks for up to them f.a.a.........., onwards to that effect — Off

Army Form C. 2118.

WAR DIARY
or
INTELLIGENCE SUMMARY.

Vol II (40)

(Erase heading not required.)

Hour, Date, Place.	Summary of Events and Information.	Remarks and references to Appendices.
5 Jan. Aumerval	Casualties — Nil	[Ref Map MARNS sheet No. 7.]
6 " do	Brig. Gen. Jacob visits the Battalion at 9.30 am	
	Casualties :— 1 sick	DRJ
7 " do	The Commander-in-Chief inspected the Bareilly and Dehra Dun (Gen. Sir John French) Bdes at 11am on the CHAUSSEE BRUNCHANT DE THERDUANNE between FERFAY and cross roads ½ mile N of first C in CAUCHY. The Battalion was drawn up in line 2 coys on the right, and 2 on the left of the road facing inwards.	
8 " do	Casualties :— Nil	DRJ
9 " do	Casualties :— 1 sick	DRJ
10 " do	Casualties :— Nil	DRJ
" do	Casualties :— 2 sick. Divine Service at 11.45 am conducted by DRJ the Rev Irwin	
11 " do	Casualties :— Nil	DRJ
12 " do	Casualties :— 1 sick	DRJ
13 " do	Casualties :— 2 sick	DRJ
14 " do	Casualties :— 1 sick	DRJ
15 Jan. do	During the period of not 16 Battalion practice trench digging found [?] that he cold [?] and the having marched from festor, clothing detained 6 marched good distances in clothing equipment etc. Ptt Casualties 1 sick.	

WAR DIARY

Army Form C. 2118.
Vol VI
(41.)
VOLUME 6.

(Erase heading not required.)

Hour, Date, Place.	Summary of Events and Information.	Remarks and references to Appendices.
1915		
16ᵗʰ JAN. AUMERVAL	Companies all bayonet fighting practise & the daily work done - Casualties 2 Sick.	[Ref Map AERIAL Sheet [?] No. 7]
17ᵗʰ JAN. —do—	Church Parade - Major A.B.H. STEWART D.S.O. is detailed to proceed at once to take temporary command of the 1st Highland Light Infantry in the trenches - Casualties Nil.	P.M.
18ᵗʰ JAN. —do—	The Battalion is issued with rounded Crown Tops BALMORAL caps (dark blue with no dicing) in place of the regimental glengarry the supply of which is presumably exhausted. Casualties 1 sick.	Ett
19ᵗʰ JAN. —do—	The following personnel have been approved in connection with the services of the Battalion in the trenches at NEUVE CHAPELLE from 30ᵗʰ October to 13ᵗʰ November 1914 — **THE DISTINGUISHED CONDUCT MEDAL** — No. 8466 C.Q.M.S. B. TENNY - 6901 C.S.M. R. SUTHERLAND - 8391 Sgt. Piper D. MATHIESON - 9393 Corporal W. McNEILL - 1203 Lance Corporal C. LEAHY	
11 A.M. 19ᵗʰ JAN. ECQUEDECQUES	An exhibition of trench attacking bomb throwing takes place under the orders of Lt. Col. C. MEERUT D'VN. 100 N.C.O.s. men of the battalion under Capt. BAILLIE HAMILTON and 2ⁿᵈ Lieut. PIGOT taking part (taking a trench from them: touch & courtly).	P.H.

Army Form C. 2118.

WAR DIARY
or
INTELLIGENCE SUMMARY. VOLUME VI. p. 42

(Erase heading not required.)

Instructions regarding War Diaries and Intelligence Summaries are contained in F. S. Regs., Part II, and the Staff Manual respectively. Title pages will be prepared in manuscript.

Hour, Date, Place. 1915	Summary of Events and Information.	Remarks and references to Appendices.
2.45 P.M. 19th JAN. FERFAY	Lt. Gen. ANDERSON commanding MEERUT DIVN. inspects all reinforcements (Ethiorie of them sick) returned to Depôt had rejoined) — Casualties Nil	[Reg. Map Appx. Depôt No. 7] Nil
20th JAN AUMERVAL	Brigade route marched 9.30am 12.30pm — VIII officers horse of active in England — Casualties 4 sick. Rain all day as usual. —	
21st JAN. do	Note: Sir John FRENCH inspected the DEHRA DUN BDE on JAN. 7th 1915 made the following remarks to the Battn. "I am pleased to hear from your corps commander and with the 1st Infantry Brigade things have done in the trenches — your Battalion has a great tradition & history and you are worthily maintaining the old tradition — You have indeed splendid and gallant service and I want all you youngsters who have joined from the 2nd & 3rd battalion to remember you belong to a famous regiment and to do all in your power to uphold its great name — I am glad to have been able to come over and see you to-day. I shall not keep you standing any longer on this very hot day but I thank you for the fine work you have put up. Your services and the fact you have displayed, you have given me assistance and from proud to have you in my command."	Ett

WAR DIARY

INTELLIGENCE SUMMARY. Volume VI p. 43

Hour, Date, Place. 1915	Summary of Events and Information.	Remarks and references to Appendices.
21st Jan. AUMERVAL	Casualties 3 sick	B.M. (Maj.) HOPPS took No. 7 to ST. OMER Sleep No. 4.] RM
22nd Jan	Afine day in return! All West back o/b leave to ENGLAND — Surplus baggage transports stored in LILLERS — Casualties 3 sick —	
9.30 A.M 23rd Jan — do —	Battalion marches viâ DEHRA DUN BDE to CALONNE and billets there (13 miles). H.Q. and 3 Coys march viâ LILLERS and CANTRAINE to L'ECLEME where they embussed (Motor lorries holding about 20 each) and continued march viâ ROBECQ arriving CALONNE 12.45 pm. 1 Coy started by lorrie and marched the second half. Transport and train followed by another road — P of 8 BDE likewise there carriable part of the distance — Afine sunny day; frozen ground. 20" frost very strong; but very few fell out, had men feet tidy and improving. Thaw at night — Casualties Nil.	RM
10.30 A.M 24th Jan CALONNE:	Battalion marches to front of The brigade to billets in LACOUTURE (about 7 miles) billets now good, and all men ½ br provided for, but 3 p.m. road surface very bad only 1 man fell out. Rest of BDE billeted in VIEILLE CHAPELLE — BDE is in reserve and Battalion detailed in "waiting" — Major A.B.M. STEWART left regime — Casualties 1 Sick —	RM

Army Form C. 2118.

WAR DIARY
or
INTELLIGENCE SUMMARY.

VOLUME VI p. 44

(Erase heading not required.)

Hour, Date, Place.	Summary of Events and Information.	Remarks and references to Appendices.
1915	NOTE. 4 men Signal returned to Duty Base on 19th inst as unfit for service at the front or on lines of communication in any capacity - There are at present 15 men in hospital at SH other than 19 Signal. 25th Jan Bn Signal G Battalion now is 12 officers (including Qrmaster but exclusive of Medical Officer & Chaplain and 2 interpreters) and 862 of other ranks (of what number 84 are away from the Battalion on Police Bde ~ Divl. employ Prison etc.), 2 officers (Lt 4th Battalion namely Lieut ABShot and 2 Lieut WS DEWAR are attached (no temporarily) so that for La Funday we have 13 officers and 712 other ranks (of this including 15 line trumpets Stretchers bearers and Qrmasters) - Casualties 4 sick. Shells fire and musketry to east and south east at 8 pm and (battalion ordered to be ready to move at short notice).— NOTE. Information was received on 22nd inst that Lt D.C. McKenzie had died of his wounds in BOULOGNE that day —(or 20th Jan. as officially reported). Battalion relieved as Battalion in waiting by 6th Jats at 5pm. RW	Ref Map see Special Bethune Content sheet to BETHUNE 1/40000

25th JAN LACOUTURE

Army Form C. 2118.

WAR DIARY
or
INTELLIGENCE SUMMARY.

Vol. VI   p. 45

(Erase heading not required.)

Instructions regarding War Diaries and Intelligence Summaries are contained in F. S. Regs., Part II, and the Staff Manual respectively. Title pages will be prepared in manuscript.

Hour, Date, Place. 1915	Summary of Events and Information. /Jouippet Trund "	Remarks and references to Appendices.
26th JAN. LACOUTURE	Each Platoon presented by Mrs Ritchie with set of hair clippers, scissors, razors — horn combs for the troops beginning to arrive instead of comforts of which we have sufficient.	[Ref. Map. BETHUNE Sheet 1: 40,000]
	The following commissions approved by the Field Marshal Com.C. the Forces in the Field (19.MR. 23/1/15/	
	No. 8248 P.M. Sgt. E. STEVENS 1st Battalion Seaforth Highlanders to be 2nd Lieut.	dated 20th JAN. 1915
	" 6884 C. Sgt Major D. LINDSAY " " " " "	
	" 8468 C. Sgt Major B. KENNY " " " " "	
	No. 8639 Sgt. J. TREDENNICK 2nd Battalion Seaforth Highlanders from 1st Bn to be 2nd Lieut.	R/R Off.
27th JAN. —do—	Casualties 1 sick —	
28th JAN. —do—	Casualties 1 sick —	
	A Draft of one officer, Lieut. J.F. GLASS and 119 men joined from the base. These men are all well exited ⟨strikethrough⟩ for the duration of the war, but a few eruptions, and all well clothed and equipped. ⟨strikethrough⟩ 10 men dispatched to Dvg. BASE as unfit for service in the trenches but ⟨strikethrough⟩ for the leute of detriment ⟨strikethrough⟩ ⟨strikethrough⟩ reenlisted him who thought they were taking on for home service 1 Off.	
	2nd Lieut Rg WALKER 3rd Gordon Highlanders joins for duty — Battalion in wating for the 24 hours commencing 10 Off. 5 P.M. — Cashier N.C.	

Gulab Singh & Sons, Calcutta—No. 22 Army C.—5-8-14—1,07,000.

WAR DIARY
or
INTELLIGENCE SUMMARY.

Army Form C. 2118.

Volume II
p. 46

Hour, Date, Place.	Summary of Events and Information.	Remarks and references to Appendices.
4.40 PM 29th Jan. LACOUTURE 1915	Battalion marched through RICHE BOURG ST VAASTE and relieved the 2/3rd Gurkhas - 9 pm - 1 pm BDE in the trenches - Relief completed by 8.30 pm - line held as under: 3 companies (HBC) with machine gun detachments & guns of 1/9th Gurkhas, 2/2 Gurkhas & 18th Cavalry T gun of 9 Gurkhas - stretching from crossroads on VSQUARE S.4.d (PORT ARTHUR) to junction of RUE DU BOIS with RUE DES BERCEAUX (1500 yds). Whole 550 yds line in horse-shoe - D company - shape (about 260 rifles) in reserve at cross roads in square S.3.C. with strand post - Hqrs. or RUE DES BERCEAUX - Whole transport in ACRE Bog ag ST VAASTE - Line of resistance the houses on the RUE DU BOIS prepared for defence with apparently completed fire trench moving on less parallel with road and anything from 20 to 680 yds from it (to the south) - barricades on road to prevent enfilade fire from NEUVE CHAPELLE - a good field of fire themselves more or less waterlogged - Each company in the front line providing piquets under officers in saver houses in our original fire trench which is in centre evening twenty some 300 (to 400 yds south of RUE DU BOIS - These piquets have to go out, get under sleep, dark are relieved every 12 hours as they get water to the knees, & there are no fires to RICHE BOURG ST VAASTE for hot baths & drying - They then join the reserve company at...	(Ref. Map BETHUNE helf sheet 1:40 000)

WAR DIARY

INTELLIGENCE SUMMARY.

VOLUME VI P. 47

Hour, Date, Place.	Summary of Events and Information.	Remarks and references to Appendices.
1915		
30th JAN. "Trenches"	Who sent him 2 officers to replace them in the front line Trop. Frost and slight frogs at night - Casualties 3 nil -	Reg. Hqrs. BETHUNE [there 1st in evening] Rft.
	Aeroplane activity with a few shells - Some shelling - How Gatlen - German balloon up - 2 GERMAN aeroplanes over - part of M.G. house set on fire (orderlies dinners in range) at 2 pm some gins [?] This lost a lot of ammunition popped off - fire eventually reaching rocket bombs taken of a store of safety! Casualties nil —	
31st JAN. do	A good deal of shelling from 8 to 10 A.M. which however did little damage; some shells hit the houses in the RUE DU BOIS, but no one was seriously hurt - One man kit overseeing from haystack in the afternoon. The man who took his place at once was killed immediately. Another man was killed trying on own extra kit after dark. The LEICESTERS who had a working party up at night had 6 casualties. In Div Section — Casualties 2 killed and 1 wounded Rft.	

War Diary
1st Seaforth Highlanders

From 1st To 28 February 1915

121/4719

WAR DIARY
OF
1st Seaforth Highlanders.
From 1st February 1915 to 28th February 1915

Army Form C. 2118

WAR DIARY or **INTELLIGENCE SUMMARY**

(Erase heading not required.)

Volume VII
P. 4 8

Stamp: ADJUTANT GENERAL INDIA — 7 MAR 1915 — BASE OFFICE

Hour, Date, Place. 1915	Summary of Events and Information.	Remarks and references to Appendices
1st FEB. "A" Trenches RUE DU BOIS	One man two wounded. One man & an officer wounded whilst on fatigue. Bn. relieved and withdrew after 8.15 p.m. by the 1/9th Gurkha Rifles and marched to billets on the outskirts of RICHEBOURG ST VAASTE, Square S.8.a. West. Digging parties of 4 officers and 350 men were furnished from behind LE TOURET firing line in Square S.10.a.r.b. about 200 to 350 yds from the GERMAN line — one officer, 2nd Lieut. E. STEVENS and 5 men were wounded. Rear parties worked from 6.30 to 12 midnight. Bn. now in Brigade support. Casualties 1 killed, 1 officer, 6 wounded. (rate: Ref. Maj. BETHUNE (Sheet 1:40,000)	Ref. Maj. BETHUNE (Sheet 1:40,000) 10ff
2nd FEB. RICHEBOURG ST VAASTE	2nd Lt. E. STEVENS died of his wounds at VIEILLE CHAPELLE at 11.30 am and was buried at LE TOURET (where 8 other 3 men killed have been buried) at 3 pm by Div. Chaplain — Carrying party of 1 officer 150 men worked from behind firing line from 5.30 pm to 11.30 pm. One man was wounded by shrapnel. Casualties 1 wounded.	10ff
3rd FEB. —do—	1 officer & 50 men worked on redoubt behind line from 9.30 am 12.30 pm. Slightly shelled, no casualties. Two reliefs of 1 officer & 100 men each worked upon the line about 200–300 yards from GERMANS from 6.30 pm & 2.30 am and lost 3 wounded, 1 officer wounded & 1 from chill & lip. Casualties 1 killed, 2 wounded — 5 sick.	10ff

Army Form C. 2118.

WAR DIARY
or
INTELLIGENCE SUMMARY.

(Erase heading not required.)

Volume VII
p. 49

Hour, Date, Place.	Summary of Events and Information.	Remarks and references to Appendices.
1915	2nd Lieut. P.B. PROTHERO & Hugh Rutherford Maffoins the Bn.	Ref. Map BETHUNE — Sheet 1:40,000
2.30 PM 4th FEB. RICHEBOURG ST. VAASTE	Battalion relieved by 2/3rd GURKHAS and marched to billets in LACOUTURE.	
5th FEB LACOUTURE	DEHRA DUN BDE being relieved in the line by the GARHWAL BDE. — RICHEBOURG was shelled that night — 2 H.E. shells pitched in LACOUTURE shortly after we arrived, killing the Divl. Chaplain's horse & R.A. trumpeter + coming from rounding women + a child — Casualties 2 sick —	Off. Off.
6th FEB.	4 Officers + 200 men proceed to LEPINETTE to work at redoubts close to firing line 8 AM. — 4 PM. — 2nd Lieut A. SHACKLEFORD joins on promotion from C.Q.M.Sgt Off. in The Welsh Fusiliers — Casualties 2 sick —	
7th FEB. — do —	Working party of same strength as yesterday at LEPINETTE 8 AM. — 4 PM. 1 Divnl Service held both for C of E + Presbyterians — Casualties 1 sick —	
11.25 AM 8th 10th FEB	Battalion with transport marches via VIEILLE CHAPELLE — FOSSE — LA CROIX MARMUSE — LE CORNET MALO to RIEZ DU VINAGE (Sq. Q.26) for a period of rest — The whole of the DEHRA DUN BDE is billeted in this neighborhood — both BDE Headquarters at CROONNE the BDE is in Corps reserve at 2 hours notice —	

WAR DIARY
or
INTELLIGENCE SUMMARY.

Army Form C. 2118.

VOLUME VII
P. 50

(Erase heading not required.)

Instructions regarding War Diaries and Intelligence Summaries are contained in F. S. Regs., Part II, and the Staff Manual respectively. Title pages will be prepared in manuscript.

Hour, Date, Place. 1915	Summary of Events and Information.	Remarks and references to Appendices.
8th FEB RIEZ DU VINAGE	The Brigade 2nd Corps of 1st/4th Seaforths 1/9th Gurkhas & 2/2nd Gurkhas, the Bns & Stats having been transferred to the Bareilly Bde – Strength of Battalion (includes all in Bde area marching in) – 18 officers (including Etchovine & P.M. Chaplain Medical officer & 2 interpreters) & 896 other ranks. Casualties 4 sick.	Ref Map BETHUNE Sheet 1. 40,000
9th FEB. –do–	Leave reopened for all ranks – 3 officers per Bn for 7 days each & 2 other ranks per Bn for 5 days each. A lot of rain – Casualties Nil.	
10th FEB –do–	"Resp" work recommences – Route marching & form an important part of days work – Casualties 1 sick.	
11th FEB –do–	Casualties Nil.	
12th FEB –do–	Battalion Route March 9.45 A.M – 1.15 P.M – Roads very bad muddy – The roots provided are in many places more of a bog like brown paper than too thick – Casualties Nil. Extract from Indian Army Corps Routine Orders d/10/2/15. The King has been graciously pleased to confer the Military Cross upon the undermentioned officer who has been duly recommended for the same under the terms of the Royal Warrant. CAPTAIN W.M. THOMSON Seaforth Highlanders u Rifles (LONDON GAZETTE 15 JAN 1915)	

Army Form C. 2118.

WAR DIARY
or
INTELLIGENCE SUMMARY.   VOLUME VII
(Erase heading not required.)   P. 51

Instructions regarding War Diaries and Intelligence Summaries are contained in F. S. Regs., Part II, and the Staff Manual respectively. Title pages will be prepared in manuscript.

Hour, Date, Place. 1915	Summary of Events and Information.	Remarks and references to Appendices.
13TH FEB. RIEZ DU VINAGE	Very heavy rain — Chaplain to Hospital.	(Ref. Map BETHUNE Casualties 1 sick—1 Officer 1:40,000)
14TH FEB. —do—	Very heavy rain — Divine Service — Casualties 3 sick — 1 Officer Captain F.G. ANSTRUTHER joins the Battalion —	
15TH FEB. —do—	Casualties 1 sick.	O.R.
16TH FEB. —do—	At 8 a.m. & 10 a.m. (Lieut J. HEMINGWAY 3rd Bn.) & 79 other ranks join the Battalion — arrived lot 6 reinforcements. Kitchener Army reported sick & wounded — Casualties 4 sick. 1 O.R.	
17TH FEB. —do—	High wind & rain. Battalion Route March 9.45 — 12 noon Casualties 5 sick. 1 O.R.	
	LIEUT. J.F. GLASS transferred to 2nd Bn. & 2nd Lieut. TREDENNICK transferred to 1st Bn. on 16th FEB. left though posted 2nd Bn. on promotion — Bn. offered a khaki cover to BALMORAL cap of the kind it reported in negative —	
11 A.M. 18TH FEB. —do—	Got MEERUT DIVN (Brig.Gen. H.B. SCOTT CB DSO acting Lt. Brig. Gen. SMO's) inspect last 9 reinforcements to — Casualties 3 sick.	1 Off.
19TH FEB. —do—	Casualties 1 sick.	1 O.R.
20TH FEB. —do—	Casualties 2 sick. 1 out of enviable looks rather serious, he being wounded — A large number being repaired by the Divt. Boot Shop at BUSNES —	1 Off.
21ST FEB. —do—	Divine Service in the open — Casualties 4 sick.	1 O.R.

Gulab Singh & Sons, Calcutta—No. 22 Army C.—5-8-14—1,07,000.

Army Form C. 2118.

WAR DIARY
or
INTELLIGENCE SUMMARY.
(Erase heading not required.)

VOLUME VII
p. 52

Instructions regarding War Diaries and Intelligence Summaries are contained in F. S. Regs., Part II, and the Staff Manual respectively. Title pages will be prepared in manuscript.

Hour, Date, Place. 1915	Summary of Events and Information.	Remarks and references to Appendices.
8.45 AM 22nd FEB. RIEZ DU VINAGE	Battalion marched to RUE M LACOUTURE via LE CORNET MALO, CROIX MARMUSE and ZELOBES. Strength in Brigade area 18 officers and 961 other ranks – (this means 18 officers and 837 other rank & file (bayonets) in the trenches – exclusive of stretcher-bearers, telephone operators etc) who also got into the trenches. Casualties 1 officer (Capt Ryan) & 9 other ranks got into the trenches wounded.	[Ref: Map BETHUNE Sheet 1: 40,000] Stretcher bearers 16 telephone operators 18 orderlies 9 Brigade employ 31 transport escort 24 O. Room, Q.M. Stores, post & orderly room 13 grooms 13 / 124
2 pm 23rd FEB. LACOUTURE	B.T.C. Coys marched from Gilbert's farm battalion to new reserve in RUE des BERCEAUX	
5.30 PM —do— —do—	A and D Coys march to RUE DU BOIS & relieve the MANCHESTER Regt. holding the line from the cross roads in centre of square. S.4.d. (PORT ARTHUR) to the ORCHARD in sq. S.10.a S.E. (20th Michigan) (B ORCHARD being prepared for all round defence – Relief Batt completed by 9 p.m. – casualties 4 trifle –	
24th FEB. RUE DU BOIS	Rain on & off all day. Enemy shell a little twn ORCHARD 11 AM - 2 pm doing no damage – 1 man killed & 2 wounded. 1 man killed & 2 wounded in B ORCHARD, all by rifle fire for No. 5 & 2 wounded in B ORCHARD, all by rifle fire for No. 5 – 2 wounded – 2 trifle –	
11.25 PM 24th FEB —do—	Information received that every three hours details of the trenches S.16.a – S.10.b – Casualties 1 killed Batt – 2 wounded – 2 trifle –	
25th FEB —do—	One of our patrols fired on 12.15 AM 7 companies stood to till 2 · 15 AM when an important guest ground white from from – The men retired by fire. No 5 advanced four – our troops accounted for 3 GERMANS –	

Gulab Singh & Sons, Calcutta—No. 22 Army C.—5·8·14—1,07,000.

WAR DIARY or INTELLIGENCE SUMMARY.

VOLUME VII p. 53

(Erase heading not required.)

Hour, Date, Place. 1915.	Summary of Events and Information.	Remarks and references to Appendices.
25th FEB. RUE DU BOIS	Lt. Col. RAWLINS C/E commanding 6th SOMERSET LIGHT INFANTRY left, having been attached to the Bn from 23rd FEB. Welcome.	(Ref. Map BETHUNE Sheet 1:40,000)
6.30 PM 25th FEB	A Draft of 30 N.C.Os & men join from HAVRE. 2nd Lieut. B. KENNY with a party of 4 men joined by a patrol from SHERWOOD FORESTERS on our left. Visit the ethine left of our line where GERMANS had been reported working by day. They got their munitions but AFT METHOD of found it isp anonymous. Tried it in returning 12 midnight. Probably it is an old top of our own, as it had been it. It is unlikely the enemy have been working here. – Cpt. Casualties 1 killed 2 sick.	
26th FEB	Some fires at night give a few shots but not to improve the trenches. 1 man wounded on fatigue at 51mm in RUE DU BOIS – Quiet day – Captain [?] wounded Cpt.	
11 AM 27th FEB	Informed that the front line by fire brigade to battalion is to be re-arranged.	
5.30 PM	A Coy in the ORCHARD are relieved by 1/9 GURKHAS. These 1 man wounded coming in from the VB Advanced Post. A Coy form Bn local Reserve & billet near junction of EDWARD ROAD with the RUE DU BOIS. Casualties 1 wounded Cpt. Le Poitre	

Army Form C. 2118.

WAR DIARY
or
INTELLIGENCE SUMMARY.
(Erase heading not required.)

VOLUME VII
P. 54

Hour, Date, Place.	Summary of Events and Information.	Remarks and references to Appendices.
6.30 – 8pm 28th FEB RUE DU BOIS	B and C Coys "Bn. took Route" into the front line and took over the Port Arthur Salient, and the road up to 200 yards North from the Port Arthur Crossroads (Square S.4.d), from the Manchester Regt. with machine gun detachment (2 guns)	[By: BETHUNE Intel. Officer 1:40000] 24th BDE.

[Hand-drawn map showing GERMAN lines, No.4 OPost, No.5 OPost 16, No.6 Post 16, No.7 OPost, No.8, No.9 Post near, PORT ARTHUR LINES, CRESCENT TRENCH, ORCHARD, ROOMES TRENCH, RUE DU BOIS, GERMAN. SCALE 1/5000]

Army Form C. 2118.

WAR DIARY
or
INTELLIGENCE SUMMARY.

VOLUME VII p. 55

(Erase heading not required.)

Hour, Date, Place.	Summary of Events and Information.	Remarks and references to Appendices.
26th FEB. In the Trenches 1915	Weather fine and frosty. In the ORCHARD south of [?] A Coy. with "A" Company. Two machine guns of 4th Cavalry were attached to the two machine CRESCENT trench with D Coy. – Battalion had as its companies in firing line and one to local reserve trenches. The 6 JATS on its left and the 119th GURKHAS to the ORCHARD. – The British corps being in depth with DEHRA DUN BDE in front line FAMOUS DUN behind the MEERUT DUN – POST ARTHUR Salient where the Battalion lost heavily from shell fire in the beginning of November 1914 – For Hty & more below in St. S. g. a. SE – One man wounded in the hand during relief (Sohdar) Forehan killed in above cold party at building. Casualties: 1 killed, 1 wounded – Diff. AM the King has been graciously pleased to approve of the undermentioned rewards for services rendered in connection with operations in the Field. Dated 18th FEB. 1915. Seaforth Highlanders. C.M.G. – Lt. Col. H. B. RITCHIE. " " MILITARY CROSS – No. 6901 Coy. Sgr. Major R. SUTHERLAND. Diff.	[?] [Ref Map.] BETHUNE [Sheet 1: 40,000]

Army Form C. 2118.

WAR DIARY
or
INTELLIGENCE SUMMARY.
(Erase heading not required.)

VOLUME VII
P. 56

Hour, Date, Place. 1915	Summary of Events and Information.	Remarks and references to Appendices.
	Extract from List No. 18 of GHR 27th FEB 1915 - Under authority granted by H.M the King to the F.M. C in C, Wt. undermentioned NCOs and men have been awarded decorations as shown :-	Ref Map BETHUNE [Sheet 1/40,000]
	THE DISTINGUISHED CONDUCT MEDAL 1st/Bn. Seaforth Highlanders	
	No. 9216 L/Sgt. P. CAMPBELL (killed)	
	" 798 L/Cpl. W. McDOUGALL (wounded)	
	" 9363 " D. SMITH	
	" 8062 Pte. J. KERRY	
	" 16840 " A. McGARRY	
	" 1392 " A. REID	
	" 1535 " C. STORRIE	
	The following NCOs and men from 26th Bn. LONDON Regiment (Artists Rifles) to be temporary 2nd Lieutenants 6/9/14/21/15 - 1st/Bn. Seaforth Highlanders	
	No. 727 Lance Corpl. C. H. KIRKALDY	
	" 1392 " J. C. EVELEGH	
	" 1185 Pte. V. ANDERSON from Hon. Arty. Coy.	"
	" 1590 " A. IRVING "	"

War Diary with Appendices
of Seaforth Highlanders
From 1st To 31st March 1915

Serial No. 280.

5 V.
32 sheets

WAR DIARY
with appendices.
OF
Seaforth Highlanders.
From 1st March 1915 to 31st March 1915.

WAR DIARY
INTELLIGENCE SUMMARY.

Army Form C. 2118.

VOLUME VIII
P. 57

Hour, Date, Place. 1915	Summary of Events and Information.	Remarks and references to Appendices.
1st MARCH. In the trenches	Enemy put 58 shells into PORT ARTHUR in the hours in the morning and 70 odd during the day. North 1 man slightly wounded (?) The shell is a very high cavity for its most part — 1 man (Stack (Bishop) in PRESENT TURN — he ___ fell out of CRESCENT TURN into DEAD MAN'S HOUSE to get wood. Three killed at once ___ Heavy rain in afternoon — Weary quiet night — Casualties 1 killed 1 wounded ORR and 2 sick.	[Ref. Map BETHUNE Sheet 1: 40000]
2nd MARCH. In the trenches	The man sniped early in PORT ARTHUR. Brigadier (Col. Jacob) visits PORT ARTHUR. for. Enemy shelled PORT ARTHUR and RUE DU BOIS in the afternoon (putting 3 shells into a house (store a platoon was billeted in latter place.) 1 man ___ kit —	ORR
6.30 — 9.15 P.M 2nd March	The Battalion relieved in the trenches by the 2nd BLACK WATCH and 1st & 56th RIFLES (BAREILLY BDE relieving DEHRA DUN BDE.) Marched to former billets in LACOUTURE — Casualties 1 Off. 1 wounded, 2 sick —	1 Off.

WAR DIARY or INTELLIGENCE SUMMARY

Army Form C. 2118.

VOLUME VIII
p. 58

1915

Hour, Date, Place.	Summary of Events and Information.	Remarks and references to Appendices.
3rd MARCH LACOUTURE	The DEHRA DUN BDE is in reserve to the BAREILLY BDE. Brigade is working party of 2 officers + 260 other ranks from behind 1st/4th/B.L.W. + the 1 wounded. My party left at 10.15 P.M. — Casualties 1 wounded —	Ref. Map BETHUNE (Sheet 1: 40 000) BHW
1.45 AM 4th MARCH —do—	3 officers and 160 men sent to ☒ RICHEBOURG ST VAASTE to escort 150 AFRIDI prisoners to LOCON —	4 trips — ☒ RICHEBOURG ST VAASTE
3.30 AM —do— —do—	Informed that working party of 2 officers + 160 O.R. had been detained in trenches at RICHEBOURG ST VAASTE.	
4.50 AM —do— —do—	3 officers and 200 O.R. sent to garrison broken ALBERT ROAD and EDWARD ROAD under orders of BAREILLY BDE. — 23rd FEB to 3rd MARCH, 40 O.R. killed, 8 O.R. wounded to 20 pistol. Casualties 2 Indian Guns with Indians, 4 drivers and 8 horses taken on the strength. Total Casualties of the Br. force landing in FRANCE are now 5 officers killed (2 died of wounds) and 10 officers killed (31 died of wounds) and 285 wounded 1116 O.R. 111 O.R. killed not heard the Pen) and 6 missing (believed killed) wounded (2336) wrong did not include Pen McNEILL, Bat not LIEUT MATLAND [officers wounded who was attached to Black Watch in our lines] NB: 5 hrs have been counted twice so that numbers and died of wounds] should really be 280 BHW	
12 NOON 4th MARCH —do— —do—	Working Party of 2 officers + 260 O.R. return —	
6 PM —do— —do—	3 officers + 200 O.R. return from RICHEBOURG —	

WAR DIARY or INTELLIGENCE SUMMARY.

Army Form C. 2118.

VOLUME VIII
p. 59

Hour, Date, Place.	Summary of Events and Information.	Remarks and references to Appendices.
4th MARCH LACOUTURE (cont) 1915	Majors ARBUTHNOT and CAMPION Captain CARDEN (MACLACHLAN & SPENCER) from 2nd Battalion, 2 other over days have been — Cancelled 1/3 Sick — Total number of Reinforcements received since arrival in FRANCE (not including personnel sick rejoining) to 15 officers and 662 other ranks. Total sick casualties since landing. So far 20 reported to Battalion is 2384 5 officers and 238 other ranks wounded not rejoined to date. 9 officers and 209 other ranks. Bn. strength leaving AGRA 17 officers & 924 O.R. (33 Batman) 17 r 924 Casualties — sick not rejoined 5 Wounded not rejoined 9 : 238 4 N.Cos & Br.H.Col. VANDELEUR 1 : 209 Lt. GLASS handpicked promoted — : 4 Killed — : 5* Left MARSEILLES not rejoined Missing — : 5 — : 6 : 11 54 — Total 21 r 576 Reinforcements not counting — 4 r 348 wounded & sick rejoined 14 : 662 Reinforcement Bn. Post SAID 2 : 4 handpicked promoted Total 25 r 666 PRESENT STRENGTH (Correct) 21 r 1014 (28 Batman)	[Ref. Map BETHUNE] [Sheet 1: 40,000] P.H N.B.* 4 of these handpicked from Orderlies from Ranks 3rd Battalion

Army Form C. 2118.

WAR DIARY
or
INTELLIGENCE SUMMARY.
(Erase heading not required.)

VOLUME VIII.
p. 60

Instructions regarding War Diaries and Intelligence Summaries are contained in F. S. Regs., Part II, and the Staff Manual respectively. Title pages will be prepared in manuscript.

Hour, Date, Place.	Summary of Events and Information.	Remarks and references to Appendices.

1915

5 MARCH LA GORGUE

3 PM LA GORGUE

6 MARCH — do —
2:45 PM —
2 officers 7:40-18 other ranks joined from base
2:30 PM — 15 men of 2nd reinforcement
A working party of 60 men supplied to R.E. for work at BAILLEUL.
3 AM — Hours of duty
temperature 40°F

7 MARCH — do —
Divine Service for Church of Scotland 10.30 A.M. Church of England 3 PM. Mass for R.C. 9 AM & Gaelic Service 4.30 PM
1 officer & 100 form working party to front line from 5-7PM. P.R.
Casualties 9 sick — Weather warm —
Cold wind arose — Working party of 100 men to 18th
Inns from 10.15 AM — 3 PM. — 2nd Lieut. I. ANDERSON & 2nd
Lt. Batchelor having done a course of instruction at BAILLEUL
L.G.C rejoined. 9 men inspected for R.E. studies at LOCON
3 officers & 200 men form working party to Breastworks at 3 PM (1st Bn as previously occupied

8 MARCH — do —
2.30 PM Bn. moved into Breastworks at 3 PM (1st Bn LONDON REGt.
by 1/2 Bn) to make room for [Connaught Ranges]

[Reg Map BETHUNE sheet 1:40,000]

[Reg Map BETHUNE sheet 1:40,000]

WAR DIARY
INTELLIGENCE SUMMARY

Army Form C. 2118.

Volume VIII
61.

Hour, Date, Place. 1915	Summary of Events and Information.	Remarks and references to Appendices.
9th MARCH LACOUTURE	Men kept to the trenches except when transport Rel[?] provided between MEERUT BUN. or canal bridges, where mule Ewy. Lance corporal - one who had been doing F.P. No 1. Baggage wagon came between 12 noon - Surplus kit stored in LACOUTURE theatre 3 pm - Casualties 4 suite - R.H.	Ref. map BETHUNE Sheet 1:40,000.
3 AM 10th MARCH —do—	A Total of 2 NCOs & 18 other ranks over stores at LACOUTURE. Bn. marched at 3 am without transport to position of assembly (Restored and reconnoitred men crossroads S.3.c.). The 4th and Indian Corps having received orders to attack NEUVE CHAPELLE (orders received by Bn. at 7.30 pm on 9th Bde. Appendix "A") - each man carried greatcoat, mess tin in haversack with 2 sandbags, waterproof sheet, 2 days rations, emergency ration in haversack & 250 rounds - In addition each company carried 40 shovels 8 picks, 4 full boxes carriers + 30 extra wire cutters - Breakfast at 2 am, before leaving. At 7.30 guns bombarded enemy trenches continuing till 8.5 & mostly the more opposing house. Some batteries lost firing short over our heads rectified some casualties from premature - Capt. P.g. ANSTRUTHER was wounded at this time by one of the few bullets coming over from the enemy- trenches standing behind the breastwork looking over it-	Appendix "F" attached Special orders 6,13 Army 9.3.15. Appendix G attached operation orders by Brig Gen. C.W. Jacob. attached. [Appendix "H" attached Sketch map of NEUVE CHAPELLE trenches] R.H.

WAR DIARY or INTELLIGENCE SUMMARY

Army Form C. 2118.

VOLUME VIII
p. 62

Hour, Date, Place. 1915	Summary of Events and Information.	Remarks and references to Appendices.
8.5am/6 MARCH NEUVE CHAPELLE	The GARHWAL BDE attacked the GERMAN trenches the objective being the breastworks Y and Z where they had been trying to headings —	Ref BETHUNE Sheet V.45000 & Sketch map opposite [attached]
9.20am	Battalion ordered to occupy the breastworks and Y + Z with 9th GURKHAS on the left. Bn. moved by EDWARD ROAD and the RUE DU BOIS, and took some time to get up as the trenches were blocked by wounded coming down and did not get into this position till about 11.15. Then Col PITMAN was ordered to go to O.C. PORT ARTHUR to reconnoitre a position in front still held by enemy between the LEICESTERS and the 1/39 GARHWAL RIFLES (roughly from C1 FC2 on Sketch map). What the LEICESTERS were trying to do was drive the GERMANS out of with partial success –	
1PM	"C" Coy (Capt. BAILLIE HAMILTON) and "D" Coy (Capt. WICKES) ordered to advance from the breastworks, pivot on the northern. Schwitz of PORT ARTHUR & advance on C near O, both the 1/39th near C2 — The 2 companies advanced on the line of O.C. — Capt. BAILLIE HAMILTON looked through to different weapons respectful ground round D + was wounded after + twelve gun fire. He headed the line D + O nearly	

WAR DIARY
or
INTELLIGENCE SUMMARY.

Army Form C. 2118.

VOLUME VIII
P. 63

Hour, Date, Place. 1915

to cooperate with Capt Wicks who was starting near X - At this point Scouts who were brought to a standstill owing to our heavy artillery shelling from W to C. - The enemy brought up a trench mortar & Wicks was wounded. The 4th Bn Black Watch were moved in amongst our advanced companies which caused some confusion. Finally both Coy reps of the Leicesters were ordered to withdraw -

4 P.M.

As it was 2.00 getting late it was decided that 1st Dehra Dun Bde should move on to attack the Bois de Biez. The Battalion was to be attached to the Garhwal Bde There to make line of protecting the line at C Securing the right flank - accordingly "A" (Major Bruce) and "B" (Capt Murray) were ordered to stalk towards point from point E, S. Coy cooperate on their right towards NC, "D" Coy to remain where it was met as a reserve - Or Port Arthur was asked to advance from C2 with the Battalion due East of the Neuve Chapelle — Port Arthur Road —

[Ref Bethune Street (moved Sketch Map)]

WAR DIARY
or
INTELLIGENCE SUMMARY.

(Erase heading not required.)

Army Form C. 2118.

VOLUME VIII
p. 64

Hour, Date, Place.	Summary of Events and Information.	Remarks and references to Appendices.
19/15	This attack was carried out, "B" Company bombing the Germans along the French front. W. 15 and Capt R.K. MURRAY was dangerously wounded, "C" were they [rushed?] up with the detachments of the 2nd LONDON Regt. who made a gallant charge from PORT ARTHUR — Our machine guns assisted in keeping the enemy heads down — 2nd Lieut. C.H. HORNOR was killed close to "C" — "A" Coys cleared the German trenches "C" Coy advancing to L.T. about 128 Germans surrendered to the Battalion — A good many also surrendered to the LONDONS — By this time it was dark the Battalion was withdrawn to the line OC with the 2nd LEICESTERS on its left — The 3rd LONDONS (2 weak coys) to the right. The 1/39th GARHWALIS on the right up to the ESTAIRES — La BASSEE road. (Col. RITCHIE being in command from then on OC 'B' — Res Poston was consolidated. Made good during the night. Their were already entrenched in the attack and [afterwards?] there more already entrenched in the attack.	[Ref?] BETHUNE 60,000 (sketch map) 2 Lt. C.H. HORNOR was buried near [Pritchen hut?] (W) with a number of others on [E.66?] Note Re fight [Capt?] Ross [Graeme?] Rogers fought [gallantly?] for Some Joue fighting [reached?] [mentioned?] Sept O. [?] [?] [?] [Goldie?]. [?] Lieut. Hon. D. BRUCE

WAR DIARY

Army Form C. 2118.

VOLUME VIII
p. 65

INTELLIGENCE SUMMARY

(Erase heading not required.)

Hour, Date, Place.	Summary of Events and Information.	Remarks and references to Appendices.
1915		
11th MARCH NEUVE CHAPELLE	2nd Lieuts. R.J. WALKER (3rd Gordons attached) P.B. PROTHERO (Reg. BETHUNE Regt. 4th A.I.F.) slightly attacked [wounded]), J.C. EVELEGH (temporary), — 1st Dragoons the C in C]. Major M. H. STEWART had his gaiters from short place to the explosion of a shell close by him. — Casualties 2 Officers 17 OR killed 75 Officers [Capt R.A.C. MURRAY died of wounds received on 11th March & OR wounded. 3 — 3 rank — (includes Officers and grounds) was buried in the Position held by 2 companies 7th in firing line, 1 in support head cemetery 7 in reserve — Held continued on parapet etc by LILLERS] day — Very little sheltering by enemy. The morning-Patrols to the early morning reported ground from M. through L and to 6th A clear of the enemy but that H was held —	
7pm — do —	Troops on our left advanced, but returned again about 9pm. — Br assisted them by firing on enemy who are not known advance on our immediate front —	
NB.	This was 10. 2/39th GORKHAS moving on LE TOUQUET of 1st GEMRA DUN BDE who had attacked the BOIS DE BIEZ — Bn. Battalion had orders to support this attack of DEHRA DUN BDE in time — They rejoined the DEHRA DUN BDE in time — BDE some guns arrived in C in the afternoon — J.R. After dark both continued consolidating position	

WAR DIARY
INTELLIGENCE SUMMARY
(Erase heading not required.)

Army Form C. 2118.

VOLUME VIII
p. 66

Hour, Date, Place.	Summary of Events and Information.	Remarks and references to Appendices.

1915

Double clothing tunics towards enemy - [Left flap BETWEEN?]
Pickets were posted at the points on the ditch [Pickets Field]
between N & B which were cut by a ditch. 2
trenches and patrols were sent out towards
L & A - ½ Lieut FERRIER never rejoined
2 Lieuts J E WAKEFIELD (3rd Royal Scots Fusiliers)
1 C BARCLAY & LA LYNDEN BELL the Battalion
after start - Casualties 5 killed (includes Wakefield & child) 14 wounded & 2 sick
N.J.R.

5AM 12th MARCH NEUVE CHAPELLE

Enemy under cover of darkness combi attack,
but not in great strength as our movement forward.
The machine guns did great execution assisted by
light from very pistols, and the GERMANS lay
pile two deep in front of our trenches - The
enemy lit were easily beaten off, only one GERMAN
(who came to bring himself up) reaching the
trenches wounded - The enemy firm any themselves
in that they could under our fire and tried to get
around our right Stars the 1/39th one - The 1/39th
lost heavily from shell fire also from bombs
[from?] which they now appear unable to
reply - A party of 'D' coy 18th FUSILIERS were sent

6.30 AM

WAR DIARY or INTELLIGENCE SUMMARY

Army Form C. 2118.

VOLUME VIII
p. 67

Hour, Date, Place. 1915	Summary of Events and Information.	Remarks and references to Appendices.
12th MARCH NEUVE CHAPELLE	Expect our men under 2nd Lt KENNY - Lt KENNY ready for us to take the trench the Germans bore through were said to be in. They found it empty. They waited and overlooked by the enemy from behind up parapet. The Germans thought our men were going to surrender & went up & shouted at once, then it turned out to be too late for the party to get clear - our men thought the enemy wished to surrender - The result was that Sgt MENEAR & men were killed, and it was impossible to return - prepared - MR BARTON started to return but was seen as he stepped by the M.L.B. & was seen as an attack by signalled and fired up & BDEs came up on left & drove food M = Mr & from head. Whole time was hot more frights - Patrols sent out before throwing the night - "D" Coy. where the 113 of GARHWALIS in the front line after dark - Couralie, Lieut FERRIER-REER 20th had wounded 6 or killed th 3 OR missing - 74 rifle - The enemy shelled actively all day -	Reg Mr P BONNE NEEDED sketch NB 1/39th sew under command of this machine gun officer - brought in 54 men in statement. NB missing probably buried Reg R.Q.†

WAR DIARY
or
INTELLIGENCE SUMMARY.

Army Form C. 2118.

Vol. VIII
68

Hour, Date, Place. 1915	Summary of Events and Information.	Remarks and references to Appendices.
13th MARCH NEUVE CHAPELLE 6.30 P.M. — 11.30 P.M. 13th MARCH	Enemy artillery very active all day. The trench held by "D" Coy from front 13 to the LA BASSÉE Road had to be evacuated by day. Bn. relieved in the trenches by the 18th SIKHS from C to the right. By the 1/39th/1/4 GURKHAS from C to the right. M Remained in German trench very nearly stopped on getting away at the end. Moved to billets in NEUVE CHAPELLE ou PORT ARTHUR, ROUGES BANCS, RUE DU BOIS FACTORY, S.B.C. and RICHEBOURG ST MARTIRE by companies - 2 machine guns kept in to slip with daylight - Battalion HQ reached NEUVE CHAPELLE 3.30 P.M. — Casualties 3 killed (includes 2nd Lieut decd of w) 21 [wounded]	Ref Report Sketch 1 & Orders [Week K] Summary of Operations 3 Suite — R.H.
14th MARCH		
12 noon 14th MARCH NEUVE CHAPELLE	2nd Lieut I.M. MATHESON (3rd Gurkhas) & a draft of 57 58 N.C.Os then joined for Bn. — The DEHRA DUN BDE — in reserve to 15 LAHORE DIVN the Bn. Bn. not to be called out — Total Casualties 13th, 14th inclusive :— 2 officers & 30 O.R. killed, 8 officers & wounded & missing Casualties :— 14 Indn. O.Rs still —	3 other ranks [killed]. 12 sick — R.H.

WAR DIARY / INTELLIGENCE SUMMARY

Vol. VIII
p. 69

Hour, Date, Place. 1915	Summary of Events and Information.	Remarks and references to Appendices.
15th MARCH VEILLE CHAPELLE	Strength of Bn. in FRANCE 18 officers (exclusive of M.O. & Surgeon) 734 O.R. [BDE] MARCH 17 officers & 843 (30 Gurkhas are employed by the BDE)	Ref: BETHUNE [Sheet 1:40,000]
10 A.M.	L.G.C MEERUT DIVN (Lt Gen Sir Charles ANDERSON) visits the Battalion, expresses Thanks & congratulations on their behaviour & during the Recent operations, & speaks of their service in FRANCE — Casualties 2 File.	[Memorandus "J" attached — copy of letter from Sir J. Willcocks Comdg I.A Corps to BDE. I.A Corps to BDE. 12th Corps to Brig Gen Cav Divn & Comdg Meerut Divn BDE]
16th MARCH —do—	Casualties 1 File	
17th —do— —do—	Sir James Willcocks Comdg I.A corps) inspects the Battalion parade at 12.30 p.m. and eulogises the behaviour of the I.A Corps during the recent operations —	[Map "K" Special order by 1st army 14.3.15]
	Maxim gun class return from ST. OMER (1 Sgt, 1 Nk, 1 L/Nk, 3 Sepoys 3 hrs at Fn to No. 2 training 10th.	
	a 14 days course — 1 Lieutenant also = Casualties 3 Files —	[Map "L" Special I.A.C Routine order 14.3.15]
18th —do— —do—	"C" Coy is billeted in a farm but a 6" gun alongside the Coy's line the latter fires short of the house falls in. Road, the men are practically the gun adj — close Round still very little room for officers though they Kept the men evacuated for a burst —	
	Casualties 2 File —	

Army Form C. 2118.

WAR DIARY
or
INTELLIGENCE SUMMARY.
(Erase heading not required.)

VOLUME VIII
P. 7.

Instructions regarding War Diaries and Intelligence Summaries are contained in F. S. Regs., Part II, and the Staff Manual respectively. Title pages will be prepared in manuscript.

Hour, Date, Place.	Summary of Events and Information.	Remarks and references to Appendices.
19th MARCH 1915 NEUVE CHAPELLE	Billets cold, windy & now all morning — ground was just drying up & now 8.30 p.m. again — the addition of gum boots, "badass" & thick liners, fresh issue 200 of "tiny" baths, fresh "thunderers" tools, every variety of periscope from 1 - 11 proving our keen recognition of friends etc — Our weekly coal have not been used for more than say 1 day the remaining 2 1/2 cwts on hand so no transport to carry them — The heavy artillery & Bn. is ordered with Both booths work "Iron boots" except a few pairs. Men pestering & kind of money — The Maxlock cafe to be very good "Flying Bug" in addition to 3 scattered fleet cycles. Bn. not known to platoon, has had a run on the divisional weekly coal. The Turkee which is generally with No. 2 (Hour) makes a fair load. During the period of dead captains surveying the attack by day & light working wire & fight interesting Gol etc. There is bog on Captain doing company duty. Most of his batteries having found 1-7 the Regiment. The have no personal knowledge of the commander — has been referred to I.A.C. Commander Nil.	[Ref BETHUNE filed 61.40350] Etc. 1/1/ X/ Special order 6 Infy. Army 14.3.15 Opl Special A.O. 15 Routine order 14.3.15 D.H.

Gulab Singh & Sons, Calcutta—No. 22 Army C.—5-8-14—1,07,000.

WAR DIARY
or
INTELLIGENCE SUMMARY.   VOLUME VIII

(Erase heading not required.)

P. 71

Army Form C. 2118.

Hour, Date, Place.	Summary of Events and Information.	Remarks and references to Appendices.
20th MARCH VIEILLE CHAPELLE	Bn. issued with KHAKI covers for SM HOODS hats — leave for officers who have not already been home & for the regiment not & change proposed — Casualties 2 sick —	Ref. map BETHUNE Sheet 1:40,000 [Appendix M.Footnote from "LILLE" WAR GAZETTE" attached]
21st MARCH — do —	Fine day with sun — country drying up — Casualties 2 sick 1 Offr.	
9.15 22nd MARCH — do — A.M.	Battalion marched to billets in PARADIS, going via FOSSE, and arriving 11 A.M. via Rantour & Main — be relieved billets with 1st & 2nd BLACK WATCH of the BAREILLY BDE. and rather slow by doing so as the billets in VIEILLE CHAPELLE were very cramped — Roads dry and quite a warm sun — Company commanders, Capt. BAILLIE-HAMILTON, Lieut. ALLANBY 2/Lieut. HEMINGWAY (3rd Pm.) & 2/Lieut. WAKEFIELD (3rd Scots Fusiliers) have to reconnoitre the trenches to be taken over at front held by the 25th British BDE. on nights 24th/25th — Casualties Nil. 1 Offr.	
4 P.M. PARADIS	Reconnaissance of trenches was cancelled last night — Draft of 150 N.C.O.s & men with 2 officers Lieut. L.D. RANKIN (3rd Bn.) & 2/Lieut. D.A.M. McDOUGALL join the Bn. at 1.30 P.M. — About 40 of these are our own men rejoining from sick movement — Col. RITCHIE 1 2 company commanders leave at 6 P.M.	
23rd MARCH — do —	for reconnaissance of line to be taken over. Casualties 1 sick 1 Offr.	

Then copies for trenches report to D.A.D.O.S. railhead.

Army Form C. 2118.

VOLUME VIII
p. 72

INTELLIGENCE SUMMARY.
or
(Erase heading not required.)

Instructions regarding War Diaries and Intelligence Summaries are contained in F.S. Regs., Part II, and the Staff Manual respectively. Title pages will be prepared in manuscript.

Hour, Date, Place.	Summary of Events and Information.	Remarks and references to Appendices
1915		
7 P.M. 24th MARCH PARADIS	The Battalion marched on a ZELOBES and NEUVE CHAPPELLE to a bivouac in bivouac M.25 north where it spent the day squatting along the hedges to the road. Baggage waggons did not accompany the Bn. [2 men to each night for tackles]	Ref BETHUNE Sheet 1:40000
6·30 PM 24th	Battalion marched into the line close over trenches from the LINCOLNS, 25 KRBE, from road junction Sg M.35 - d. 4/9 b a point about Sg M.29 d 5/2 - 2 companies in firing line with 4 machine guns, 1 coy in support close behind right of firing line, 1 coy and Bn H.Q. N Sg M.28, d along the road - trenches very wet, untraversed - impossible to get at by day without going right across the open - Germans roughly 200 - 250 yards in front - 16 officers - 50 hun held an advanced post intn., 150 yds. of enemy at road junction Sg M.36 a.1/2 in an orchard - no communication between right & left of advanced post, nor between right flank firing line company and between firing line & supports by day, 200 from firing line to advanced post except by running across the open -	

Army Form C. 2118.

WAR DIARY
or
INTELLIGENCE SUMMARY.
(Erase heading not required.)

VOLUME VIII   p 73

Hour, Date, Place.	Summary of Events and Information.	Remarks and references to Appendices.
1915	The line is that reached by the BRITISH in the attack on 10th MARCH. There are still many unburied British and hun. BRITISH & GERMAN lying about and the whole area is littered with ammunition, rifles, equipment, entrenching tools, grenades etc. Reliefs complete by 9.15 p.m. Companies all worked hard during the night improving trenches etc. Enemy also working hard, very little firing.	[Ref. BETHUNE Sheet (1: 40000)]
4 am 25th MARCH "In the Trenches"	Brigadier visits the firing line – heavy rain during the night – stay – hardly any shelling, very little sniping – we hold "A" Sub section Southern section of Indian corps line – our front is protected by wood and cleared de fuse. The enemy to front putting up his wire obstacle. Division wire "wood frames removed for front GERMAN position." Whiskey here is a strong moon all night. Very cold tonight. Col. Ritchie visits the GLOUCESTER HQs, a hostile round the trenches. The GLOUCESTERS are on our right and the 2nd GURKHAS on our left. Casualties NIL	Casualties / Sick / Off. R.H.

Army Form C. 2118.

WAR DIARY
or
INTELLIGENCE SUMMARY.
(Erase heading not required.)

VOLUME VIII
p.74

Hour, Date, Place.	Summary of Events and Information.	Remarks and references to Appendices.
1915.		
3.30 A.M. 26th MARCH in the Trenches	Patrols report enemy in house 130 yds in front of our right company, from which SOP runs to enemy main line. All companies working had all night. Reserve company sheds the remainder & takes up their sentries etc. Collected 730 boxes S.A.A lying near the reserve trench. Very little "sniping" by enemy during day - kept up from stelled our trenches and advanced post. Towards 8 men slightly in the latter, they half the stand range & damaged the parapets -	Ref: BETHUNE Sheet 1:40,000
2.30 P.M.	A platoon under an officer from the reserve Company relieves the advanced post the Coy in support relieves the company in our right fire trench - Casualties 1 killed 5 wounded 10/4. (3 very slightly return to duty.) INDIAN corps cables that the F.M.C in C has awarded the following decoration - The Military Cross	
7.30 P.M.	CAPTAIN R. LANG 1st Bn Seaforth Highlanders 10/4. (for services on 20 - 22 DEC.)	

WAR DIARY or INTELLIGENCE SUMMARY

Army Form C. 2118.

VOLUME VIII
75

Hour, Date, Place.	Summary of Events and Information.	Remarks and references to Appendices.
27th March "In the Trenches" 1915	Nos. 83, 84 & 85 Batteries R.F.A are in close support to the Bn. and their observing officers are during the night. – No 2 Siege Battery to shell house in front our right company commencing 8 A.M. and we evacuated right company fire trench – advanced post – every 2nd rifle average fire was 20 to find till 8.45 A.M. 11 shells have been fired – a large portion of the house was blown away. The Brigade took 6 guns against garrison. I advanced post reduced to 16 men by day on account of shell fire – Every odd day with high explosive shrap – 2 green rockets fired in rapid succession from fire trench agreed upon as signal for artillery support by night if telephone trunks blown – Trenches being much drier – Left Company 250 yds has 3 sections in support and 150 yds in rear fire trench by day accommodated much less from trench in reserve 2 machine guns 114 & separatists brought into our line in addition to our 4th – Casualties 3 wounded 1 sick. Ptt	[Ref] BETHUNE Sheet [(1: 40,000)]

WAR DIARY
or
INTELLIGENCE SUMMARY
(Erase heading not required.)

Army Form C. 2118.

VOLUME VIII
p. 76

Hour, Date, Place.	Summary of Events and Information.	Remarks and references to Appendices.
28th March in the trenches	Very cold at night with frost – likely be frozen. Many stand-to waterproof sheets & some blankets. The trenches when we came in – it is now possible to visit the trenches by day, they are all screened – communication is often between all trenches and the advanced posts, and a lot of work has been done. Temp. 2nd Lieut. J.D. MARVIN (from 28th Bn. LONDON REGT, ARTISTS RIFLES) joins the Battalion – The reserve company and the machine guns stay in the trenches the rest of the Battalion is relieved by the 1/4th SEAFORTHS (Major CUTHBERT) from 8.30 to 10.15 – and marches to Gillebekhead CROIX BARBEE 'a' trench M.33.a.0/3 – Roft. Casualties 1 wounded (arm)	BETHUNE Sheet 1:40,000
29th March CROIX BARBEE	Very cold again, frost – ditto by day – working parties finds 300 men provided at each – "Affair with infection leaves at 5.45 p.m. to garrison a redoubt when this brigade area attacks Canache, 5 trench Roft. Source M.22.	

Army Form C. 2118.

WAR DIARY
or
INTELLIGENCE SUMMARY.

(Erase heading not required.)

VOLUME VIII
77.

Instructions regarding War Diaries and Intelligence Summaries are contained in F. S. Regs., Part II, and the Staff Manual respectively. Title pages will be prepared in manuscript.

Hour, Date, Place.	Summary of Events and Information.	Remarks and references to Appendices.
1915 24th – 28th March In the Trenches.	Rough Sketch of Sub Section "A" Southern Section Indian Corps 24th – 28th March.	

GERMAN LINE ——
BRITISH LINE ——
(1) Taken over
(2) added by Bn
wire
barricades
M. Guns
listening post

200x   50   0   200x
R. des Layes.

GERMAN LINE

1 officer 50 men

Sap House

BREASTWORK

3/4 Coy

1 Coy

½ Coy

Water

½ Coy

from Reserve Coy
Bn. H.Q.
500 yds.

Army Form C. 2118.

WAR DIARY
or
INTELLIGENCE SUMMARY.
(Erase heading not required.)

VOLUME VIII
78.

Hour, Date, Place.	Summary of Events and Information.	Remarks and references to Appendices.
30th MARCH 1915 CROIX BARBEE	Still cold and frost - leave granted for officers except commanding officers. The general recommended on the score of health efficiency & present strength of battalion in FRANCE; 22 officers & 1057 other ranks. With the battalion 21 officers & 943 o.r. (16 of the same importation the Reveiss, 78 in prison, 116 on father). 9 on central duty (1 of type), 33 on division of Staff; 23 in brigade area), Officers & Burma (21), 15 are 2 Lieuts, 3 Lieuts, 2 Captains & 1 Lt. colonel. Our Indian A.T. carts (16) have now been returned replaced with 7 officers in Turkey but have been replaced with 7 & Khurbust wagons referred. These will be of great hardship as the A.T. carts have been most useful, they have gone to Peshawar - they have been used always been greater personnel I reckon. - My infantry have been kept been sick or sorry. V2 have always been rewarded for their behaviour under fire. Lieut. RAWKEN apptd. (?) transport officer. Re Guardroom - has been doing this in addition to his other duties since Lieut. SWARD McKENZIE was wounded in November. Captain BAILLIE HAMILTON leaves McANNBY & ANDERSON proceed on leave tel April 4th - 2Lt. I. ANDERSON takes over charge of machine guns from Lt. K. ANDERSON. Casualties 1 wounded, 2 sick - D.H.	BETHUNE sheet 1:40,000 / Working parties of 500 officers provided at dusk D.H.

WAR DIARY
INTELLIGENCE SUMMARY.

Army Form C. 2118.

VOLUME VIII
p. 79

Hour, Date, Place. 1915	Summary of Events and Information.	Remarks and references to Appendices.
31st MARCH - CROIX BARBEE	The DEHRA DUN BDE is relieved in the front line by the FEROZEPUR BDE -	[BETHUNE Sheet 1:40000]
9.15 P.M. —do— —do—	The Battalion marches to billets in VIEILLE CHAPELLE. The Machine guns & "A" Coy. rejoin the battalion in the early morning of the 1st from the firing line, (killed one of the Machine gunners two killed - Casualties 1 killed - 1 sick - Total Casualties from 24th to 31st. 2 O.Rs killed 10 wounded (3 reported 1 died of wounds) 10 sick - ROH.	ROH.
3.45 P.M. 1st APRIL VIEILLE CHAPELLE		

Special Order.

To the 1st Army.

We are about to engage the enemy under very favourable conditions. Until now in the present campaign, the British Army has, by its pluck and determination, gained victories against an enemy greatly superior both in men and guns. Reinforcements have made us stronger than the enemy in our front. Our guns are now both more numerous than the enemy's are, and also larger than any hitherto used by any army in the field. Our Flying Corps has driven the Germans from the air.

On the Eastern Front, and to South of us, our Allies have made marked progress and caused enormous losses to the Germans, who are, moreover, harassed by internal troubles and shortage of supplies, so that there is little prospect at present of big reinforcements being sent against us here.

In front of us we have only one German Corps, spread out on a front as large as that occupied by the whole of our Army (the First).

We are now about to attack with about 48 battalions a locality in that front which is held by some three German battalions. It seems probable, also, that for the first day of the operations the Germans will not have more than four battalions available as reinforcements for the counter attack. Quickness of movement is therefore of first importance to enable us to forestall the enemy and thereby gain success without severe loss.

At no time in this war has there been a more favourable moment for us, and I feel confident of success. The extent of that success must depend on the rapidity and determination with which we advance.

Although fighting in France, let us remember that we are fighting to preserve the British Empire and to protect our homes against the organized savagery of the German Army. To ensure success, each one of us must play his part, and fight like men for the Honour of Old England.

(Sd.) D. HAIG, General,
Commanding 1st Army.

9th March, 1915.

1st Printing Co., R.E. G.H.Q. 673.

Operation Order No 22
by
Brigadier General C.W. Jacob
Commanding Dehra Dun Brigade

Copy No. 3

Appendix "G"

LA COUTURE 9th March 15.

Information 1. (a). The 4th and Indian Corps are to attack NEUVE CHAPELLE on March 10th. Further objectives will be East Edge of BOIS DE BIEZ and the high ground AUBERS to LIGNY LE GRAND.

(b). The dividing line between the Corps is :— point where where the dividing line between the Squares M and S NEUVE CHAPELLE cross roads in S.6.a/9 – cross road at LA CLIQUETERIE FE

(c). The Garhwal Bde is to assault the trenches extending from the front of PORT ARTHUR to opposite the left of the line now held by the Meerut Division at 8-5 am. The Dehra Dun Bde is to be in support and the Bareilly Bde will continue to hold the present line of trenches

(d). The 1st Corps is undertaking an offensive North East of GIVENCHY.

Intention. 2. The Dehra Dun Bde. will be prepared to attack the BOIS DE BIEZ as soon as the Garhwal Bde attack has succeeded.

Orders to troops 3. Battalions will move into the positions of assembly already indicated as under :—
1st Seaforths route via X.5.a road south of the LA LOISNE river – RUE DES BERCEAUX to pass road junction X.5.a. S.W at 3 am.
2nd Gurkhas Route R.34 b and d – LA COUTURE Church then road South of LA LOISNE river to pass road junction X.5.a S.W at 3-30 am.
9th Gurkhas. Route R.35 a and d – X.6.a – S.1.b – S.2.a and b – S.3.a – S.3.c to pass road junction R.35.d.5/5 at 3 am.
4th Seaforths route R.34. a, c and d – road

Road South of LA LOISNE River - road junction S.2.c S.W. - S.1.b. SE - S.2.a 3/2 to pass Road junction X.5.a S.W at 3-15 a.m.

S.A.A. 4. As opportunity offers the S.A.A which has been placed in the positions of assembly should be moved up nearer the front as the advance progresses. It is possible that the rear Companies might be able to carry up some boxes and form a Depot further ahead.

Medical. 5. Wounded will be collected at the existing Reg'tl Aid Posts in RUE DES BERCEAUX (S.8.b and S.3.c). Ambulances will be at VIEILLE CHAPELLE and ZELOBES. Line of evacuation Northern RICHEBOURG road to VIEILLE CHAPELLE thence via FOSSE.

1st line Transport. 6. (a) First line Transport will remain in present billets. Quarter Masters of battalions will keep in close touch with the Staff Captain at present Bde Headquarters.
(b) Units will use their own discretion as to how far Machine gun mules can be taken.

Tools 7. Shovels and some picks in charge of battalions should be carried to some convenient spot in area of assembly and, if possible, should be carried further forward during the advance and left in some convenient place.

Prisoners. 8. Any prisoners will be handed over to the Bareilly Bde for disposal. Bareilly report centre is at S.2.d.10/0.

Reports. 9. Report centre will be, in first instance, defended house, M.32.d.8/2 which will be connected to present H.Q by telephone.

H.R. Walker
Major
Brigade Major Dehra Dun Bde

Issued at   pm
Copy 1 and 2 War Diary
" 3   1st Seaforths   Copy 8. 128 JFA
" 4   4th Seaforths   " 9. Meerut Div.
" 5. 9th Gurkhas   " 10. Garhwal Bde
" 6. 2nd Gurkhas   " 11. Bareilly Bde.
" 7. 19 BFA

Appendix "H"

NEUVE CHAPELLE

2/Lr Protheroe wounded
2/Lr Eveleigh wounded
Lr Bryce wounded
Capt. Wicks wounded
2/Lr Walker wounded
Capt Anstruther wounded
Capt Murray wounded
2/Lt Kirkpatrick
Maj. Stewart

2nd attack
1st attack
PORT ARTHUR
Orchard
Orchard

F. E. P. O. N. M. L. K. B. C. A.

- - - Original British Line
--- " German Line
— Water channels

Scale 1/5000
100 50 0 100

Appendix "J"

Head Quarters Dehra Dun Brigade.

12th March 1915

Copy of a letter from Sir James Willcocks, Commanding Indian Army Corps, to Brigadier General C.W. Jacob, Commanding Dehra Dun Brigade, dated the 12th March 1915.

....

Please convey to all your gallant Officers, Indian Officers, N,C,O's and men my very hearty thanks and congratulations on their splendid behaviour in the Field at NEUVE CHAPELLE. I am indeed fortunate and proud to be associated with such good soldiers - I am confident all ranks are ready for immediate further efforts.

Sd James Willcocks, Lieut General.

To.
The Officer Commanding

1st Seaforths.
4th Seaforths.
9th Gurkha
2nd Gurkhas.
39th Garhwalis.

Major
Brigade Major Dehra Dun Brigade.

Appendix "F"

SPECIAL ORDER
TO THE 1st ARMY.

I have received the following message from Field Marshal Sir John French:—

"At the conclusion of the four days fighting which marks the first stage of the operations entrusted to the 1st Army, I am anxious to express to you personally my warm appreciation of the skilful manner in which you have carried out your orders, and my fervent and most heartfelt appreciation of the magnificent gallantry and devoted tenacious courage displayed by all ranks whom you have ably led to success and victory. My warmest thanks to you and all."

I desire to express to all ranks of the 1st Army my great appreciation of the task accomplished by them in the past four days of severe fighting. The 1st Army has captured the German trenches on a front of two miles, including the whole village of Neuve Chapelle and some strongly defended works. Very serious loss has been inflicted on the enemy; nearly 2,000 prisoners are in our hands, and his casualties in killed and wounded are estimated at about 16,000.

I wish also to thank all concerned for the very careful preparation made for the assault. Much depended on this thoroughness and secrecy. The attack was such a complete surprise to the enemy that he had neither a Corps nor an Army Reserve at hand, and had to draw on the adjoining Army for help.

The absolute success of the operation of breaking through the German lines on the first day is not only a tribute to the careful forethought and attention to detail on the part of the leaders, but it has proved beyond question that our forces can defeat the Germans where and when they choose, no matter what mechanical contrivances or elaborate defences are opposed to their advance.

The results of the successful action just fought are not, however, confined to the material losses sustained by the enemy. The organization of the German forces from Ypres to far South of the La Bassee canal has been thrown into a state of confusion. Reinforcements available to oppose the French in the battle which is taking place at Notre Dame de Lorette or destined for other parts of the line, have been drawn into the fight opposite the 1st Army, and, in many cases, very severely handled.

The losses sustained by the 1st Army, though heavy are fully compensated for by the results achieved, which have brought us one step forward in our efforts to end the war; and the British soldier has once more given the Germans a proof of his superiority in a fight, as well as of his pluck and determination to conquer.

The spirit and energy shown by all ranks augur well for the future, and I feel confident that the success achieved by the 1st Army at Neuve Chapelle is the forerunner of still greater victories which must be gained in order to bring the war to a successful conclusion.

(Sgd.) D. HAIG, General,
Commanding 1st Army.

14th March, 1915.

Appendix "L"

INDIAN ARMY CORPS ROUTINE ORDERS

BY

LIEUT.-GENERAL SIR JAMES WILLCOCKS, K.C.B., K.C.S.I., K.C.M.G., D.S.O., COMMANDING.

Dated 14th March, 1915.

445. SPECIAL. The G.O.C. Indian Corps has had great pleasure in to-day publishing for the information of all ranks a highly complimentary order received from the Field Marshal Commanding-in-Chief regarding the fighting of the Corps at Neuve Chapelle from 10th to 13th March.

On his own behalf General Willcocks wishes to congratulate and thank most heartily the Divisional and Brigade Commanders, the Army Corps, Divisional and Brigade Staffs, the Commanders and Staffs of the Royal Artillery and Royal Engineers, and the Administrative Services, but above all the magnificent British and Indian Units who have for 5 months past so nobly and unflinchingly done their duty culminating in this last victorious engagement at Neuve Chapelle.

The work of the Artillery has been most admirable and very largely contributed to the success of every operation.

With such officers and men all work has been a pleasure and no task can be too difficult to achieve.

446. OFFICERS—POSTINGS. The following postings have been approved :—

Captain T. Luck, 67th Punjabis, Lieut. W. C. Cooper, 53rd Sikhs, Captain C. A. James, 126th Infantry, and Captain C. A. G. Money, 130th Baluchis to 1st Bn., 39th Garhwal Rifles. Dated 12th March, 1915.

A. S. COBBE, BRIGADIER-GENERAL,
Deputy Adjutant and Quartermaster General.

Appendix "M"

TRANSLATION FROM "LILLE WAR GAZETTE," 3rd MARCH, 1915.
(This is a weekly newspaper, issued by the Germans in LILLE, in German).

FIRE.

(By Lieutenant-Colonel Kaden.)

As children many of us have played with it: some of us have seen an outbreak of fire. First a small tongue-like flame appears, it grows into a devastating fury of heat. We out here in the field have seen more than enough of it.

But there is also the fire of joy, of sacred enthusiasm! It arose from sacrificial altars, from mountain heights of Germany, and lit up the heavens at the time of solstice and whenever the home countries were in danger. This year fires of joy shall flare from the Bismarck Columns throughout the length and breadth of Germany, for on 1st April, just one hundred years ago, our country's greatest son was born. Let us celebrate this event in a manner deep, far-reaching and mighty! BLOOD AND IRON.

Let every German, man or woman, young or old, find in his heart a Bismarck Column, a pillar of fire now in these days of storm and stress. Let this fire, enkindled in every German breast, be a fire of joy, of holiest enthusiasm. But let it be terrible, unfettered, let it carry horror and destruction! Call it HATE! Let no one come to you with "Love thine enemy!" We all have but one enemy, *England!* How long have we wooed her almost to the point of our own self-abasement. She would none of us, so leave to her the apostles of peace, the "No-War" disciples. The time has passed when we would do homage to everything English—our cousins that were!

"God punish England!" "May He punish her!" This is the greeting that now passes when Germans meet. The fire of this righteous hate is all aglow!

You men of Germany, from East and West, forced to shed your blood in the defence of your home-land through England's infamous envy and hatred of Germany's progress, feed the flame that burns in your souls. We have but one war-cry "GOD PUNISH ENGLAND!" Hiss this to one another in the trenches, in the charge, hiss as it were the sound of licking flames.

Behold in every dead comrade a sacrifice forced from you by this accursed people. Take ten-fold vengeance for each hero's death!

You German people at home, feed this fire of hate!

You mothers, engrave this in the heart of the babe at your breast!

You thousands of teachers, to whom millions of German children look up with eyes and hearts, teach HATE! unquenchable HATE!

You homes of German learning, pile up the fuel on this fire! Tell the nation that this hate is not un-German, that it is not poison for our people. Write in letters of fire the name of our bitterest enemy. You guardians of the truth, feed this sacred HATE!

You German fathers, lead your children up to the high hills of our home-land, at their feet our dear country bathed in sunshine. Your women and children shall starve; bestial, devilish conception. England wills it! Surely, all that is in you rises against such infamy?

Listen to the ceaseless song of the German forest, behold the fruitful fields like rolling seas, then will your love for this wondrous land find the right words, HATE, unquenchable HATE. Germany, Germany above all!

Let it be inculcated in your children and it will grow like a land-slide, irresistible, from generation to generation.

You fathers, proclaim it aloud over the billowing fields, that the toiling peasant below may hear you, that the birds of the forest may fly away with the message: into all the land, that echoes from German cliffs send it reverberating like the clanging of bells from tower to tower throughout the country-side: "HATE, HATE, the accursed English, HATE"!

You masters, carry the flame to your workshops; axe and hammer will fall the heavier when arms are nerved by this HATE.

You peasants, guard this flame, fan it anew in the hearts of your toilers, that the hand may rest heavy on the plough that throws up the soil of our home-land.

What CARTHAGE was to ROME, ENGLAND is to GERMANY. For ROME as for us it is a question of "to be or not to be." May our people find a faithful mentor like Cato. His "ceterum censeo, Carthaginem esse delendam" for us Germans means.—

"GOD PUNISH ENGLAND."

N.B.—A copy of this newspaper was found on a German prisoner captured during the recent fighting at NEUVE CHAPELLE. It is of interest as showing the hatred for Great Britain which is being sedulously cultivated in Germany. This hatred is being encouraged and fostered officially by every possible means.

War Diaries with Appendices
of 1st Seaforth Highlanders
From 1st To 30th April 1915

121/5504

Army No. 260

WAR DIARY
with appendices.
OF
1st Seaforth Highlanders.

From 1st April 1915 to 30th April 1915

6.T.
17 sheets

WAR DIARY
INTELLIGENCE SUMMARY

Army Form C. 2118.
VOLUME IX
p. 80

(Erase heading not required.)

Hour, Date, Place. 1915	Summary of Events and Information.	Remarks and references to Appendices.
1st APRIL VIEILLE CHAPELLE 3.45 PM	Battalion marched to billets in L'EPINETTE St. R. 7:- Close billets. Every available troops have been employed by native troops for some time and are very insanitary indeed, (tumble down houses etc.) Casualties Nil.	[BETHUNE Sheet 1:40000] Btt.
2nd APRIL L'EPINETTE	Lt Col RITCHIE and medical officer Capt. NEWTON go on 7 days leave – Casualties 2 rick –	Btt.
10.40 AM 3rd APRIL	L.G.C. DIVN (Sir Charles ANDERSON) inspects the reinforcements which joined the Battalion on the 14th & 23rd March – Rain all day – 2 officers of the 72nd Highlanders of CANADA ride over & see the Battalion – Casualties 3 rick –	Btt.
4th APRIL do	Rain all day – 4 trained Telegraphists leave the Battalion (1 for Meerut Signal Company's & 3 for Aldershot) – Company training continues during this period. Regt (Sikh) route marches, Bomb throwing, attack practice etc.) Casualties Nil	Btt.
5th APRIL do	Rain all day – Casualties 3 rick –	Btt.
6th APRIL do	10 reinforcements join from the BASE. Pay Btt to black of 1st R.S.C. drives this cargo for gun Alas gs light 6 knapsacks that tested. Pouring rain - Afrine day, Rain again at night – Casualties 2 rick – Btt.	Btt.

WAR DIARY or INTELLIGENCE SUMMARY

Army Form C. 2118.

VOLUME IX
p. 81

Hour, Date, Place.	Summary of Events and Information.	Remarks and references to Appendices.
1915		
7th April L'EPINETTE	Showery – Casualties Nil	WD [BETHUNE Staff Rft 1:40,000]
8th April –do–	Casualties 2 sick	
9th April –do–	Lt.Col. RITCHIE returned o/l 7 days leave – Captain D.H. DAVIDSON reported the Battalion – Showery all day – Sir John FRENCH was to have inspected the DEHRA DUN Bde at 4 p.m. but postponed his visit – Casualties Nil – Rft	
10th April –do–	One company sent to a cinematograph entertainment at FOSSE in the morning (2nd entrt) The battalion marched to LESTREM where the Field Marshall Commander in Chief (Sir John FRENCH) inspected the DEHRA DUN BAGADE – Sir John addressed each battalion separately.	
4pm –do–	Orders received for return to the trenches on the night of 12th/13th inst. During the attack on 10th March some of our men who were with the Brigade bombing partys collected a number of German helmets worthless the other troops who were engaged with the enemy. They afterwards disposed of these at francs 10/- each, thousands being purchased by men in Field Ambulances Cyclists etc to send to the line –	

Gulab Singh & Sons, Calcutta—No. 22 Army C.—5-8-14—1,07,000.

WAR DIARY or INTELLIGENCE SUMMARY

Army Form C. 2118.

VOLUME IX
P. 82

Hour, Date, Place.	Summary of Events and Information.	Remarks and references to Appendices.
1915		
10 APRIL L'EPINETTE	Casualties	
11 APRIL —do—	Divine Service for R.C., C of E & Presbyterians. Casualties.	BETHUNE SHEET 1/40,000 Map 25 Infantry Bgd. for John French Sgt. Dpn Bay M. Norto? NY
12 APRIL —do—	2nd Lieuts. R.B. CONDUITT and 9.F. WILSON from 1st Res 14 Rn 1st London Regt joined R Battalion. 1st Lt of R.B. with 3 companies took over trenches at NEUVE CHAPELLE from the Commanding and 1 platoon took over trenches at NEUVE CHAPELLE to be taken over tonight. — Casualties 1 sick —	
9 P.M. —do— —do—	The Battalion trenches run:— CROIX MARMUSE – FOSSE – BOUT DEVILLE – CROIX BARBEE and CROIX ROUGE to NEUVE CHAPELLE; and takes over from the NORTHAMPTONS the line from LA BASSÉE – ESTAIRES road (etchonne) to the next parallel road to the East of it. Exactly the same line occupied by the Battalion & 1 Company of the 3rd LONDONS when we left the trenches last on March 14th. Nothing much has been done to the trenches since the parapets & traverses are largely composed of sandbags. The Germans are	D. of R.
5·45 pm —do— —do—		

Gulab Singh & Sons, Calcutta—No. 22 Army C.—5·8·14—1,07,000.

Army Form C. 2118.

VOLUME IX
p 83

WAR DIARY
or
INTELLIGENCE SUMMARY.
(Erase heading not required.)

Hour, Date, Place.	Summary of Events and Information.	Remarks and references to Appendices.
12th APRIL 1915	The trenches to there distant abt (500-500 yds) except on the right where it approaches to about 350 yds. There have been 2 advanced posts dug but (24 hours relief) the furthest being only abt 80 yds. from a bit of the enemy trench which projects. 16 Companies are in the firing line on a frontage in our 2nd position at PONT MATTHEW (with Bn H.Q.) and 1 company in reserve behind in ELGIN road known to FORESTERS LANE, this is the line our 18 November to the West of "Q" LA B— ESTAIRES road. Bn H.Q. has telephonic communication with each Company in the firing line to with FR 145 BTY. forming station in LA RUE DU BOIS — O.R. BDE H.Q. THIS FR Bn on the right (2/8 GURKHAS) FR Bn on the left (2/2 GURKHAS) — 4 B1.8 the Brigade are in the firing line today, the very broken oak (6th JATS) in reserve — one Indian back in MERVILLE CHAPELLE. Went to examine from our left — our 2nd front "E" (Sketch map.) — No cut	[BETHUNE ROAD] 1:40,000 & sketch map to = 14 March

WAR DIARY
or
INTELLIGENCE SUMMARY
(Erase heading not required.)

Army Form C. 2118.

VOLUME IX

Hour, Date, Place. 1915.	Summary of Events and Information.	Remarks and references to Appendices.
12th APRIL in the trenches (cont.)	being still of value. About 10 to 10:30 the enemy's rifle fire almost ceased though we could not be caught up close enough to hear approaching steps on the first line trenches we felt out in the open to see if such there were & took lifeges on infantry between the trenches. The situation remained between the lines — at 9 P.M. with intervals of five left CROIX BARBEE at 9 P.M. with intervals of 5 minutes between companies, carrying four days provisions. Very rifle ammunition (6000) & entrenching tools & 200 rounds for him a whole G. ravement disabled & they in the back — the Regt was completed by 11:15 p.m. — Trenching & any communication trenches rather muddy & had been improved by Butts Engineers — Casualties NIL.	Appendix "N" Appendix "N" march of Regiment to the front line. of British Prisoners of war in Germany which were circulated & Regimenter before they left their earlier billets in the front line to them for the splendid fighting they have done and for

NB. Sir John French in the 15th April addressed the O.C. to the following effect: "I have spoken to the officers of their having been

WAR DIARY or INTELLIGENCE SUMMARY

Army Form C. 2118.

Volume IX
p. 85

Hour, Date, Place: 1915

Summary of Events and Information:

Splendid feat they [performed] in the glorious battle of NEUVE CHAPELLE. Such is a glorious feat not only because of the gun, through we have [gained] the enemy's position and [driven] the enemy for a [long] [distance], for it is because it has [shown] [that] he cannot hold his [position] [against] [you]. [whenever] asked to [do] so — [you] all that [anyone can ask] of [you] — [it may] [confidently] [be] known [hereafter] [that] [having] been further than the enemy's [line] has [become] [easy]...

There is no use dwelling on the [past] [battles] [of] so glorious a regiment. The feats are known to every soldier. We know [that] [you] have upheld the glorious traditions — and [won] many honours on the colours of your regiment but the battle of NEUVE CHAPELLE is no greater [than] [any] [other] [that] [you] [have] [taken] [part] [in] — [of] [the] [other] [glorious] [fights] [which] [will] [be] [added] [to] [your] [colours] [after] this war — [you have] [just] [now] [to] [know] [how] [well] [it]

Remarks and references to Appendices:

BETHUNE Road
L/40,000 sheet
Map app "H III"

WAR DIARY

or

INTELLIGENCE SUMMARY.

(Erase heading not required.)

Army Form C. 2118.

Volume IX
p. 86

Instructions regarding War Diaries and Intelligence
Summaries are contained in F. S. Regs., Part II,
and the Staff Manual respectively. Title pages
will be prepared in manuscript.

Hour, Date, Place. 1915	Summary of Events and Information.	Remarks and references to Appendices.
	well I understand all that you have done – I am sure your Country will be grateful to you. I hope it will make mention of – Remember – your splendid work ~~~~~~ (Rev. J A McN.)	BETHUNE Sheet 1:40000 + Sketch map appendix "H"
13th APRIL "in the trenches"	The enemy landed 40 light shells in PORT ARTHUR between 9 & 10 A.M. & did no damage – one of the same got a direct hit on "B" Coy. Signallers dug out & killed 3 out of 4 smashing the instrument, the 4th man was unhurt – Some more shelling at 1 pm – man badly shot in the neck through a loophole Casualties 8 killed (shell) & 6 wounded (1 from shell) – CH	
14th APRIL –do–	Enemy landed 27 Crumps (6") in + around PORT ARTHUR from 7.15 A.M. – 8 A.M. (1 man slightly wounded) – They gave us plenty of light shells in the afternoon + our own guns were active too – Work continued on trenches, but the supply of Sandbags in inadequate – The advanced posts in front of the right are dangerous places to visit by daylight – There are numbers of partially buried British germans + natives especially on our right + we are trying to bury them – Casualties 1 wounded, 1 sick – CH	

Army Form C. 2118.

WAR DIARY
or
INTELLIGENCE SUMMARY.

(Erase heading not required.)

Volume IX
p 57

Hour, Date, Place.	Summary of Events and Information.	Remarks and references to Appendices.
15th APRIL in the Trenches	A quiet night. During morning companies took advantage of mist by 10.30 a.m. fog. 3 line took shelter about. Dead was brought down by stretcher — CSM WHEELER was killed trying to get in. — Corpl ROSS (without permission) — Men went to Mthby without permission — Ration parties behind the line no fatal T casualty. The 2nd Royal Scots in the firing line have been relieved by the 2nd R Sussex Regt from 7.30 — 11 p.m. Our Headquarters was moved out of POST ARTHUR to point "E" (on sketch) — The O.C. former HQ tried to use 500 yards communication trench. Casualties killed 3 wounded Officer R.St.	Lieut BETTHUNE killed. Woooo effect 15/- Rip "A" to
16 APRIL	A quiet night throughout — R.F.A. afternoon be guns to both fields were very lively — 2nd R.B. CONDUITT was killed by a direct hit on his dugout (he had just been knocked out by standing smoking just before by a bullet Shock — Another man ofhis have at about a day after smoking — 2 men wounded but not struck their own. Casualties — damaging any of them — 1 officer killed, 3 O.R. wounded (1 Steel), 1 sick R.H.	N.B. 2nd Lieut CONDUITT was buried at VEILLE CHAPELLE & military cemetery on 18th R.H.

Army Form C. 2118.

WAR DIARY
or
INTELLIGENCE SUMMARY.
(Erase heading not required.)

15 June IX
P 88

Hour, Date, Place.	Summary of Events and Information.	Remarks and references to Appendices.
17th April. In the Trenches	Battalion relieved 4th Yorkshires. Can be stated that a very quiet night — few men so casualties known up to evening — afternoon had 7 shelling & 2nd Lieut Borland killed & Lt 22 22nd return from hospital & knowing at 12-30 pm. Their Brevial at 1 pm — 13th Cornwallis I wounded	BETHUNE Trench [WOOD] Off.
18th April —do—	Very cold day with rain — Some bodies developed cases over our lives — 1 man wounded in the advanced post at 11am killed during the relief of the 2 companies in the firing line by their [?] 3 days in Casualties 2 killed 1 Off. Off.	
19th April —do—	Very fine morning — 2 Infantries been for the Dwe. Signal company (compulsory) 1 NCO & 2 men leave for their course of Rocket gun Practice at J.H.R. Sometiming 3rd Londons relieve the 2/8 A.J.V.R.C on 18th night — Casualties shrapnel	
20th April —do—	very fine day again — Conference at BDE HQ — 2/tie 3 of the evacuation orders up in Brenning— Casualties 1 wounded 1 to shell	Off. NB Lieut V. BORLAND RAMC joins on 20 Oct. Takes over medical Off. charge of Battalion from Capt F M HEWSON
21st April —do—	Very heavy [?] with all night — Casualties 1 wounded 1 Sick — Half wounded 1 sick 10ff. Company change over again at night —	who takes us sick.

Gulab Singh & Sons, Calcutta—No, 22 Army C.—5-8-14—1,07,000.

Army Form C. 2118.

WAR DIARY
or
INTELLIGENCE SUMMARY.

(Erase heading not required.)

Volume IX
p. 89

Instructions regarding War Diaries and Intelligence Summaries are contained in F. S. Regs., Part II, and the Staff Manual respectively. Title pages will be prepared in manuscript.

Hour, Date, Place. 1915	Summary of Events and Information.	Remarks and references to Appendices.
22nd April In the Trenches	River wounded in advanced post early. If storm day – Port Arthur shelled by heavies [5-9 inch] intended by us by day permanently. It has moved out the trench works to the east and during at night – Port Arthur got it again in the evening – Enemy appeared to be laying fair guns as all fell just in every direction all day, some on trench + some Trenches + he racked closer especially the Rd Lines or Posin 68 in road trench held on normal point. Hostile Trine No. C on fire – Fire of Trm had impossible to identify, some have been very 7.8. In some cases our original places removed. Our men have been very calm; guns credits acting up. The force has very collected. 2 wounded. Look Rd. Casualties. 1 killed 2 wounded.	BETHUNE Sheet 1: 40 000
23rd April – do –	Very cold day. No shelling by enemy at all. Caşn-ates 2 Sick.	Rd.
24th April – do –	Very cold day but wind again. Not much hostile Shelling – Withdraw our Reserve (6) holfd of Bn. on 25th/26th with a 200 CarriKed – Other have been. Long enough & in Trench in and Bun. No thought we who are the officers Who are suffering from extreme cold. Attended of Officers. Rd. Casualties, 1 wounded. 24 sick. Rd.	

Gulab Singh & Sons, Calcutta—No. 22 Army C.—5-8-14—1,07,000.

WAR DIARY or INTELLIGENCE SUMMARY.

Army Form C. 2118.

VOLUME IX p. 90

(Erase heading not required.)

Hour, Date, Place.	Summary of Events and Information.	Remarks and references to Appendices.
25th APRIL In the trenches	Some rain at night. Work on parapets etc limited owing to shortage of sandbags which cannot at present be supplied in sufficient quantities. I had hopes of pushing a few snipers (German) - a very quiet day - Casualties 1 wounded 8 sick. Off.	Ref 6E/44245 [6] 1:40,000
26th APRIL do	First day. Man hit in the advance poor (buttock). Addition of rake reconnoitred to take place ready in all trenches & troops prepared to combat the asphyxiating gases which the enemy are said to employ against us - 6 pm night for duty in the trenches deputed to J.H.Q. Company officers of SUPPORTERS sent out this way to every 12 hours - 5 hrs leave to another machine gun NISQUES - 25 OR 5 hrs leave to fire 175.2 Trenching Company N.Z. at LESTREM (miners). A draft of 20 OR joined the 1 Sikhs. Transport yesterday 25th. Orders received to relieve of 6 on night of 29/1/30th. Casualties 1 wounded 8 sick. Off.	
27th APRIL do	Very lively night with hostile guns making for an heavy & sniped - a fine day with good deal of wind, the sort of level in trenches sinking daily. Some hostile shelling. Companies charge normal again after 3 days in - our machine gun Reg.	

Gulab Singh & Sons, Calcutta—No. 22 Army C.—5-8-14—1,07,000.

Army Form C. 2118.

WAR DIARY
or
INTELLIGENCE SUMMARY.
(Erase heading not required.)

VOLUME IX
p. 91

Instructions regarding War Diaries and Intelligence Summaries are contained in F. S. Regs., Part II, and the Staff Manual respectively. Title pages will be prepared in manuscript.

Hour, Date, Place.	Summary of Events and Information.	Remarks and references to Appendices.
27th April 1915 (cont.)	Relieved by two of 2/3rd Gurkhas of 9th Bhopal Brigade. Enemy fire reported to be low at the top layer of sandbags & to advance from with reduced fire. Never known to this effect to push an urgent demand to sandbags & replace them. 3 men were killed. Casualties 4 wounded 4 sick.	Maj BETHUNE then [I.A.40000] N.R.
28th April "In the Trenches"	Very fine cloudless day — been blossoming strong from the night — was much disturbed by heavy musketry fire — Reinforcements of 2 officers and 2/8 of transport joined the 14th line transport yesterday 27th (Lieut. J.A.C. INGLIS & Lieut. 2nd Lieut. F.H. MAITLAND). Hostile biplane usually comes over 30th line between 9 to 9.30 AM. 3 of Br machine guns go into the line again in the Sikh section (Regt. du Bois) — Sikh reserve trench. Uman Kup his in the reserve trench. Casualties 1 wounded.	N.R.
29th April do	Very fine for day without a cloud in the sky — some heavy De Shelling from aero directions — In fact our fire into trenches at 2.30 again he left our fire about 6.30 AM — then his.	R.F.

Gulab Singh & Sons, Calcutta—No. 22 Army C.—5-8-14—1,07,000.

Army Form C. 2118.

VOLUME IX
p. 92

WAR DIARY
or
INTELLIGENCE SUMMARY.
(Erase heading not required.)

Hour, Date, Place.	Summary of Events and Information.	Remarks and references to Appendices.
9.30 PM 29 APRIL in the trenches 1915	Battalion relieved by 2nd LEICESTERS. Battalion withdrawn by 3.45 AM & clear BDE Trenches to Billets in LACOUTURE BIS (1/40,000). CROIX BARBEE — Carrying out as usual 2 new rounds to bomb totes per coy, periscopes & Verey pistols, exchanging entrenching tools with relief. Relief complete by 11.15 PM — 1 machine gun withdrawn again from southern section of line, leaving 2 in. — 2nd Lieut Pt CUMMINGS joins the Battalion coming from 1/4 London Regt (London Scottish) — Casualties 4 wounded RFP— The following had been awarded the Distinguished Conduct Medal for their actions at NEUVE CHAPPELLE from 10th—14th March — by PM C in C— No. 9198 Sergt D. McRAE 10622 L/Cpl J. MUIR 1084 Pte A. BROWN 328 Pte A. HUNTER 10873 Pte D. McLEOD 10068 Sgt T. PORTER 6875 Pte J. WARD (Bomb gun section) 742 Pte ... (Bomb gun section) The following officer has been awarded the Distinguished Service Order by the C in C Captain H.W.C. WICKS 1st Seaforth Highlanders	1st Seaforth Highlanders (1/40,000) 1st Seaforth Highlanders

Captain H.W.C. WICKS 1st Seaforth Highlanders

WAR DIARY or INTELLIGENCE SUMMARY

VOLUME IX P. 93

Army Form C. 2118.

(Erase heading *not required*.)

Hour, Date, Place.	Summary of Events and Information.	Remarks and references to Appendices.
30th APRIL. LACOUTURE	Mostly cloudless hot day. The strength of the Battalion now is 27 Officers (Lt Colonel, 3 Captains, 4 Lieuts & 18 2nd Lieuts, 1 Quartermaster) and 1239 OR of the latter 116 are employed outside the Bde (rear (Divl employ) 24 ; BDE employ 10 ; Police 16 ; Prison 14 ; Band 23 ; 176th Tunnelling Coy 24 ; I.W.T. wipers 5) leaving strength in BDE AREA as 1 1 2 3 — Casualties incurred by the Battalion in the trenches from night (12th/13th to night of 29/30th held (including 1 officer) ; 34 wounded (8 of whom died of wounds) & 27 sick — Casualties on 30th Nil. Enemy shelled our billets (5 Shells) in the evening	1st/4th BATTALION ORDERS 13 also 600 Lt. R/R.

Appendix "N"

TREATMENT OF BRITISH PRISONERS IN GERMANY.

The following are extracts from the official White Book published by the British Foreign Office (and republished by the *Daily Telegraph*), describing the treatment of British prisoners of war in Germany:—

One of the communications forwarded to the United States Ambassador (Mr. Page) by Sir E. Grey was an account by an American of a visit paid by him to the camp at Döberitz, near Berlin. There were, he wrote, 9,000 "very miserable men" in the camp.

These men are sleeping—200 to 500 to the tent—in horse tents which have been cast off by the German cavalry. These tents are very old. Some of them have been patched and thatched with torn and discoloured bits of canvas. The present camp is only a makeshift, intended to bridge over the time until the winter barracks shall be completed. By this time they may be housed in these permanent huts.

Not one has had a bath since he was first brought to the camp. It isn't likely that one will have a bath while the war lasts. When winter comes, and they move into the permanent wooden barracks which have been provided for them, conditions must grow worse. They will be huddled about stoves then, and in the lack of proper clothing will not keep in the open air.

When a man can stand the torture no longer he is sent to the hospital. There he gets—not a bath—but a thorough daubing with a vermin-killing ointment. His clothes are disinfected. He is sent back to be reinhabited.

Some of them do their best to keep clean. In the centre of the camp is a horse-trough, perhaps 50 ft. long, into which water may be turned from a tap. It stands in the open air. Men who have money and can buy soap at the canteen wash their clothes in this trough. If they are particularly particular they strip themselves and take an ice-water bath. The winter climate of Northern Germany is very severe. We were shivering in our overcoats. But we saw half-a-dozen men naked to the waist, rubbing themselves down with water at the horse-trough.

"Seems to me a great many of the Englishmen are very pale," I said to the guard. "Do they get enough to eat?"

He said they did, but that they didn't like it. The men receive a hunk of war bread, made of rye and potato flour, with a cup of tea in the morning, and the same thing at night, with an occasional chunk of sausage added. The one hot meal of the day is at noon, when each gets a pannikin full of a soupy stew of cabbage and carrots and potatoes, or whatever other vegetable may be handy, plus some meat.

"The Russians like that soup," said the guard. "The Englishmen and Frenchmen do not. They are always complaining."

I saw that stew in the rough. Perhaps I was influenced by my dislike for cabbage and carrots, but it seemed to me it was a mighty unappetising mess. I began to understand why so many of the Tommies looked so pale.

The men sleep in pairs in the tents on straw ticks. When we were there it had been raining for days. The dirt floor of the tents was a mass of mud. The straw gave off a sour and musty odour. But the guards say that the animal heat of so many men sleeping under a single canvas roof keeps them warm. Perhaps that is true. It is very certain that the atmosphere in the tents in which the inhabitants were largely Russian was abominable. The English and French lashed back the tent flaps and ventilated the sleeping places during the day.

Another American observer, in a statement made to the Army Council on Dec. 20, asserted that "British prisoners, and especially the officers, are kept on very short commons. There is a dearth of blankets and clothes amongst the prisoners. Many of them are in possession only of the clothes in which they were originally captured."

MAJOR VANDELEUR'S INDICTMENT.

One of the communications forwarded to Mr. Page was a report by Major C. B. Vandeleur, 1st Cameronians, attached to the Cheshire Regiment, who was taken prisoner on Oct. 13 close to La Bassée, and who subsequently escaped from Crefeld, where he was interned. Describing his journey to Germany Major Vandeleur writes:

At about two p.m. we were all marched off to the railway station, being reviled at and cursed all the way by German officers as well as by German soldiers. One of our officers was spat on by a German officer.

At the station we were driven into closed-in wagons, from which horses had just been removed, fifty-two men being crowded into the one in which the other four officers and myself were. So tight were we packed that there was only room for some of us to sit down on the floor. This floor was covered fully 3 in. deep in fresh manure, and the stench of horse urine was almost asphyxiating. We were boxed up in this foul wagon, with practically no ventilation, for thirty hours, with no food, and no opportunity of attending to purposes of nature.

All along the line we were cursed by officers and soldiers alike at the various stations, and at Mons Bergen I was pulled out in front of the wagon by the order of the officer in charge of the station, and, after cursing me in filthy language for some ten minutes, he ordered one of his soldiers to kick me back into the wagon, which he did, sending me sprawling into the filthy mess at the bottom of the wagon. I should like to mention here that I am thoroughly conversant with German, and understood everything that was said. Only at one station on the road was any attempt made on the part of German officers to interfere, and stop their men from cursing us.

Up to this time I had managed to retain my overcoat, but it was now forcibly taken from me by an officer at a few stations further on. On reaching the German-Belgian frontier, the French prisoners were given some potato soup. The people in charge of it told us that none was for us, but that if any was left over after the French had been fed we should get what remained. This is in accordance with the general treatment of British prisoners by the Germans, who always endeavour to attend to our necessities last, and to put us to as much inconvenience and ill-treatment as possible. We subsequently got a little soup and a few slices of bread amongst twenty-five British prisoners in the same wagon with me.

On Oct. 18, early, we arrived at Cologne, and the four officers and myself were removed from the wagon, and after some delay, sent on to Crefeld.

It is difficult to indicate or give a proper idea of the indescribably wretched condition in which we were in after being starved and confined in the manner stated for three days and three nights. What with the filth of the interior, the number of people confined in it, and the absence of ventilation, it seemed to recall something of what one has read of the Black Hole of Calcutta.

I found out that the wagon in front of us was full up with English soldiers. This particular wagon had no ventilation slit of any sort or description, and men were crowded into this even worse than they were in the wagon in which I was. They banged away continually on the wooden sides of the van, and finally, as I supposed the Germans thought that they might be suffocated, a carpenter was got, who cut a small round hole in one of the sides.

I am strongly of opinion myself that this brutal treatment of British officers and men on their way to a place of internment is deliberately arranged for by superior authority with the object of making us as miserable and despicable objects as possible. The French officers were treated quite differently.

I also wish to state that———, who arrived at Crefeld about December, told me that all the Irishmen at his camp were collected together shortly before he left, and were harangued by the commandant, who stated that the Emperor was aware of the down-trodden state of Ireland, and now wished that the Irishmen should be placed in a separate camp, where they would be better fed and treated differently from the Englishmen. He further stated that subsequently they went in a body to the commandant, and said they did not wish to have any different treatment from their compatriots.

To his account of the barbarities to which British soldiers are subjected, Major Vandeleur adds that the men are used solely for all menial duties and dirty work connected with the camps, such as cleaning out latrines and such-like; also every other unpleasant fatigue duty.

In connection with this the French orderlies at Crefeld stated to me that they were very sorry indeed to see the British soldier treated in such an ignoble and disgraceful manner, being, in fact, more like slaves, the idea being to create ill-feeling between the French and British soldiers by this means.

In his covering letter to Mr. Page, Sir E. Grey calls attention to the fact that when Major Vandeleur was a prisoner, the German authorities refused to allow him to communicate to the American Ambassador in Berlin a list of the British prisoners.

He had written soon after his internment to the Prisoners' Help Society at Berlin, and received a letter in reply from Mr. Gerard on Nov. 3, in which he was asked to furnish a complete roll of the British prisoners. He replied on Nov. 5 enclosing the roll, and thanking the Ambassador for his interest. On Dec. 6 this letter was returned to Major Vandeleur by the commandant, who stated that he had orders to prevent its being delivered.

A further letter from Mr. Gerard was handed to Major Vandeleur a few days after this, which had been addressed by Mr. Gerard to the commandant of the camp, again asking for a complete list of prisoners. Major Vandeleur was asked by the commandant to prepare the list, which he at once did, but the list was handed back to him a few days later, with the statement that it would not be sent. Your Excellency, who has, I believe, received several communications from Germans interned in Great Britain, will, I am sure, properly appreciate this incident.

A Russian Medical Officer, who was detained at Strolsünd, made the following statement, forwarded by the British Minister at Petrograd, on December 9th, 1914:—

The British officers are not as well treated as the Russian officers. They are classed among the less educated Russians, who speak no language other than Russian, so that they cannot talk. The Russians are allowed to buy books, but the British officers are not allowed to do so. The German Lieutenant in charge is openly insulting and hostile towards the British prisoners. One British officer complained of his conduct, and expressed the opinion that the German officer was acting on his own feelings, and that the German authorities were not aware of his conduct towards the British officers; but the doctor did not entirely share that view.

With regard to the food, the doctor said it was very bad both in quality and quantity. The coffee was bad and made with dirty water. The officers were given three pieces of bread a day made with potato meal. Lunch consisted mostly of potatoes. In the evening they received bread and a small slice of sausage. The cost of the above was 1.50 marks. A lieutenant was allowed 60 marks a month, but from this was deducted 45 marks for the above food.

On Dec. 26 Sir E. Grey forwarded to Mr. Page various communications with regard to the bad treatment of British prisoners, and stated that information on the subject had reached the Government from a variety of sources.

A French priest, who has returned to Rome from Minden, where a number of British prisoners of war were confined, is reported to have given an account of the cruelties practised upon the British prisoners by their guards. While "the French prisoners were very well treated and the Russians not so badly," the British were singled out for ill-treatment. According to the French priest "the German soldiers kick the British prisoners in the stomach, and break their guns over their backs; they force them to sleep in marshy places, so that many are now consumptive. The British are almost starved, and such have been their tortures that thirty of them asked to be shot."

After quoting further testimony of similar character Sir E. Grey added:

Speaking generally, the reports of ill-treatment to which I have the honour to draw your Excellency's attention, corroborated as they are from so many independent sources, show, as I am sure your Excellency will agree, that the German authorities are in many cases entirely neglecting the provisions of the articles dealing with the treatment of prisoners of war. His Majesty's Government feel bound, therefore, to protest in the strongest manner against the inhuman treatment to which it is unfortunately evident that many of the British prisoners of war in Germany are being subjected, and I shall be grateful if your Excellency will cause this protest to reach the German Government with as little delay as possible.

His Majesty's Government are all the more concerned by the reports which have reached them of the manner in which British prisoners of war in Germany have been singled out for ill-treatment, in that they have, on their part, interpreted the above-mentioned provisions of The Hague Convention in a liberal spirit, and have, as your Excellency is aware, communicated to the German Government a full statement of the treatment shown to German prisoners of war in the United Kingdom.

. . . . Owing to the terrible distress evidently prevailing among our soldiers who are prisoners, I venture to express the earnest hope that the United States Government will be willing at the earliest possible moment to cause a sum of money to be expended on providing money, clothing, extra food, and other things which seem necessary to raise the present standard of the prisoners to one of decent human existence.

On Dec., 30, Sir G. Buchanan forwarded from Petrograd the statement of a second Russian medical officer, who had been detained at Dänholm. It was to the effect that English private soldiers there were subjected to a régime of extreme harshness.

A graphic account of the conditions prevailing among the civilian prisoners at the Ruhleben camp, supplied apparently by an inmate, was sent to Mr. Page by the Foreign Office on Jan. 19. The following is an extract:

There is a canteen, where at exorbitant prices such luxuries as sugar, white bread, condensed milk, butter, chocolate, cigars, &c., can be bought by those who can afford it. Those who cannot afford to buy these luxuries are in a very bad plight. They are not actually dying of starvation, but they can only just keep themselves alive and no more. About eight at night we begin to go to "bed" as best we can, and at nine there must be dead silence. All this, as related here, does not sound so very terrible, but in practice, for those who have to go through it, it is "hell."

Six men abreast in a space of about 10ft 6in means that they are packed like sardines in a box, and no one can move. They are supplied with only one poor blanket each, and those who have none of their own are in a sad plight. If one man in the line attempts to turn he disturbs all the others. Young men in the full vigour of life may be able to stand it, but for elderly men it simply means, if not immediate death, then certainly a shortened life and broken health for the rest of their days. The coughing which starts shortly after they have all turned in, and which is apparently caused less by colds than by foul air and the dust, is awful to hear.

On Feb., 20, Sir E. Grey transmitted to Mr. Page information showing that twenty-three British officers confined at Burg, near Magdeburg, were given very little food, and were all herded together without light or warmth, their condition being such that they were apparently being gradually starved to death.

Similarly, prisoners at Ulm were reported, on March 13, as receiving very little food, and to be prematurely aged as the result of their treatment.

EXTRACT FROM DIARY OF GERMAN OFFICER.

The following extract, dated 19th December, 1914, from the dairy of an Officer of the 13th German Regiment, 13th Division, VII. Corps, is published in the Official Bulletin of the V. French Army:—

"The sight of the trenches, and the fury—not to say the bestiality—of our men in beating to death the wounded English affected me so much that for the rest of the day I was fit for nothing."

I.A.C.
17-4-15.

Appendix "O"

No B.M.9.   Head Quarters Dehra Dun Brigade.
                                    9th April 1915.

From.
    The Brigade Major.
        Dehra Dun Brigade.

To.
    The Officer Commanding
        1st Seaforth Highlanders.
        4th Seaforth Highlanders.
        6th Jat Light Infantry
        9th Gurkha Rifles.
        2nd Gurkha Rifles.

1.   In accordance with Meerut Divisional Operation Orders, the Dehra Dun Brigade is to take over the front now held by the 2nd Infantry Brigade.

2.   The front extends from the LA BASSEE-ESTAIRES Road exclusive to the point where the right of the Brigade rested during the last tour of duty in the trenches.

3.   Four Battalions will be in the line and one in Reserve.

4.   The reliefs are to take place during the Nights 11th/12th and 12th/13th April - two Battalions moving in on each night. The Reserve Battalion moving on second date.

5.   The probable distribution will be :- Right to Left:-
1st Seaforths - 2nd Gurkhas - 4th Seaforths - 9th Gurkhas, with 6th Jats in reserve. The two left Battalions will probably move in first.

6.   Operation Orders will issue tomorrow, (10th April).

7.   Battalions are not likely to move from present billets before 3.p.m. on date they take over post in line or Reserve.

                                        n   Major.
                        Brigade Major Dehra Dun Brigade.

Head Quarters Depot and Brigade.
No. B.M.2.

94/173 1915.

From:
The Seaforths

To:
The Officer Commanding
1st Seaforth Highlanders.
2nd Seaforth Highlanders.
4th Seaforth Highlanders.
5th Seaforth Highlanders.
6th Seaforth Highlanders.
and Depot Seaforths.

Depot and Brigade.

1. In accordance with Regular Battalions Operation Orders, the Depot and Brigade is to be moved from Wick by the L.N.W.R. PASSENGER-CARRIAGE ROAD and Infantry Brigade.

2. The Train Start from the L.N.W.R. PASSENGER-CARRIAGE ROAD exchange to the Depot, where the start of the Brigade moves during the last four of duty in the present.

3. Four Battalions will be in one line and one in reserve.

4. The Railway one to take place during the night 11th/12th and the next one on the same night.

5. The Brigade distribution will be:- Right to left:- 1st Seaforths - 2nd Seaforths - 4th Seaforths - and Curkhas, with the 5th in reserve. The two last Battalions will probably arrive in time in reserve.

Move in first.

6. Operation Orders will issue tomorrow, (10th April).

7. Battalions are not likely to move from present billets before 9 a.m. on late trek lake over road in line of reserve.

Depot and Brigade Major Seaforths.
Major.

No B.M.5.   Appendix "P"   Head Quarters Dehra Dun Brigade.
                                          10th April 1915

From.
    The Brigade Major.
    Dehra Dun Brigade.

With reference to my No B.M. 9 dated 9th April 1915
1. The Officers Commanding and Company Commanders of the 4th Seaforths and 9th Gurkhas will report to Head Quarters 2nd Infantry Brigade, RICHEBOURG ST VAAST (House where Dehra Dun Bde Head Quarters were) at 10 a.m. tomorrow the 11th April 1915, where they will receive instructions and be shown round the front to be taken over.
2. The 9th Gurkhas will be on the left. Each Battalion will have two Companies in front line and support and two in Local Reserve.
3. As the above front is held by one Battalion and a Company of the 2nd Brigade at present, it may be necessary for both the 9th Gurkha and 4th Seaforth Head Quarters to be in the same locality until some more satisfactory arrangement can be made, i.e. a second Battalion Head Quarters is found.
4. The 9th Gurkhas will march via CROIX MARMUSE - ZELOBES - VIEILLE CHAPELLE - BOUT DEVILLE and PONT DU HEM so as to arrive at Road junction M.27.d. at 9-15.p.m. 11th April, where the Battalion will be met by guides from the Unit to be relieved.
5. The 4th Seaforths will march via same route so as to arrive at M.27.d. at 9-45 p.m. 11th April.
6. It is suggested that there should be an interval of three minutes between Companies after passing PONT DU HEM.
7. 1st Line Transport of 4th Seaforths and 9th Gurkhas will billet for night 11th/12th at les 8 Maisons, R.23.d. Orders for billets on following nights will be issued later by the Staff Capt.
8. Commanding Officers and Company Commanders of the 2nd Gurkhas and 1st Seaforths will report to Head Quarters 2nd Brigade RICHEBOURG ST VAAST at 10 a.m. on 12th April where they will receive instructions and be shown round the front to be taken over.
9. Further orders as to march of 2nd Gurkhas, 1st Seaforths and

and 6th Jats and billets for first line transport will issue later.

10. Commanding Officers will use their own discretion as to whether Officers will return to present billets or await arrival of Battalions at the rendezvous after reconnoitring front. (vide paragraphs 1 and 8).

                                            Captain for.
          Brigade Major Dehra Dun Brigade.

To.

    The Officer Commanding

        1st Seaforth Highlanders.
        4th Seaforth Highlanders.
        6th Jat Light Infantry
        9th Gurkha Rifles.
        2nd Gurkha Rifles.

later issue will be first line-firstserve and the date and
time printing Officers will use their own discretion as to
issuing flags to shifts present billets or swap around. (Also
of battalions at the Longarone Steel Decompiling Plant.)

The Officer Concerning

Supreme Highjack 1st,
Acrophobia Highjackers,
The Bearlooby Highjackers,
The Bearlooby Highjack the
Any supreme Niters,
And Supremo Niters.

to.

Bureau Major Henry Tom Supreme.
Galbraith Tor.

(42)

/ A Seaforth

(5 par 1 sinistralad

Appendix "R"

Head Quarters Dehra Dun Brigade.

16th April 1915

Copy of a letter from the General Staff Meerut Division To the General Officer Commanding Dehra Dun Brigade. No G-377/38. dated the 16th April 1915.

.....

It appears that the orders issued not long ago that the troops in the first line were to keep the enemy engaged both by day and night by sniping and the use of rifle grenades and mortar bombs have been allowed to fall into abeyance. The G.O.C. desires Brigade Commanders to have this order in remembrance constantly and to notice if there is a falling off in activity in the front trenches. If the enemy find they can harass us with impunity they will regain morals which they lost considerably as a result of the recent action of NEUVE CHAPELLE.

No B.M.17.

From.
    The Brigade Major Dehra Dun Brigade.

To.
    The Officer Commanding

        1st Seaforth Highlanders.
        4th Seaforth Highlanders.
        6th Jat Light Infantry
        9th Gurkha Rifles.
        2nd Gurkha Rifles.

Forwarded for information and guidance.

Major.
Brigade Major Dehra Dun Bde.

Head Quarters Benes and Brigade.
14th April 1915

Copy of a letter from the General Staff, Meerut Division No G-745/29.

To the General Officer Commanding Bareilly Brigade.

Dated the 14th April 1915.

OF HEAVY CASUALTIES.

.....

It appears that the officers trained for this war have not the necessary knowledge of map reading and forget that the floors in the first line were to keep the crews supplied both by men and that by putting on blankets will rest of men and reinforcements have been drawn to fill the gaps. The G.O.C. desires that [illegible] to have this order in remembrance considering duty to notice if there is absence. In the event of casualties to the front, billets a return of the actual strength of the front line is at once made this immediately after each action. This

[signature: H. Stafalis]

To: The Officer Commanding,
    1st Seaforth Highlanders,
    4th Seaforth Highlanders,
    69th Punjab Infantry,
    58th Wilde's Rifles,
    2nd Rifles Brigade.

Forwarded for information and guidance.

[signature]

Brigade Major Bareilly Brigade.

War Diaries with Appendices

1st Seaforth Highlanders

From 1st To 31st May 1915

7.V.

WAR DIARY
With appendices.

1st Seaforth Highlanders.

From 1st May 1915 To 31st May 1915

WAR DIARY
or
INTELLIGENCE SUMMARY.
(Erase heading not required.)

Army Form C. 2118.

VOLUME I
94

Instructions regarding War Diaries and Intelligence Summaries are contained in F. S. Regs., Part II, and the Staff Manual respectively. Title pages will be prepared in manuscript.

Hour, Date, Place. 1915	Summary of Events and Information.	Remarks and references to Appendices.
4.15 AM 1st MAY LACOUTURE 5.10 AM	Enemy started shelling our front line. Received message from Bde HQ to advance. Road junction in Square R.35.A.4/2 – at the same time enemy shells began falling in billets. The companies were companies but scattered into their platoons then dog led on getting the order to fall in. It took some time to form them out as they had to look for their equipment (in doing so 4 Sepoys were killed & 3 wounded in one "C" Company's billets.) Several forces was damaged including 10 C.B.s to the inhabitants – 3 gunners wounded on collecting in alarm post whilst parading to form up attacking –	10/1 BETHUNE SHEET 1. 40,000
6.30 PM —do— —do—	Received orders to return to billets as enemy has not tried attacking – A very fine day. – Casualties 4 killed 30 wounded – No shelling in billets – Divine Service held – Casualties 2 sick –	"A" Companies "Q" & "R" "Q" & "R" attached for Batt. infantry
2nd May —do—	Several companies slept in the open for greater security both on night of 30/1 & 1/2 & 2/3. As it is now much warmer –	Batt. infantry
11 AM 3rd MAY —do—	The Lt Col Lt Gen ANDERSON inspected 15 Capt NCOs lots of reinforcements viz. 3 officers = 236 O.R.	Batt

Gulab Singh & Sons, Calcutta—No. 22 Army C.—5-8-14—1,07,000.

WAR DIARY or INTELLIGENCE SUMMARY.

Army Form C. 2118.

VOLUME X
P. 95

(Erase heading not required.)

Hour, Date, Place. 1915	Summary of Events and Information.	Remarks and references to Appendices.
3rd MAY LACOUTURE	1 NCO & 2 men despatched to join the Carrier Pigeon Section of Divl. Signal Company — Casualties 3 sick —	Ref. BETHUNE Sheet 1/40000 Ptt.
4th MAY —do—	Thunderstorm in the evening — The Trot Boots again allotted to the battalion at VIEILLE CHAPELLE for the first time since December. These are very necessary although it is 2½ hours business for a man to get into them in canvas etc. They do not weigh 5 lbs more than the change, as they used 6 lbs of the hot baths. But newly soaked then underground — "B" Company supplied a digging party behind the front line in the RUE DU BOIS from 7 pm to 6.30 am. Lost 1 man killed — Casualties 1 killed 2 sick	
5th MAY —do—	"A" Company with 2 machine guns relieve the 2nd Gurkhas in the trenches in the immediate neighbourhood of LA-V ISNEE road. Being first been relieving K1 2A-V road, and being billets at 7 P.M. They at LT Col. ROCHE & 4 JATS with BAISEE road. Command of 2 Lt Col. ROCHE & 4 JATS with LEICESTERS of MARSHAL B.E. on them opposed 4 R. Seyforth on then rights—	

Gulab Singh & Sons, Calcutta — No. 22 Army C. — 5-8-14 — 1,07,000.

Army Form C. 2118.

WAR DIARY
or
INTELLIGENCE SUMMARY.

VOLUME X
P. 96

(Erase heading not required.)

Hour, Date, Place.	Summary of Events and Information.	Remarks and references to Appendices.
6th MAY /1915	Enemy shelled our billets at 12 noon, 4 p.m. and 6 p.m.; 8 men wounded, of whom 2 died of wounds. A Coy. in the trenches, lost 4 wounded & 1 died of wounds. Fine day. Casualties: 3 died of wounds, 4 wounded, 4 sick.	HQ/Hd BETHUNE [Sheet 1. 5,000]
7th MAY	Fine & quiet day. Casualties (A Coy.): 2 wounded (G.S.J) 3 sick	
8th MAY	Very fine day. Btn., less A Coy., left billets at 7 p.m. to take up its position in the trenches astride the LA BASSÉE – ESTAIRES road S. of Port Arthur, preparatory to an attack at dawn on the enemy's lines. "B" Coy. was east of the road for some 150 yards, "C" occupied the reclaimed fire trench for a similar distance; "A" was in the Pioneer trench and "D" in half the Grescent trench.	[Appendix "S" attached for information]

Gulab Singh & Sons, Calcutta—No. 22 Army C.—5-8-14—1,07,000.

Army Form C. 2118.

VOLUME X

97

WAR DIARY
or
INTELLIGENCE SUMMARY.

Hour, Date, Place.	Summary of Events and Information.	Remarks and references to Appendices.
9th MAY		Before 9 am light
5 A.M.	The men had hot tea & some food in early morning. Before down A Coy. packed greatcoats by platoons & left a man in charge. The artillery bombardment began at 5 A.M. and lasted 40 mins. in all; an enemy maxim fired intermittently during the bombardment and there was even	
5.25 A.M.	considerable rifle fire. At 5.25 A.M. B & C Coys. went over the parapet and lined out, being fired on by maxims & rifles during the process; at the same time the guns fired high explosive at the German parapet. At	
5.40 A.M.	5.40 A.M. the guns lengthened range, but it was noticed that but few heavy shells had touched the parapet; the shelling had been short & uncomfortably near our men, some shells falling amongst them, so that they were unable to creep up appreciably nearer the enemys' line. On attempting to advance as ordered at 5.40 A.M. the enemy's line was well manned and heavy maxim and rifle fire stopped the attempt.	

Army Form C. 2118.

Volume X 98

WAR DIARY
or
INTELLIGENCE SUMMARY

(Erase heading not required.)

Hour, Date, Place	Summary of Events and Information	Remarks and references to Appendices
9th MAY (Cont.)	During a fresh bombardment 2 platoons of "D" and "A" Coys. respectively went over the parapet and supports "B" and "C". A second attempt to advance failed owing to heavy maxim & rifle fire, although a little more ground was gained. After further bombardment and reinforcement by the remaining two platoons of "D" and "A" Coys., a third attempt to advance was made which was checked after a few yards for a similar reason. At 9 a.m., seeing the task was not feasible and that the men had lost most of their Officers, and were continually being sniped by maxims & rifles & were under the heavy artillery fire of both combatants; the Commanding Officer ordered all who were able to do so to get back when they saw a reasonable chance. A good few succeeded in doing so, but many had to lie out, some getting back at 3.40 p.m., when the Bareilly Brigade attacked, and the remainder came in under cover of darkness. Both the front and support trenches were under a heavy shrapnel and high explosive fire all day.	[Ref. BETHUNE sheet 1/40,000]
9 A.M.		

Army Form 2118.

Volume X 99

WAR DIARY
or
INTELLIGENCE SUMMARY

(Erase heading not required.)

Instructions regarding War Diaries and Intelligence Summaries are contained in F. S. Regs., Part II. and the Staff Manual respectively. Title pages will be prepared in manuscript.

Hour, Date, Place	Summary of Events and Information	Remarks and references to Appendices
9th MAY Cont: 2 P.M. 8 P.M.	At 2 p.m. the 41st DOGRAS arrived to relieve us and the battalion was taken out of the trenches to bivouac near CROIX BARBÉE and later on in the evening to billets at RIEZ BAILLEUL, which we reached at 8 p.m. Our losses were: 7 officers killed 10 wounded Other ranks 131 killed 346 wounded ---- missing Officers killed Capt. D. H. DAVIDSON Capt. A. B. BAILLIE HAMILTON Lt. J. A. G. INGLIS (4th H.L.I.) 2/Lt. J. HEMMINGWAY 2/Lt. A. SHACKLEFORD 2/Lt. D.A.H. McDOUGALL 2/Lt. D. MARVIN Officers wounded Lt. R.H. ALLANBY Capt. & Adjt. R. HORN Lt. G.E. WAKEFIELD (3rd Scots Fusiliers) Lt. A. IRVINE 2/Lt. I.G. BARCLAY (shock) 2/Lt. J.A.SpL.TREDENNICK 2/Lt. P.H. CUMMINGS 2/Lt. I.M. MATHESON 2/Lt. D. LINDSAY 2/Lt. F.H. MAITLAND	[Ref. BETHUNE Sheet 15 A.0000]

WAR DIARY
or
INTELLIGENCE SUMMARY

(Erase heading not required.)

Army Form C. 2118.

Volume X

Hour, Date, Place	Summary of Events and Information	Remarks and references to Appendices
10th MAY	Hunter parade for all Companies at 11 A.M., and Companies were reorganized as much as possible, temporary Platoon Commanders etc. appointed. Strength of battalion (including transport etc.) 10 officers 601 other ranks Very fine day. Orchestra & a small party returned to them his & buried some of our men too.	[Ref. BETHUNE sheet R.10000]
11th MAY	Marched at 2 p.m. to billets in area LACOUTURE – VIEILLE CHAPELLE (along road running from R 28 d 6/8 – R 35 a 5/2). Very crowded & most men in bivouac. Fine & hot.	
12th MAY	Very hot. Took over 2 small farms from 1/4th SEAFORTHS and one from 107th PIONEERS. Bn. is in Corps reserve at 1 hr.s notice.	
13th MAY	Very wet. Warned to be ready to move at 20 mins notice after 11.30 pm, but order cancelled later.	
14th MAY	Cleared up in afternoon. Coys. paraded in mornings at Physical drill & route marching. A small draft of 28 men arrived at 5 pm.	

Army Form C. 2118.

Volume X
101

WAR DIARY
or
INTELLIGENCE SUMMARY

(Erase heading not required.)

Instructions regarding War Diaries and Intelligence Summaries are contained in F. S. Regs., Part II. and the Staff Manual respectively. Title pages will be prepared in manuscript.

Hour, Date, Place	Summary of Events and Information	Remarks and references to Appendices
15th MAY	Showery weather. Bn. warned to be in constant readiness from 5 A.M. to-morrow (16th inst.). Heavy bombardment all night; a night attack was launched at 11.30 p.m. by 2nd Division and GARHWAL BDE.	[Ref. BETHUNE sheet 11.0000]
16th MAY	Reveille 4.30 A.M. and Bn. stood to arms at 5 A.M. When all had been arranged the for an instant move the men fell out and cooked breakfasts. We remained in this state all day, listening to the bombardment and without news, except that the INDIAN CORPS attack had failed while the others had succeeded. Order received at 6 p.m. to return to normal state of readiness, but the men slept with boots on. Casualty — 1 sick.	
17th MAY	Heavy firing all night. Again ordered to be in constant readiness from 11 a.m.; this order once more cancelled at 8.30 p.m. No definite news. Rained in evening and continued all night. Sent off 6 unfits to act as orderlies at G.H.Q. Casualties — 3 sick.	

Army Form C. 2118.

Volume X 102

WAR DIARY
or
INTELLIGENCE SUMMARY.
(Erase heading not required.)

Instructions regarding War Diaries and Intelligence Summaries are contained in F.S. Regs., Part II. and the Staff Manual respectively. Title pages will be prepared in manuscript.

Hour, Date, Place	Summary of Events and Information	Remarks and references to Appendices
18th MAY	Dull and rainy day. At 6 P.M. we were ordered to get ready to move, and the baggage wagons were called up. At 7 P.M. Capt. THOMSON, Lt. BRODIE, Lt CALL, 2Lt BUCHANAN and 2Lt KILGOUR (3rd A & S Highrs) arrived. The Btn. marched at	[Ref. BETHUNE sheet 1:40000]
9 P.M.	9 P.M. to the gridiron reserve trenches near CROIX BARBÉE at M 32 b 4/7. The guns were firing most of the night. Casualties — 4 sick.	
19th MAY	Col. RITCHIE came to see the Btn. at 9 A.M. and made the men a short speech before leaving to take our Command of the 26th Brigade, 9th Division. Capt. THOMSON takes over command of the Btn. The men had a short run, but otherwise did nothing. Wet day. One shell burst fairly near us but Casualty — 1 wounded.	
20th MAY	Finer weather. Men were not allowed to move about. At 10 P.M. a party of 240 men carried R.E. material down to the RUE DU BOIS. Casualties — 1 wounded, 2 sick.	

Army Form C. 2118.

Volume X
105

WAR DIARY
or
INTELLIGENCE SUMMARY.
(Erase heading not required.)

Instructions regarding War Diaries and Intelligence Summaries are contained in F. S. Regs., Part II. and the Staff Manual respectively. Title pages will be prepared in manuscript.

Hour, Date, Place	Summary of Events and Information	Remarks and references to Appendices
21st MAY	Rainy morning, but cleared up. Ordered to return to billets recently vacated near VIEILLE CHAPELLE; the companies marched back at short intervals commencing at 3 P.M. Returned to 1 hours notice. Lt. DAVIDSON and 2/Lt MALTBY (3rd R. Scots) joined.	[Ref. BETHUNE sheet 1:40,000]
3 P.M.		
22nd MAY	Fine & hot. Men spent morning cleaning up and bathing. A party of 40 men, 2 full ranks, the Bttn. SERGT-MAJOR, & 2/Lt. WILSON handed under Lt. RIGBY and marched to	
5 P.M.	Hd. Qrs. 152nd Brigade, Highland Division at 5 P.M. They are attached to the Brigade to help and explain matters, as the Highland Division have never been in the trenches before. A draft of 5 officers	
8 P.M.	and 86 other ranks arrived at 8 P.M.; the officers being:—	
	Lt. R.M. ROSS	
	Lt. R.G. MAXWELL	
	2/Lt. J. MACLEOD	
	2/Lt. G. WILKINSON-BROWN (3rd Royal Scots)	(3rd Royal Scots Fusiliers)
	2/Lt. J.S.D. DIXON (4th A & S Highrs)	

WAR DIARY
or
INTELLIGENCE SUMMARY.
(Erase heading not required.)

Army Form C. 2118.

Volume X

Hour, Date, Place	Summary of Events and Information	Remarks and references to Appendices
MAY 23rd	Fine & hot. Presbyterian Church parade in fields at 10 A.M.s G 64 E at 10.15 A.M. at Hd. Qrs. 7th Seaforths.	[Rest BETHUNE Sheet]
2.30 P.M.	Moved off by platoons at 2.30 P.M. to relieve 15th SIKHS in reserve trenches near WINDY CORNER (Square S.3. c ½). Last party delayed ½ an hour owing to shelling. Relief completed.	
5.30 P.M.	Our four machine guns went up into the front line trenches occupied by 4/7TH SEAFORTHS. Companies worked at night improving Breastwork. Very hot day. Casualties — 3 sick. 2/Lt. S. R. ROBERTSON 3rd Royal Scots joined	
MAY 24th	Showed all day in hot sun. A few shells fell near us but no damage done. Lt. ROSS and Lt. BUCHANAN left in coming for 24 hrs. instruction in trenches and were attached to 1st Bn. Heavy firing and bombing at full midnight but nothing came of it. Casualty — 1 2/Lt. G. WILKINSON-BROWN sick (3rd Royal Scots)	

Army Form C. 2118.

Volume X 105

WAR DIARY
or
INTELLIGENCE SUMMARY.
(Erase heading not required.)

Instructions regarding War Diaries and Intelligence Summaries are contained in F. S. Regs., Part II. and the Staff Manual respectively. Title pages will be prepared in manuscript.

Hour, Date, Place	Summary of Events and Information	Remarks and references to Appendices
MAY 25th	Hot day again. Some bomber shells fell very near in morning. Lt. GULL and 2nd Lt. KILGOUR attached to 4th SEAFORTHS for 24 hrs. instruction in trenches. Casualties: 7 wounded, 4 sick.	[Ref: BETHUNE Sheet 1:40000]
MAY 26th	O.C. Companies visited trenches to be taken over from 1/4th SEAFORTHS. Relief commenced 8.45 P.M. and completed 10.45 P.M. D Coy. occupied firing line, C and A in support and B in local reserve. Bn. Hd. Qrs. at house S.9.a.9.1. 2nd GURKHAS occupied line on our right and GARHWAL BDE on our left. Trenches horribly smelly and a great deal of improvement required. Numerous bodies were buried and front line parapet & parados strengthened. Commanding Officer went round line at night. Lt. RIGBY and party rejoined from 152nd Brigade. 2Lt MAITLAND rejoined from hospital. Casualties - nil 2 men rejoined from piece hospital	[Appendix T attached for information] yes
10.45 P.M.		yes

Army Form C. 2118.

Volume X 106

WAR DIARY
or
INTELLIGENCE SUMMARY.
(Erase heading not required.)

Instructions regarding War Diaries and Intelligence Summaries are contained in F.S. Regs., Part II. and the Staff Manual respectively. Title pages will be prepared in manuscript.

Hour, Date, Place	Summary of Events and Information	Remarks and references to Appendices
MAY 27th	Our support trench was fairly heavily shelled but very little damage done. Strong wind and much cooler, which greatly spoiled the shell. Parapets straightened and work started on a new communication trench to Contention at LINDER TRACK. 2/Lt. G.E. MACKLIN (3rd Royal Irish) joined. Casualties — 1 wounded.	[Ref: BETHUNE sheet 1:40000]
MAY 28th	Still windy and cool. Front line and supports again shelled. One of our own 18 pr. shells hit H.Q. Sgt. and wounded one man.	
8.30 P.M.	B Coy. relieved D Coy. in front line at 8.30 P.M.P.D. returning to reserve. Commanding Officer visited line in evening. Worked all night & practically no trench mortar [illegible] (ours or theirs). Casualties — 6 wounded.	
MAY 29th	Had a hot day. Usual amount of shelling. Commanding Officer went up to line as much work on trench etc. continued. Casualties — 1 wounded, 1 sick.	

Forms/C. 2118/10

Army Form C. 2118.

Volume X 107

WAR DIARY
or
INTELLIGENCE SUMMARY.
(Erase heading not required.)

Instructions regarding War Diaries and Intelligence Summaries are contained in F. S. Regs., Part II. and the Staff Manual respectively. Title pages will be prepared in manuscript.

Hour, Date, Place	Summary of Events and Information	Remarks and references to Appendices
MAY 30th	All day. At 8.30 P.M. C Coy. changed from support trench to reserve; A Coy. relieved B in firing line and B & D held support line. Owing to a change in the frontage to be held by MEERUT DIVN. we are to be relieved to-morrow. Work on trenches and communication trench almost completed.	[R.H.Q. BETHUNE. Strength 11.0000]
12.15 A.M.	Completely cut owing to own Artillery firing at 12.15 A.M. and the Germans replying. We had 2 seas. Casualty — 1 wounded	[To]
MAY 31st	Heavy shelling by both sides about 1 A.M. Officers of the CONNAUGHT RANGERS visited line in morning with a view to taking over. Heavy shelling all morning. Relief started 9.30 P.M. and on completion Battalion marched to Gullets & Bivouacs in Northern Road between LACOUTURE and RICHEBOURG. Casualties — 1 killed (shell) 4 wounded, 1 sick	[Appendix "X" attached for information] [To]

Strength of Battalion:—
24 Officers (including Quarter Master)
561 Other Ranks (approximate numbers)
654 " " (Brigade Orders) |

Operation Order No 37.
by
Brigadier General L W Jacob
Commanding Dehra Dun Brigade
X.12.a.9/8 May 5th 1915.

Information 1. The Dehra Dun Brigade is to be relieved by the Garhwal Bde on May the 7th 1915.

Orders to troops 2. (a) Units will move in accordance with attached Table.

(b) Details of reliefs in trenches to be arranged between Commanding Officers concerned.

(c) The Brigade Machine Gun Officer, Garhwal Brigade, will arrange for relief of Machine guns with the Officers Commanding the two Subsections. On relief the detachment No 5 Motor Machine Gun Battery will rejoin its own Unit.

Routes 3. As 1st Seaforths and 6th Jats have to use the same route for part of their respective marches - special precautions must be taken to avoid congestion and small parties (e.g Platoons) should be got on the move as soon as relieved.

Bomb guns 4. Bomb gun Section will move to billetting area 4th Seaforths under arrangements to be made by O.C 4th Seaforths and Bde Bomb gun Officer.

Reports 5. Report Chateau LES LOBES after all reliefs are completed - until then to farm X.12.a.9/8.

Issued at 1.30 pm

H A Walker Major
Bde Major Dehra Dun Bde

Copy 1 and 2 Retained   Copy 9 to 6th Jats
" 3 to Meerut Div   " 10 to 9th Gurkhas
" 4 to Garhwal Bde   " 11 to 2nd Gurkhas
" 5 to Bareilly Bde   " 12 to 13th Bde RFA
" 6. to Sirhind Bde
" 7 to 1st Seaforths
" 8 to 4th Seaforths

Relief May 7th 1915 "Dehra Dun and Garhwal Bdes"

Unit	Centres and be relieved by	From	To	Route	Remarks
4th Rifles	3rd Londons	Bivouac about X.6.a.	Billets in VIEILLE CHAPELLE West of Bivouac.	R.35.d and a — Cross roads R.28.d	Londons will arrive about 4 p.m.
9th Gurkhas	8th Gurkhas	Bivouac about X.5.d.	VIEILLE CHAPELLE road if cannot send about cross roads R.28.d.	X.6.a.2½ – R.35.c.5½ – R.34.d and a.	8th Gurkhas will arrive about 3 p.m.
1st Seaforths	2nd Leicesters	Trenches	Billets about R.25. and R.31.a and b.	ALBERT Road – Southern roads to LACOUTURE and VIEILLE CHAPELLE – ZELOBES.	Leading Unit of Leicesters will arrive at road junction S.2.b. at 8.45 pm.
2nd Gurkhas	3rd Gurkhas	Trenches	Billets about X.3.d and H.a.	CHOCOLAT MENIER corner – LE TOURET – (Road junction X.16). Road junction X.4.d.4/7.	Leading Unit of 3rd Gurkhas will arrive at CHOCOLAT MENIER CORNER at 8.15 p.m.
1/th Joats	Garhwal Rifles	Bivouac S.8.b.	Billets R.29.	Road junction S.8.b – S.2.a.s.w – R.35.a.9/2.	Leading Unit of Garhwal Rifles arrives road junction S.8.b. at 9.45 p.m.

SECRET

OPERATION ORDER NO M1.
by
Brigadier General C.W.JACOB.
Commanding Dehra Dun Brigade

M.31.d. 6th May 1915.

Reference map of Assembly forwarded under my No B.M.22 of 5th May.

1. The Brigade will move into Position of Assembly by 11.p.m. on May 7th preparatory to an attack at dawn.
2. All movements will be via ST VAAST Corner M.32!d - track alongside Trolley line - past LANSDOWNE POST to RUE DU BOIS. The only communication trench to be used between LANSDOWNE POST and RUE DU BOIS is that known as ORCHARD Communication trench.
3. The 1st Seaforths will pass ST VAAST POST, Companies at 10 minutes interval, commencing at 8.p.m. and will enter the Assembly area from the RUE DU BOIS by the three first Communication trenches crossing the RUE DU BOIS west of PORT ARTHUR cross roads i.e PIONEER Communication Trench - CRESCENT Communication trench and the trench leading to centre of CRESCENT trench.
4. The 2nd Gurkhas will leave FORESTERS LANE by Companies at 10 minutes interval commencing at 8.p.m. Companies marching from billets not to pass ST VAAST POST before 8-30.p.m. and will enter the Assembly area by the Communication trenches leading into and through the ORCHARD.
5. The 4th Seaforths will pass ST VAAST POST by Companies at 10 minutes interval, commencing at 9.p.m. and will enter the Assembly area by the two Communication trenches leading into centre of CRESCENT Trench and the new trench near West end of CRESCENT Trench.
6. The 9th Gurkhas will pass ST VAAST POST by Companies at 10 minutes interval commencing at 9-40 .p.m. and will enter the assembly area by the same communication trenches as the 1st Seaforths.
7. The 6th Jats will pass ST VAAST POST in two parties at 10-20 10-30.p.m. and will enter the Assembly area via the Communication trenches leading from RUE DU BOIS towards North end of ORCHARD.
8. Ladders and Bridges will be carried up by Companies.
9. The importance of absence of noise both during the march and when in the Assembly area is to be impressed on all ranks. Also the vital necessity of men keeping hidden from view as much as possible after dawn while the Artillery is registering and cutting wire.
10. Brigade Report Centre will be established at "96 Picadilly" after 8-30.p.m. on May the 7th.

Issued at 7.p.m.
Sd H.A.WALKER Major
Bde Major Dehra Dun Brigade.

Copy No 1 to Meerut Division.
Copy No 2 to JULLUNDER Brigade
Copy No 3 to Garhwal Brigade.
Copy No 4 to Bareilly Brigade.
Copy No 5. to 1st Seaforths.
Copy No 6 to 4th Seaforths.
Copy No 7. to 6th Jats.
Copy No 8. to 9th Gurkhas.
Copy No 9. to 2nd Gurkhas.
Copy No 10 to Bde Bomb Gun Officer.
Copy No 11 to 4 Trench Battery R.F.A.
Copy No 12 to Section Mountain Battery.
Copy 13 and 14 retained.

S E C R E T

OPERATION ORDER NO 32.
by
Brigadier General C.W. JACOB.
Commanding Dehra Dun Brigade.

7th May 1915.

Information. 1 (a). The 1st Army is attacking on May the 8th.
(b) The 1st Corps retaining right on GIVENCHY is to advance on RUE DU MARAIS -LORGIES and ILLIES.
(c). The Indian Corps is to operate so as to cover the left of the 1st Corps capturing the FERME DU BOIS BIEZ and advancing on line LIGNY-LE-GRAND - LA CLIQUETERIE FERME.
(d). The 4th Corps is to turn the AUBERS Defences by an attack from North East and subsequently to gain touch with the Indian Corps at LA CLIQUETERIE FE.
(e). The Meerut Division is to make the attack to be delivered by the Indian Corps.
(f). The Lahore Division is to hold the front allotted to the Indian Corps less that portion from which the Meerut Division is to attack. It will assist the left flank of the Meerut attack by fire. It will also open a communication trench from the Listening Post at Point 61 to connect up with attack if this becomes desirable.

Intention. 2. The Dehra Dun Brigade will break the enemy's line from Point V.6. to 56 and establish itself on the front Distillery (Square S.17.a.c.) - FERME DU BIEZ - Point 53.

Orders to Troops. 3. (a). The 2nd Gurkhas will break the enemy's line between Point V.6. and the ditch which runs at right angles to the German trenches about Point 52. Subsequently working in conjunction with the right of the 4th Seaforths. The Battalion will push on towards the line R.16.E -LE TOURELLE cross roads . The Left Flank should reach the ESTAIRES-LA BASSEE Road near Point V.9.E. whence it should push up the road clearing the houses on West side.

The Battalion will establish itself on the above line but if circumstances permit will push forward a detachment to seize and occupy the DISTILLERY.
(b). The 4th Seaforths will break the enemy's line from east of ditch mentioned in (a) and the LA BASSEE Road. Subsequently working in conjunction with the left of 2nd Gurkhas, the Battalion will push on to the line LE TOURELLE Cross road - Point V.8. where it will establish itself. The Main LA BASSEE Road should be crossed in the vicinity of Point V.9.E. and the right flank should clear the houses on the East side of road.
(c). The 1st Seaforths will break the enemy's line between the LA BASSEE Road and Point 56. Subsequently the Battalion will push on towards Point V.8. and road junction immediately east of V.12. A protective flank is to be established facing the BOIS DU BIEZ along the road leading from Point 53 to V.12. The Battalion will establish itself in the above line, but if circumstances permit will push forward a detachment to seize and occupy the FERME DU BIEZ.
(d). The 6th Jats will support the 2nd Gurkhas and as soon as the latter Battalion has reached its objective will push forward and occupy the DISTILLERY. It will move forward to the trenches vacated by the 2nd Gurkhas as soon as the latter advance to the assault.
(e). Two Companies 9th Gurkhas will support the 1st Seaforths and as soon as the latter Battalion has

has gained its object will push forward and occupy the FERME
DU BIEZ. They will move forward to the trenches W of LA
BASSEE Road vacated by 1st Seaforths as soon as the latter
battalion advance to the assault. 9th Gurkhas (less 2 Coys)
will act as Brigade Reserve and will occupy the front line of
trenches vacated by the 4th Seaforths as soon as the latter
move forward, sending a British Officer to Brigade Head Quarters
to await any instructions.

(f). During night 7th/8th May officers Commanding Assaulting
Battalions will arrange to cut the wire in their front to
allow of exit and will place bridges in position as far as
possible. Every effort should be made to conceal the Bridges.
This work should be done before the moon rises 2.7.a.m.

(g). The 3 Assaulting Battalions will form up in front of our
advanced trenches after the wire cutting portion of the
bombardment is completed at 5-30.am. and before the bombardment
of the enemy's trenches ends at 5-40.a.m. The assaulting line
will, during the bombardment, move up as close to the enemy's
line as our shell fire permits, and will reach the enemy's
front line trenches at the earliest possible moment after this
bombardment is lifted to more distant objectives at 5-40.a.m.

(h). The following points as captured will be held by
garrisons and strengthened. Parties of Sappers and pioneers will
be sent under orders of C.R.E. to assist. :-
 (a). South end of LE TOURELLE Village.
 (b). Distillery.
 (c). Road junction in S.11.a (Points 52 and 53).
 (d) Group of houses near Point 50.
 (e). FERME DU BIEZ.

Ammunition

4. (a) Men will carry 200 rounds on the person.

(b). Part of the Regimental Reserve S.A.A. should be
collected at convenient places in the forward line of trenches
and Units should endeavour to have these carried forward behind
the attack and to establish a forward Depot. This can be done
either by detailing the rear Company to carry forward a certain
number of boxes or by leaving parties from each Company with
orders to follow some distance behind or when they see the
Distinguishing flags hoisted in certain localities.

(c). A Depot of S.A.A. has been established in the RUE DU
BOIS near the R.E. Depot shown on the Assembly map. All
Officers and N.C.O's should know where this is.

(d). The two supporting Battalions, 9th Gurkhas and 6th Jats
will arrange to carry forward additional boxes of ammunition
to some forward locality.

(e). Depots of ammunition have been or will be established
as shown on Assembly map at Head of Communication trenches
and also in the Listening Post East of PORT ARTHUR.

Grenades and Bombs

5. A Reserve of Grenades and Bombs has been collected in
dug outs as shown on the Assembly map, and all concerned should
know the exact locality.

Sandbags. 6. Every man will carry two sandbags.

Distinguishing Flags

7. (a). Flags 3' X 3' - Red and black divided diagonally
and with a white diagonal cross have been issued and should
be stuck up on the reverse side of prominent points gained
to mark the progress of the attack.

(b). Troops of the 8th Division will show a Red Flag
2'-6" square with a white or yellow diagonal ~~square~~ stripe.
~~in centre~~ Blocking parties of Bombers will show a red flag
1'-3" square.

(c). Troops of 7th Division will show a flag 3' long
by 2' Broad with three horizontal stripes two red and one white.

(d). Troops of 1st Division will show a red flag with
white vertical stripe in centre.

(e). Lahore Division will show a yellow flag.

Masks 8. Masks will be kept in readiness soaked in the solution,
by all troops in the front trenches and will be worn by

by assaulting troops.

No 4 Trench Battery R.A and Bomb Guns.
9. No 4 trench Battery R.A. after the Artillery has cut wire and while the bombardment of trenches is going on will fire on V.6.. Brigade Bomb Gun Officer will detail two guns to proceed with each assaulting Battalion. These will be used to bomb localities which hold out obstinately.

Signals 10. Each Unit will carry two helios in addition to other Signal Equipment.

Medical 11. A collecting Station will be established between LANSDOWNE POST and the Tramway where it crosses FORESTERS LANE. Route for wounded returning from the front will be by the ORCHARD Communication trench which runs from RUE DU BOIS to FORESTERS LANE along the North West side of the Tramway.

Prisoners 12. Prisoners will be handed over to LAHORE Division at Dehra Dun Bde Report Centre.

Official time. 13. Official time will be given to Units at Brigade Head Quarters after 5.p.m. on May the 7th - two watches to be sent by each representative.

Reports 14. RUE DU BOIS near Communication trench leading into ORCHARD.

Issued at 9.a.m.   Sd H.A.Walker Major
                    Brigade Major Dehra Dun Brigade.

Copy 1 and 2 retained.
Copy 3 to Meerut Division.
Copy 4 to Jullunder Brigade.
Copy 5 to Bareilly Brigade.
Copy 6 to Garhwal Brigade.
Copy 7 to 1st Seaforths.
Copy 8 to 4th Seaforths.
Copy 9 to 6th Jats.
Copy 10 to 9th Gurkhas.
Copy 11 to 2nd Gurkhas.
Copy 12 to Bde Bomb Gun Officer.
Copy 13 to No 4 trench Bty R.A.
Copy 14 to Section Mountain Artillery.

No B.M.10.   Head Quarters Dehra Dun Brigade.
                                            25th May 1915.

From.

    The Brigade Major

        Dehra Dun Brigade.

To.

    The Officer Commanding

            1st Seaforth Highlanders.
            4th Seaforth Highlanders.
            9th Gurkha Rifles.
            2nd Gurkha Rifles.

The 1st Seaforth Highlanders will relieve the 4th Seaforth Highlanders and the 2nd Gurkhas the 9th Gurkhas during the night of the 26th/27th May 1915 under mutual arrangements by Commanding Officers.

                                            H.A.Walker
                                                    Major.
                                    Brigade Major Dehra Dun Brigade.

Appendix T

Operation Order 36 Appendix "U"

by

Brigadier General C. W. Jacob
Commanding Dehra Dun Bde

3

[Ref: FESTUBERT sheet 1:8000]

RICHEBOURG ST VAAST
31st May 1915.

Information 1.(a). The front held by the Indian Corps is to be readjusted.

(b). The Dehra Dun Bde will hold the Northern Section of the Meerut Div.

(c). Bareilly Bde will be on our right and Ferozepore Bde on our left.

(d) The Northern Section extends from a point about midway between V.1 and R.6 to the communication trench inclusive 100 yards S of Q.7

(e). The 9th Gurkhas took over from R.3 to Q.7 from 152nd Bde on night 30/31st May.

Subdivision of Northern Section 2. The Section will be subdivided into two Subsections Right and Left, dividing line the bend in trench about 60 yards South of present right of 6th Gats.

Orders to Troops 3.(a). On night 31st May/1st June the 1st Seaforths and Machine guns of 4th Seaforths will be relieved by Ferozepore Bde under arrangements to be made with by C.O. of battalion concerned, and will move into billets and bivouacs on the Northern road from LA COUTURE to RICHEBOURG. Billeting Officer to report to Staff Capt at road junction B.35.d.8/3 at 11 am on 31st May.

(b). At 8-30 pm on 31st May the 2nd Gurkhas will move into billets and bivouacs in same vicinity. Billeting Officer to report to Staff Capt as mentioned in (a) above.

(c). The 4th Seaforths will move into bivouacs vacated by 2nd Gurkhas after 8-30 pm

(d) On night 1st/2nd June the 6th Jats will take over the extra piece of trench on their right referred to in para 2. from 9th Gurkhas.

(e) On night 1st/2nd June the 9th Gurkhas will take over the extra piece on their right referred to in para 1 (d) from 154th Bde details to be arranged with battalion of 154th Bde concerned.

Reports H. Reports to RICHEBOURG ST VAAST.

Issued at 5-30 am.   H.H. Walker
                                    Major
              Bde Major Dehra Dun Bde

Copy 1 and 2 War Diary
  "   3   to 1st Kafirs
  "   4   to 4th   "
  "   5   to 6th Jats
  "   6   to 9th Gurkhas
  "   7   to 2nd Gurkhas
  "   8   to 13th Bde RFA
  "   9   to Meerut Div
  "   10 to Ferozepore Bde
  "   11 to 154th Brigade.

War Diary with Appendices

1st Seaforth Highlanders

From 1st To 30 June 1915

Army Form C. 2118.

Vol. XI 108

WAR DIARY
or
INTELLIGENCE SUMMARY.
(Erase heading not required.)

Instructions regarding War Diaries and Intelligence Summaries are contained in F. S. Regs., Part II. and the Staff Manual respectively. Title pages will be prepared in manuscript.

Hour, Date, Place	Summary of Events and Information	Remarks and references to Appendices
JUNE 1ST	Strength of Btn. March 5th 1915 — 21 officers 1014 O.R. Reinforcements, including sick and wounded rejoined 35 " 612 "	[Ref. BETHUN sheet 1:40,000]
	56 " 1626 "	
	Casualties 26 " 883 "	
	30 " 743 "	
	(Subtract REV. MACNEILL, M.O. and M. WALKER & MAITLAND slightly wounded & rejoined)	
	Present strength 26 " 743 " in France (one O.R. Cooper)	
	Btn. strength in Brigade Area 26 officers 646 other ranks	
	Btn. strength for trenches 16 officers 527 other ranks (including A-Adj & -Mj)	
	Officers consist of: CAPT. THOMSON in command, 1 other captain, 7 Lieutenants, 16 2nd Lieutenants, Quartermaster & Medical Officer. Other ranks 1 S.M., 1 Sergeant Major, 4 C-S-Majors, 4 C-Q-M-Sergts., include; 44 full ranks.	
2.30 A.M.	Relief completed late owing to late arrival of CONNAUGHT RANGERS, and delayed by shrapnel fire; reached billets at 2.30 A.M. — no casualties on the way.	

Army Form C. 2118.

109

WAR DIARY
or
INTELLIGENCE SUMMARY.
(Erase heading not required.)

Hour, Date, Place	Summary of Events and Information	Remarks and references to Appendices
1ST JUNE	We are billeted in houses just outside RICHEBOURG on Northern road to LACOUTURE (Sq. S.1.b.); D being nearest RICHEBOURG, C further along the road, then B and lastly A Coy. in trench (running from S.1.b. 2/7 to X.6.a.3). Fine hot day, then bathed in canal near NEUVE CHAPELLE, taking turns to go. Bttn is in Brigade Reserve and at one hour's notice. 2nd Line brought up about 7 P.M. 2Lieut R.T. STEWART 2Lieut I. CAMPBELL (3rd A&S Hrs) joined. Casualties nil	[Ref. BETHUNE SHEET 1:40,000]
2nd JUNE	Big-gun JACOB came round after breakfast and saw all the new officers one by one. Another hot day and the men again bathed in canal. "C" Coy. provided a carrying party	
8 P.M.	at 8 P.M. — 40 men under 2Lt. LYNDEN-BELL; back by	
11 P.M.	2Lt S.R. ROBERTSON (3rd R. Scots) sick Casualties 2 sick	

WAR DIARY or INTELLIGENCE SUMMARY

Army Form C. 2118.

1/0.

Hour, Date, Place	Summary of Events and Information	Remarks and references to Appendices
3rd JUNE	Hot & sunny. G.O. and Q-M. motored to BAILLEUL in morning to see Brig Gen RITCHIE & returned at 6 P.M. Battn parades as usual. "D" Coy provided small carrying party of 20 men under Lt. DAVIDSON at 6 P.M. — back by 8 P.M. One case of measles in G Coy, so moved one platoon into trenches alongside A and disinfected the house. Casualties — 2 sick.	[Ref: BETHUNE sheet 1:40000]
4th JUNE	Fine but cooler. A F.G.C.M. sat in our Hd. Qrs. at 11 A.M. on 6 of our men (all drunks). Some shells dropped in & around RICHEBOURG at intervals during day but no damage to us. Casualties — 1 wounded, 2 sick.	
5th JUNE	Voluntary C of E Communion Service at 8 A.M. by Rev. IRVIN. A/Sgt RAMAGE & C/M ROBERTS left to rejoining by with our & attend machine gun course at WISQUES, with a view to becoming instructors. Adjt visited 4th SEAFORTHS Hd. Qrs in morning re billets for C.O, and Coy. Commanders at 6 P.M.	
6 P.M.	G.O. and Coy. Commanders at 6 P.M. Relief started 8.15 P.M. at which hour B Coy. marched from billets, followed by C, D and A at ½ hr intervals all in single file. Two machine guns following B Coy	

Army Form C. 2118.

WAR DIARY
or
INTELLIGENCE SUMMARY.
(Erase heading not required.)

Hour, Date, Place	Summary of Events and Information	Remarks and references to Appendices
5th JUNE (Cont:) 11 P.M.	Relief was completed at 11 p.m. D, C and B Coys. were in front line and support and A in local reserve Bn. Hd-Qrs. in a small house at S.8.d.9/3 on ALBERT ROAD. The section of line held by the DEHRA DUN BRIGADE is known as the Northern Section of which the Battalion holds the Northern, or D, sub-section. The trenches on the whole are slightly better than what we have taken over lately, but both the front and communication trenches are not dug deep enough to afford sufficient protection. G.O. visited line on completion of relief. Before leaving RICHEBOURG, at about 4 P.M. the enemy began shelling the billets occupied by C and D Coys. who were very lucky in escaping with no casualties; about 30 shells were sent over, but the men soon scattered and no damage was done. A draft of 86 O.R. under 2/Lt G.P. STEVENSON (4th A.I.S.H) arrived at 6 P.M. and were temporarily attached to A Coy... Casualties: 7 sick x 2 wd...	Ref: BETHUNE Sheet [1/40000]
6th JUNE	Officers of the 2nd LEICESTERS arrived at 6 A.M. and went round the trenches with a view to relieving us to-morrow. Gen. JACOB came down in the morning. Hot, and fairly quiet day.	

Army Form C. 2118.

3/1/2

WAR DIARY
or
INTELLIGENCE SUMMARY.
(Erase heading not required.)

Instructions regarding War Diaries and Intelligence Summaries are contained in F.S. Regs., Part II. and the Staff Manual respectively. Title pages will be prepared in manuscript.

Hour, Date, Place	Summary of Events and Information	Remarks and references to Appendices
6th JUNE (Cont)	G.O. visited trenches after dinner. Work was continued on improving the parapets and deepening the R.2 communication trench. 2/Lt T. G. CHRISTIE (A & S Hrs) arrived. Casualties: 2 sick & Pte STONE accidentally drowned.	Ref. BETHUNE sheet [1/40000] also [Trench Map VIOLAINES/ESTAIRES sheet 1:5000] Appendix "A" attached.
7th JUNE	Very hot. Quiet day. Relief was started by the machine guns at 1 P.M. The LEICESTERS were late and did not arrive till 9.30 P.M. Relief completed 12 midnight. Companies marched independently to billets near ZELOBES, via southern road through LACOUTURE and VIEILLE CHAPELLE: East Company, B, did not arrive till 3 A.M.	
3 A.M.		
8th JUNE	Billets are very scattered indeed, but quite good on the whole. Hd-Qrs. are in a barn at R.28.b.3. and the Companies in houses scattered over squares R.25 and R.31.a. and b.. Bn. is in divisional reserve and at 2 hrs. notice. Broiling hot day, which developed into a thunderstorm at 1 P.M. B and D Coys. bathed in canal at VIEILLE CHAPELLE in morning, and A and C went in afternoon. 2/Lt G. MACLEAN (1st A & S Hrs) and 2/Lt R. H. HADOW (1st A & S Hrs) joined. Casualties: 3 sick	

Army Form C. 2118.

E/I/3

WAR DIARY
or
INTELLIGENCE SUMMARY.
(Erase heading not required.)

Hour, Date, Place	Summary of Events and Information	Remarks and references to Appendices
9th JUNE	Another steamy hot day. Brig. Gen. Jacob met all the officers and full ranks of Brigade HdQrs at 9.30 A.M., and made a short speech congratulating them & us on its work in the past & expressing confidence that the same standard of excellence would be maintained in the future. Bde. beyond Major SUTHERLAND granted the D.G.M...	[Ref: BETHUNE Sheet 11:40000]
10th JUNE	A dull day. Companies carried out ordinary parades. Brig-Gen. RITCHIE & Lt-Col. GAISFORD arrived in? ??? ??? a short visit in the afternoon. The ??? party sent to LESTREM for instruction in the Vickers light gun returned in evening. A trial football match was held in evening, with a view of choosing a team to represent the Btn. 2/Lt G. McLEAN BM to join his regiment the 1st A & S Hrs. Gen Sha--- nil.	[Appendix "B" attached]
11th JUNE	Another cloudy day. Gen. Sir James Willcocks inspected A Coy at 3 P.M. B.E. was drawn up in quarter column, the Genl. & staff in rear. Present on parade 2 officers and 3 N.C.O.s...	

WAR DIARY
or
INTELLIGENCE SUMMARY.
(Erase heading not required.)

Army Form C. 2118.

3/1/4

Hour, Date, Place	Summary of Events and Information	Remarks and references to Appendices
11th JUNE (cont.)	After inspection the General spoke to each officer and also to all N.C.O.'s and men who were under him in the ZAKKA KHEL and MOHMAND expeditions. 7 days leave to U.K. Lt. RIGBY and 2/Lt KENNEDY. Leave from Madras gun course at LUCTREN. 2/Lt. J. ANDERSON rejoins from Casualties: 1 sick	[At: BETHUNE street PHOTO] [Appendix "C" attached]
12th JUNE	Fine day. Court-Martial held at 2nd Welsh Hdqrs at 10.30 A.M., on two of our men. at one of our gunners Capt BRODIE attended. A football match against the 4th Bn. kick-off 5.30 P.M. — result 3-1 in our favour. Match was followed by tea & an open air concert at which men from the 4th & 5th Bns. and the 2nd M.A.G. performed, the latter very kindly bringing a piano. Concert ceased at 9 P.M. Casualties: 2 sick (including W.O.3. MALTBY).	
13th JUNE	Presbyterian Church parade at 10.30 A.M.. Quiet day. One officer & 49 men, draft for 2nd Black Watch, attached to us for 3 days. Casualties: nil	
14th JUNE	Fine but cool. The men Battled in the hot Battles at VIEILLE CHAPELLE on the 12th & 13th, but most of the benefit was lost as except for A Coy, the hurricator was not working. Football match v. 2nd Ammunition Column (result	Casualties: nil

Army Form C. 2118.

WAR DIARY
or
INTELLIGENCE SUMMARY.
(Erase heading not required.)

[Ref. BETHUNE sheet 1:40000]

Hour, Date, Place	Summary of Events and Information	Remarks and references to Appendices
14th JUNE (cont.)	A party of 25 men from G Coy, under 2/Lt STEVENSON, left at 5 p.m. to report to S. & T. Corps officer at the rail-head on KING'S ROAD, for helping with the removal of surplus stores etc. A concert was held in the evening, A Coy. entertaining G Coy. Casualties: nil	
15th JUNE	Fine but cool. G and D Coys again went to the 1st Battn at VIEILLE CHAPELLE and this time had their clothes & kilts fumigated. Gen. Snow came round in morning and told us what he knew about the attack timed to begin at 6 p.m. The Officers played the M.G. O's at football, & lost 4-2. Heavy firing in evening. 2/Lt J.S.D. DIXON (A. & S. Hrs) sick. Casualties: 1 sick	
16th JUNE	Very hot day. Fatigue parties of 30 men under an Officer employed at FOSSE for loading stones in carts at 8 a.m., 6.30 p.m. & 7.30 p.m. Cinematograph show in open air at 9 p.m. Casualties: 1 sick	
17th JUNE	Fine. Battn marched to billets & bivouac from X.11.d.2/6 along road to X.11.b. Paraded at 4.30 p.m. by Coys. and marched off	

Army Form C. 2118.

WAR DIARY
or
INTELLIGENCE SUMMARY
(Erase heading not required.)

Hour, Date, Place	Summary of Events and Information	Remarks and references to Appendices
17th JUNE (cont:)	from crossroads at ZELOBES by 5.15 P.M. Bn. relieved the 41st DOGRAS. Almost everyone is in the Breastwork running parallel to the road. Bn. is in a state of constant readiness (i.e. ready to turn out at 10 mins. notice). In evening O.C. Companies reconnoitred the road to the firing line.	[Ref: BETHUNE sheet 1/40000] (Appendix "D" attached) Casualties: 2 sick
18th JUNE	Stood to arms at 3 A.M. as the 4th Corps on our right were expected to attack, but nothing happened. The men spent the day making dug-outs, latrines etc. and generally improving their G positions. A & D Coys moved from the open Breastworks & bivouacked in orchards. A digging party of 4 officers & 100 men under 2Lt. WILSON paraded at 8.30 P.M. and worked on front breast held by 1/4th SEAFORTHS. 15 men on fatigue for unloading carts under orders of S & T CORPS. Casualties: 1 wd. 1 sick	
19th JUNE	Fine day. Our guns bombarded the German lines at 3 A.M. heavily for 3/4 hour, but no attack followed. Another fatigue party of 4 officers & 100 men under Lt MAXWELL moved off at 8.30 P.M. as before. Lt. RIGBY & 2Lt. KENNEY rejoined from leave. Casualties: 1 wd. 2 sick.	

WAR DIARY or INTELLIGENCE SUMMARY.

Army Form C. 2118.

(Erase heading not required.)

Hour, Date, Place	Summary of Events and Information	Remarks and references to Appendices
20th JUNE	Hot & quiet day. The mortar bombers were shelled in morning & 2 of our men were wounded. Three others wounded owing to a bomb accident. Casualties: 5 wd. 2 sick	(Ref. BETHUNE Sheet 13 40000)
21st JUNE	Fine & quiet. Men continued digging dug-outs etc. Casualties: 5 sick	
22nd JUNE	Fine & hot. Capt. Sir JOHN FOWLER (Adjt. 1/4th SEAFORTHS) killed by a shell in morning. Court-Martial on two of our men held at Hd. Qrs. 2/2nd GURKHAS at 10 A.M. A party of 30 men under 2/Lt. McLEOD carried sandbags to 6th JATS at 9 P.M. Casualties: 4 sick	
23rd JUNE	Shower in morning. 2/Lt. STEVENSON and party rejoined, handed at 10.15 P.M. to relieve 1/4th SEAFORTHS. Machine guns pack heavier & shorts exchanged. As we are stronger than 4th Bn. only 3 Coys. went up — "C" remaining behind in Brigade reserve at KING'S ROAD. Relief completed 1 A.M. "A" Coy. hold firing line, D in support and B in reserve. Trenches good throughout, but require deepening. Draft of 46 O.R. arrived and attached to Companies; 5 sick 1 wd. (accident to leg)	(Appendix "E" attached)

Forms/C.2118/10
Draft of 46 O.R. arrived

WAR DIARY or INTELLIGENCE SUMMARY.

Army Form C. 2118.
118

Hour, Date, Place	Summary of Events and Information	Remarks and references to Appendices
24th June	Sultry day. Slight shelling of front line. Flies very bad indeed. Deepened & cleaned trenches & put down lots of Chloride of Lime. Brigade Major came round in morning. 2/Lt. O.B. MALTBY rejoined. Following mentioned in dispatches: Lt-Col. A.B. RITCHIE C.M.G. Capt. & Adjt. R. HORN Maj. A.B.A. STEWART D.S.O. Capt. R. LAING Capt. A.B. BAILLIE-HAMILTON Capt. Hon. G.H.M. ST-CLAIR Qr.Mr. & Hon. Lt. J. MACRAE 3913 Reg-Sergt-Major A. SUTHERLAND 996 Pte. S. DORMAN 8978 Act-Sergt J. McINTOSH 10659 Pte. S.N. McEACHEARN 637 L/Cpl. J. FIELD 581 Dmr. J. NEILL Casualties: 5 sick	[Ref. BETHUNE sheet 1:40000]
25th June	Dull day with drizzle & heavy rain in evening. Trenches v. muddy. Worked hard at cleaning & deepening them. Two Saps for machine guns started. Brigadier came round line in morning. Lt-Col. RITCHIE promoted to Brevet Colonel Capt. & Adjt. R. HORN granted Military Cross. Casualties: 4 sick	

WAR DIARY
or
INTELLIGENCE SUMMARY.
(Erase heading not required.)

Army Form C. 2118.

Hour, Date, Place	Summary of Events and Information	Remarks and references to Appendices
26th JUNE	Fine & hot. Trenches dried up quickly when the wind was turned. Men worked all night & during day on improving the lines. One H.E. shell fell on supports — no casualties. Started cutting grass in front of our line. G Coy. provided a working party. Casualties: 5 sick	[Ref. BETHUNE sheet] 1A.0000]
27th JUNE	Showers in evening. Work continued. G Coy. came down again on fatigue. Draft of 56 O.R. arrived at 1st Line. Casualties: 3 wd., 2 sick	
28th JUNE	Dull & cloudy; more showers. Firing line & supports shelled with pip-squeaks. Work continued & both saps completed. Casualties: 1 wd.	
29th JUNE	All reliefs are now changed, and the Brigade is to stay in longer. We are to hold "B" Sub-section with 2 Coys., the other two being in reserve on KINGS ROAD. This leaves line weaker but still it should be strongly enough held. A & D marched back to KINGS R.D. The firing line is held by 3 platoons of G; support by 2 platoons of B & one of G; by 2 platoons of B & 4 machine guns in front line.	(Appendix "F" attached)

WAR DIARY or INTELLIGENCE SUMMARY.

Army Form C. 2118.

B/100

Hour, Date, Place	Summary of Events and Information	Remarks and references to Appendices
29th JUNE (cont.)	We got our own guard back from 4th Bn. Hd. Qrs. to remain in reserve line. Relief to be carried out every 4 days. Two demonstrations on how to use gas helmets held at LES 8 MAISONS at 9 A.M. and 10.30 A.M., 10 men attended each under 2/Lt WILSON & 2/Lt CAMPBELL. Casualties: 2 wd. 1 sick.	[Ref. BETHUNE sheet 1:40000]
30th JUNE	Wet morning. Act/Adjt. went to KINGS R.D. for day. Worked at clearing trenches, which have now been improved a hundredfold. The 1/4th SEAFORTHS are on our right and next to them the 7th SEAFORTHS under Lt. Col. GAISFORD. The draft of 46 O.R. joined their bays. to-day. Casualties: 1 sick 1 wd (accidentally)	

No B.M.3. "B" Head Quarters Dehra Dun Brigade.
8th June 1915.

From.
    The Brigade Major.
        Dehra Dun Brigade.

To.
    The Officer Commanding
        1st Battalion Seaforth Highlanders.

The Field Marshal, Commanding in Chief has, under authority granted by His Majesty the King, awarded the Distinguished Conduct Medal to :-

No 5913, Regimental Sergeant Major A. SUTHERLAND, 1st Battalion Seaforth Highlanders.

2. He should be informed, and his name will be published in the List of "Appointments, Commissions, Rewards etc" as soon as practicable.

Captain
/n Brigade Major Dehra Dun Brigade.

S. M. Sutherland

THE HYMN OF HATE.

HASSGESANG GEGEN ENGLAND.
Ernst Lissauer.

Was schiert uns Russe and Franzos',
Schuss wider Schuss und Stoss um Stoss,
Wir lieben sie nicht, wir hassen sie nicht,
Wir schützen Weichsel und Wasgaupass,—
Wir haben nur einen einzigen Hass,
Wir lieben vereint, wir hassen vereint,
Wir haben nur einen einzigen Feind:
Den Ihr alle wisst, den Ihr alle wisst,
Er sitzt geduckt hinter der grauen Flut,
Voll Neid, voll Wut, voll Schläue, voll List,
Durch Wasser getrennt, die sind dicker als Blut.
Wir wollen treten in ein Gericht
Einen Schwur zu schwören, Gesicht in Gesicht,
Einen Schwur von Erz, den verbläst kein Wind,
Einen Schwur für Kind und Kindeskind,
Vernehmt das Wort, sagt nach das Wort,
Es wälze sich durch ganz Deutschland fort:
Wir wollen nicht lassen von unserm Hass,
Wir haben alle nur einen Hass,
Wir lieben vereint, wir hassen vereint,
Wir haben alle nur einen Feind:
    England.

In der Bordkajüte, im Feiersaal,
Sassen Schiffsoffiziere beim Liebesmahl,—
Wie ein Säbelhieb, wie ein Segelschwung,
Einer riss grüssend empor den Trunk,
Knapp hinknallend wie ein Ruderschlag,
Drei Worte sprach er: "Auf den Tag!"
Wem galt das Glas?
Sie hatten alle nur einen Hass.
Wer war gemeint?
Sie hatten alle nur einen Feind:
    England.

Nimm Du die Völker der Erde in Sold,
Baue Wälle aus Barren von Gold,
Bedecke die Meerflut mit Bug bei Bug,
Du rechnetest klug, doch nicht klug genug.
Was schiert uns Russe und Franzos',
Schuss wider Schuss und Stoss um Stoss,
Wir kämpfen den Kämpf mit Bronze und Stahl,
Und schliessen Frieden irgend einmal,—
Dich werden wir hassen mit langem Hass,
Wir werden nicht lassen von unserm Hass,
Hass zu Wasser und Hass zu Land,
Hass des Hauptes und Hass der Hand,
Hass der Hämmer und Hass der Kronen,
Drosselnder Hass von siebzig Millionen,
Sie lieben vereint, sie hassen vereint,
Sie haben alle nur einen Feind:
    England.

The following free translation of The Hymn of Hate appears in the "Toronto Daily Star," with "no apologies to Herr Lissauer":—

A HYMN OF HATE.

Carrrots or beets we hate them not,
We love them not, we hate them not.
Of all the things that land on our plate,
There's only one that we loathe and hate;
We love a hundred, we hate but one,
And that we'll hate till kingdom come—
    Sauer Kraut.

It's known to you all, it's known to you all,
Pilgrims on this terrestrial ball;
Full of vinegar in distress,
Making a most unsavoury mess.
Come, let us stand in our eating place,
An oath to swear to, face to face;
An oath of bronze no wind can shake,
An oath for all sons of guns to take.
We will never forego our hate;
We have all but a single hate.
We love as one; we hate as one.
And we'll hate that dish if we do it alone—
    Sauer Kraut.

Wienerwurst, liverwurst, lager beer,
Many a time hath given us cheer;
Not so bad if made just right;
Bad to take going to bed at night;
Better by far to lunch in—"The Day."
Then there won't be the devil to pay.
But you we hate with a lasting hate;
We will never forego our hate;
Hate of the stomach and hate of the tongue.
Hate of the senses every one;
Hate of millions who've choked it down;
Hate of the country and hate of the town.
We love a thousand; we hate but one,
And that we'll hate with hate of Hun--
    Sauer Kraut.

Indian Army Corps,
5th June, 1915.

"D"

Operation Order No 38
by
Brigadier General C. W. Jacob.
Commanding Dehra Dun Brigade

No 5

LES LOBES
16th June 1915.

1. The DEHRA DUN Brigade will relieve the BAREILLY Brigade in the trenches on the 17th Instant.

2. Hours of march and location of Units as per attached table.

3. The Motor Machine Guns now in the trenches will remain in until the evening of 19th June, when they will return to No 5 Motor Machine Gun Battery.

4. The 1st. Seaforths will find a Section on the right of the Brigade line for liaison with the 51st Division.

5. Reports to WHITE HOUSE VIEILLE CHAPELLE after 10 pm on 17th Inst.

Issued at 10-30 a.m.
                              Major
Brigade Major Dehra Dun Bde.

Copy 1 and 2 retained
" 3 to Meerut Div
" 4 to Bareilly Bde
" 5 to 1st Seaforths
" 6 to 4th Seaforths
" 7 to 6th Jats
" 8 to 9th Gurkhas
" 9 to 2nd Gurkhas
" 10 to 2 Coy M.D.T.

Unit	Route	Location	Time of arrival	1st Line Transports	Remarks
1st Platoons	VIEILLE CHAPELLE — PONT LEVIS — LA COUTURE.	X.11.d.2/6 from R on RUE northwards to X.11.b.	6-30 pm	R.34.c.9/4	By platoons at suitable distance after leaving R.34.d.
4th Platoons	Shortest	Trenches	9-45 pm	R.34.c.9/4	Time given is for arrival at DEAD COW HOUSE
10th Plat	Shortest	Trenches	9 pm	R.34.d.2/3	Time given is for arrival at DEAD COW HOUSE
9th Platoons	LA COUTURE	X.11.d.3/6 South-wards to X.11.c.10/0	6 pm	R.34.d.2/3	By platoons at suitable distance after leaving R.34.d.
2nd Platoons	VIEILLE CHAPELLE — PONT LEVIS — LA COUTURE	X.4.d along road into LA COUTURE and thence to X.5.a.4/3.	5 pm	R.34.d.2/3	By platoons at suitable distance after leaving R.34.d.

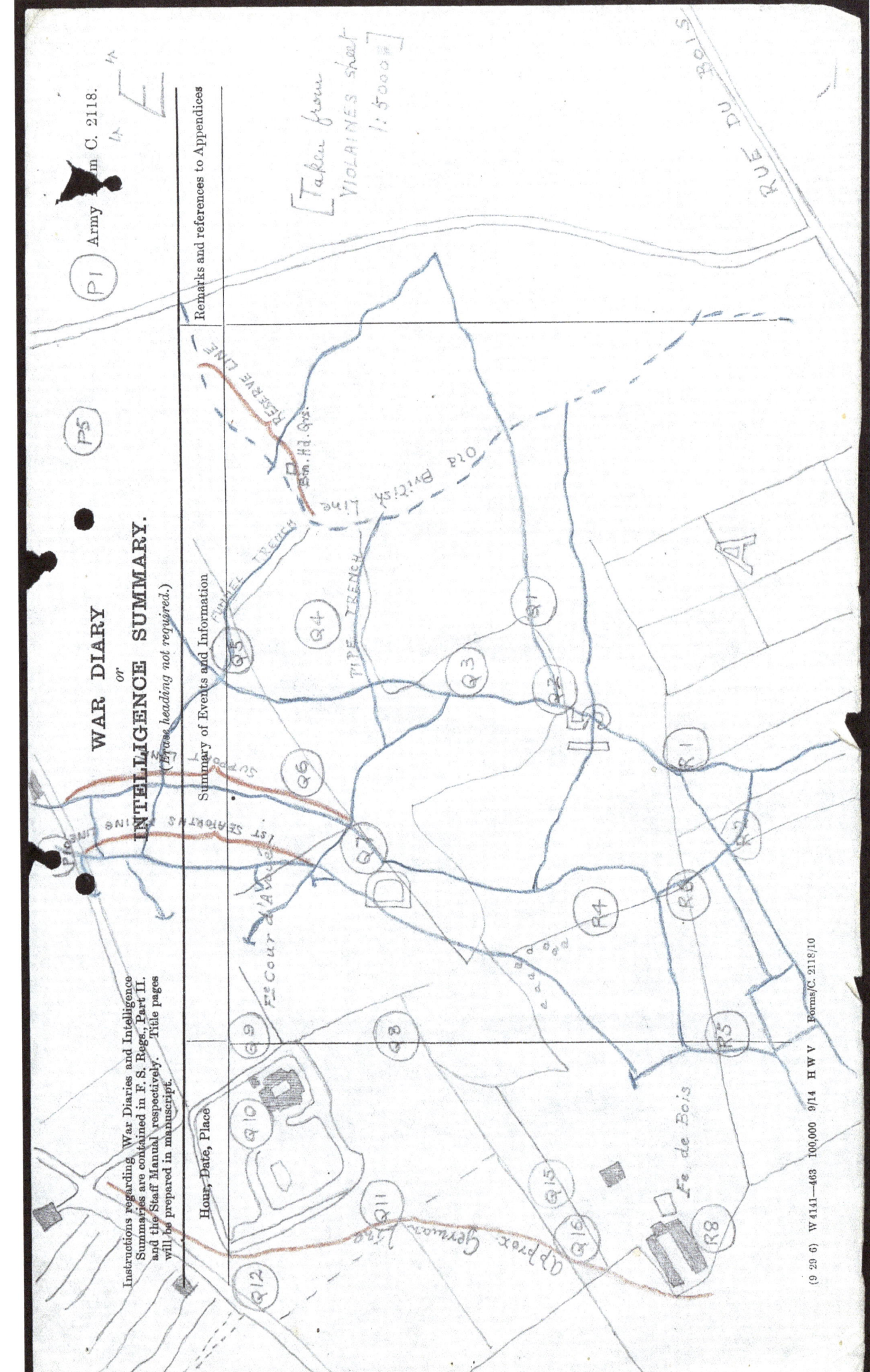

Operation Order No 39   Copy No. 3
by
Brigadier General C. W. JACOB. C.B
Commanding Dehra Dun Brigade

"F"

VIEILLE CHAPELLE
28th June 1915.

1. Reliefs as under will be carried out on night 29th/30th June 1915. Details of reliefs to be arranged between Commanding Officers concerned:-

4th Seaforth Highlanders to relieve "A" Subsection.
1 Coy 1st Seaforths now in Brigade Reserve to relieve two Companies in "B" Subsection.
6th Jats to relieve "C" Subsection.

2. Billets of relieved Units:-
   2 Companies 1st Seaforth Highlanders   KING'S ROAD.
   9th Gurkha Rifles . . . . KING'S ROAD.
   2nd Gurkha Rifles . . . . . KING GEORGES ROAD.
All Units in constant readiness.

3. Reports to WHITE HOUSE VIEILLE CHAPELLE.

Issued at 8.30 pm.

B.E. Anderson Major.
Brigade Major Dehra Dun Bde.

Copies 1 and 2 Retained   Copy 9 to Bareilly Bde
Copy 3 to 1st Seaforths   Copy 10 to Garhwal Bde
Copy 4 to 4th Seaforths   Copy 11 to 21st Bde.
Copy 5 to 6th Jats   Copy 12 to 2 Coy Train.
Copy 6 to 9th Gurkhas
Copy 7 to 2nd Gurkhas
Copy 8 to Meerut Div

Meerut Division

Seaforth Highlanders

From 1st To 31st July 1915

Serial No. 26

121/6502

WAR DIARY
with appendices
OF
Seaforth Highlanders.

From 1st July 1915 To 31st July 1915

9.V.
20 sheets

Army Form C. 2118.

VOL XII page 2V22

WAR DIARY
or
INTELLIGENCE SUMMARY.
(Erase heading not required.)

Instructions regarding War Diaries and Intelligence Summaries are contained in F.S. Regs., Part II. and the Staff Manual respectively. Title pages will be prepared in manuscript.

Place	Date	Hour	Summary of Events and Information	Remarks and references to Appendices
	1ST JULY		Dull & cloudy day. Work continued. C.O. visited coys. in Brigade reserve during day. Draft of 56 O.R. which reached the 1st Line on 27th JUNE has now joined the companies. Casualties: 2 wd. (1 accidental)	Bethune sheet 36cSW3
	2ND JULY		Dull day again. Worked on communication trenches which are now very good. Lt.-Gen. Sir CHARLES ANDERSON went round the line. Casualties: 1 wd. 4 sick	
	3RD JULY		Fine & hot. Act/Adjt. visited the coys. in Brigade Reserve. A and D Coys. relieved C and B at 10 P.M. Three platoons of A being kept one platoon of A and two of D in support; two platoons of D in reserve. Casualties: 1 wd. 3 sick	
	4TH JULY		Very hot indeed. Lt. MACRAE and 2Lt. 1. ANDERSON and WALKER start on a week's leave. A party of 80 men worked under R.E. officers on the flank defences to FUNNEL trench. Casualties: 3 sick	

Army Form C. 2118.

Vol XII
Page X

WAR DIARY
or
~~INTELLIGENCE SUMMARY.~~
(Erase heading not required.)

Instructions regarding War Diaries and Intelligence Summaries are contained in F.S. Regs., Part II. and the Staff Manual respectively. Title pages will be prepared in manuscript.

Place	Date	Hour	Summary of Events and Information	Remarks and references to Appendices
	5th JULY		Cloudy day. C.O. acted as President of a F.G.C.M. at the Bareilly Brigade. Three men went on a week's leave. Quiet day and work was continued on improving the trenches. 2/Lt. MACKLIN (3rd Royal Scots) sick. Casualties — 5 sick	[Ref BETHUNE Sheet 1: 40000]
	6th JULY		Hot day and rain in afternoon. A Coy. moved back into reserve and D Coy. took over the firing line. C Coy. provided 100 men for digging at 9.30 P.M., but owing to rain not much was done. Lt. DAWSON (medical officer) left on a week's leave. Lt. RANKIN evacuated sick to the base for deafness. Casualties — 8 sick	
	7th JULY		Showery day but quiet. 2/Lt. McLEOD and 4 N.C.O's left for a short refresher course on machine guns at MOLLINGHEM. Casualties — 3 sick	
	8th JULY		We were to have been relieved, but owing to changes relief is postponed till 10th inst. A list was submitted to the Brigadier showing all our men who came from India & who have not been home — in some cases for many years — with a view to their being granted leave. Casualties — 2 sick	

Army Form C. 2118.

WAR DIARY
or
INTELLIGENCE SUMMARY.
(Erase heading not required.)

Vol XII Page 122

Place	Date	Hour	Summary of Events and Information	Remarks and references to Appendices
JULY	9th		Cloudy day, but evening not very active — shelling normal. We are to be relieved tomorrow by the 7th Division, and are to be temporarily attached to the JULLUNDUR BDE of the LAHORE DIVN. All the native units are being taken out for a 3 weeks rest, but the British troops (not H attd) are all to join the LAHORE DIVN and to remain in the line. Work continued, and our trenches are now quite 100% better than when we took them over; the men have worked very hard. A draft of 53 O.R. under 2Lt. G.W. BROWN arrived. Casualties: 4 sick	Rd. BETHUNE Sheet 1: 40000 APPX 'G' or 4th attd.
JULY	10th		The Officers of the 2nd YORKSHIRE REG. arrived at 11 A.M. to look over the trenches; they are to relieve both ourselves and also the 4th Battalion. Our line was somewhat heavily shelled about 3 P.M. The relief started at 9.15 P.M. and was completed by 12 midnight without hitch. B and C Coys. marched at 8.45 P.M. from KINGS RD. A and D and the machine guns arrived at billets at 3 A.M. The machine guns and Hd. Qrs. have been in the trenches for 18 days on end!	

Army Form C. 2118.

Vol XII Page 23

WAR DIARY
or
INTELLIGENCE SUMMARY.
(Erase heading not required.)

Place	Date	Hour	Summary of Events and Information	Remarks and references to Appendices
	JULY 10th (Cont.)		The billets are at L'ÉPINETTE (R.7.G) — the same ones we occupied in April. The draft joined us from PARADIS. Casualties; 1 wd., 1 sick	Ref. BETHUNE Sheet 1/40000
	JULY 11th		Dull & windy day. Posted draft to companies. New billets are good, but the officers are v. crowded. Voluntary Presbyterian Service at 6.30 P.M. Casualties; Sick 3.	
	JULY 12th		Lt. MACRAE, 2/Lt. I. ANDERSON and 2/Lt. WALKER returned from leave. 2/Lt. KENNEY together with C-Q-M-S CAMPBELL & Sgt SCOTT left at 1 p.m. for the Base for "training duties"; these three were sent as requiring a rest. The Baths are open at PONT RIQUEUL and A. Coy. provided 2 batches of 75 men each in the afternoon. A clean change of clothes being provided from the Corps laundry. Casualties: Sick 2	
	JULY 13th		C.O. and Coy. Officers visited the trenches to be taken over to-morrow from the Seaforth Brigade. The baths are open again, both at PONT RIQUEUL and at LA GORGUE — every man having a bath. A cinematograph show was held at Hd. Qrs. last night & was a great success. Lt. K. ANDERSON, 2/Lt. WILSON & 5/Lt LYNDEN-BELL on leave. Casualties: 3 Sick	Appendix I attached to

Army Form C. 2118.

VOL XII Page 124

WAR DIARY
or
INTELLIGENCE SUMMARY.
(Erase heading not required.)

Place	Date	Hour	Summary of Events and Information	Remarks and references to Appendices
	1915			REF. BETHUNE (SHEET 1:40000)
	14th July		Captain ᴬ Thomson appointed temporary Major.	
			Capt E.G. Rigby appointed Temporary Capt.S dated April 10th and June 10th respectively.	
			2nd Lieut. B. Kenny, appointed Temporary Lieut. dated 10th June 1915.	
			8 men considered unfit for the Trenches were inspected by the C.O.C. Lahore Division, and was recommended to be sent home, the remainder was recommended for employment on the L.O.F.C.	
			B.n proceeded for the Trenches at 6.30 P.M., raining hard, & arrived at Rue Biche to take over the line at Neuve Chapelle on the 15th March from the 15th Sikhs. the Germans at Neuve Chapelle on the 10th March. The Battalion took over from the Seaforths, relief was not completed about 2 A.M. owing to the heavy rain relief was not completed about 2 A.M. Trenches very muddy and in some places both sides & walls. Nil. Firing line and Supports A. B.Y.C. Coys Local Reserve D Coy Port Arthur 50 Rifles of A Coy. Machine Guns hrs in Firing Line and two in Port Arthur. Casualties 9 men	
	15th July.		Dry and windy, C.O. 6 Jullunder Brigade visited Bn Headquarters. worked all day to pump out the mud in Trenches and improving communicating Trenches, blowing of Trenches, Dugouts Trenches	

Army Form C. 2118.

WAR DIARY
or
INTELLIGENCE SUMMARY.
(Erase heading not required.)

VOL XII Page 65

Place	Date	Hour	Summary of Events and Information	Remarks and references to Appendices
Continued				
	15th July		continued up party will during the day. Pte LOVE. D Coy was killed about 11 PM by a Rifle Bullet while out with a party digging a communication Trench.	[REF. BETHUNE SHEET 1.400]
	16th July		Lieut Davidson and one man proceeded on leave. BRIGADIER visited Subsection. Enemy shelled the vicinity of Subsection Head Qrs into Lgt Light Field Guns (Pip Squeaks) Mles Pte LOVE Buried at VILLE CHAPELLE. Rained in the evening. 10.45 PM Heavy Bombardment was heard to our right.	Casualties Killed 1 {Lieut & NCR Casualties= 1 Officer and 3 men sick
	17th July		Cloudy with strong wind. Our 60 Pounders Bombarded Houses No 53 in front of our line. No direct hit. But Enemy's works in the vicinity damaged. Mles One German 8" Bright Shell damaged our parapet opposite PORT ARTHUR. No casualties.	Casualties 1 sick

Army Form C. 2118.

WAR DIARY
or
INTELLIGENCE SUMMARY.
(Erase heading not required.)

Instructions regarding War Diaries and Intelligence Summaries are contained in F. S. Regs., Part II. and the Staff Manual respectively. Title pages will be prepared in manuscript.

VOL XII Page 136

Place	Date	Hour	Summary of Events and Information	Remarks and references to Appendices
	1915			REF. 36 NING SHEET 1/40000
	18TH July		Dry and windy. BRIGADIER visited and inspected Trenches. PADRIE Marker to Redforths went round the Trenches. Lig. men of B. company wounded by a shell, in man went on leave for 7 days. Hostile artillery shell during the day.	
			Casualties:— Wounded 6, Sick 3	
	19th July		Very hot. GEN. SIR JAMES WILLCOCKS inspected the front line Trenches and PORT ARTHUR. Lt-Colonel's Lynalter wounded at PORTHED Quarter by SHRAPNELL. D Coy relieved C. the front line and B Coy came back in Reserve. PORT ARTHUR garrison changed Lieut MAXWELL relieving 2ND Lt Buchanan with 50 men of D coy	
			Casualties Wounded 1, Sick 4	

Army Form C. 2118.

WAR DIARY
or
INTELLIGENCE SUMMARY.
(Erase heading not required.)

Vol XII Page 27

Place	Date	Hour	Summary of Events and Information	Remarks and references to Appendices
REF. BETHUNE SHEET 36A NE 1/40,000	20th July		Fine. Enemy bumped "A" Coy's Trenches. Corpl. Dawson and Pte. Bison were buried in their dug-outs. Corpl. Dawson was killed and Pte. Bison died in the Field Ambulance the same day. Other men wounded. Artillery duel during the day.	
			Casualties: Killed 1, wounded 4.	
			Died of wounds 1, List 4	
	21st July		Hot & sunny. Enemy shelled right of our line with Field Guns used H.2 Howitzers, no damage. At 12 M.N. Enemy threw a Bomb into the (POPE'S NOSE.) our advance post on left of LA BASSEE road Square S.11.a.9/ wounding 6 men of "A" Coy who were out on listening Guard. Draft of 39 n.c.o's & men arrived at 1st Line Transport.	
			Casualties wounded 6	
			Sick 4	

Army Form C. 2118.

Vol XII Page 198

WAR DIARY
or
INTELLIGENCE SUMMARY.
(Erase heading not required.)

Place	Date	Hour	Summary of Events and Information	Remarks and references to Appendices
	22nd July		Fine windy but warm. Normal shelling in the morning, but man wounded in support line by G.S. bullet, fired 3 rounds at pair V.10.A. 4th Br. were relieved by 125th by 111th SIKHS. Br. Head Quarters moved to the Trenches known by the Bn in November near PORT ARTHUR. Heavy Artillery firing to the South of our lines. 2nd Lt. LINDEN Bell returned off leave.	REF. BETHUNE SHEET 1. 40,000 /// ///
			Casualties wounded	/// Sick 3
	23rd July.		Capt. Anderson and 2nd Lieut. Wilson returned off leave. "B" Company moved into the Fire Trench while "A" Company came into Road reserve. Draft of 70 N.C.O.s & men joined the 1st line transports.	///
			Casualties wounded 1 Sick ni	///

Army Form C. 2118.

VOL. XII Page 134

WAR DIARY
or
INTELLIGENCE SUMMARY.
(Erase heading not required.)

Place	Date	Hour	Summary of Events and Information	Remarks and references to Appendices
	24th July		Hot. German airoplane over our lines. Bad Shooting by our Anti Aircraft Guns. Shelling normal. Draft of 39 men arrived and posted to Coys. Casualties Sick 2.	REF. BETHUNE SHEET 7. 1/40000 /MR
	25th July		May Hot. very little shelling. Coy Sergt-Major Meadows reported from hospital after being wounded on 9th May & posted to "C" Coy. 2nd LIEUT. DAVIDSON returned off leave. 2nd Lieut. MILLER rejoined from Hosp. & 96 PATTERSON B Coy accidentally killed in the front-line by a rifle Bullet. Casualties 1 Killed 1 Sick	MR MR
	26th July		Windy but warm. Hot Artillery duel first in the morning. 2nd LIEUT STEWART. and 6 other ranks recommenced for a Machine Gun course. Casualties 1 wounded 3 Sick	MR

Army Form C. 2118.

WAR DIARY
or
INTELLIGENCE SUMMARY.
(Erase heading not required.)

VOL. XII Page 130

Place	Date	Hour	Summary of Events and Information	Remarks and references to Appendices
	27th July		Heavy showers of rain in the morning. Artillery on both sides very active for about an hour. Draft of 70 N.C.O.s & men joined and posted to Coys. About 12 M.N. enemy shelled the vicinity of RICHEBOURG ST VAST with heavy guns and PONT LOGY with field guns. One unexploded German heavy shell in support trench, doing however no damage.	REF. BETHUNE SHEET 1:20,000 Casualties 2 sick Unknown
	28th July		Windy with occasional showers. G.O.C. JULLUNDUR BRIGADE inspected the Trenches at 11 A.M. Lively shelling with trench mortars about Sub Section Head Quarters for about 2 an hour. 7th Division on our right opened a heavy burst of field guns & rifle fire on German Trenches. Unexpected German heavy shell sent to Bn Head Qrs	Casualties 2 sick

Army Form C. 2118.

VOL XII Page 30 & 31

WAR DIARY
or
INTELLIGENCE SUMMARY.
(Erase heading not required.)

Instructions regarding War Diaries and Intelligence Summaries are contained in F. S. Regs., Part II. and the Staff Manual respectively. Title pages will be prepared in manuscript.

Place	Date	Hour	Summary of Events and Information	Remarks and references to Appendices
	29th July		Very hot with light breeze. The Oreilly's dug-out was broken in PORT ARTHUR by a shell, no damage. Shelling in other places normal. B&E H.E. M.D. THUNDER occurred no more live shells to be cut there.	REF BETHUNE SHEET 1/40,000
			Casualties 4 sick.	
	30th July		Light Breeze and warm. 65 Hostile 5.9 Gun shells were fired into an orchard behind PORT ARTHUR REDOUBT. no one there as our saumap attacked done during. Thirteen shells did not explode. Officers of the 4th Kings who relieved us tomorrow night came up and are now in the Trenches. 2nd Lieut STEWART and 6 N.C.O's & men left for a machine Gun course at MELLINGHEM. 2nd Lieut LINDEN BELL promoted Lieut dated 1st May 1915.	APPX "J"
			Casualties nil	
	31st July		Very warm. 45 Hostile 5.9 Gun shells were fired into the vicinity	

Army Form C. 2118.

VOL XII Page 132

WAR DIARY
or
INTELLIGENCE SUMMARY.
(Erase heading not required.)

Place.	Date	Hour	Summary of Events and Information	Remarks and references to Appendices
Continued	31st July		of NEUVE.CHAPELLE. Our N.C.O and 10 MEN went to No 173 TUNNELLING Co R.E. A, B & C Coys were relieved by three Companies of the 14th KINGS. D Company being relieved the same time by the 89th PUNJABIS. Reliefs completed about 11.30 P.M. Coys assembled at PONT.DU.HEM. ESTAIRES-LA BASSIE road, and marched to LA GORGUE where we were billeted. Even Pioneer Officers but indifferent to the heat. To our satisfaction we now joined our own One, The DEHRA.DUN. having been attached to the JULLUNDUR B.de LAHORE DIVISION for 23 weeks. Through being attached to that division the Battalion occupied the front line as follows= West of LE EPPINETTE next 33 days in Brigade reserve, 3 days at rest in LE EPPINETTE next 42 days we had 6 days in front trenches. Letter from General Stuckland commanding JULLUNDUR BRIGADE, as to the work performed by the Battalion attached as APPENDIX.	REF BETHUNE SHEET 7 No 1971 "K" esta. APPENDIX Casualties 4 Sick

Operation Order No 43
by
Lieutenant-Colonel G.T. WIDDICOMBE
Commanding Dehra Dun Brigade.

APPX
'G'
Copy No. 2

VIEILLE CHAPELLE.
9th July 1915.

1. The Dehra Dun Bde will hand over to the 21st Infantry Bde the front now held between LA QUINQUE RUE and R.5.

2. The Yorkshire Regiment will relieve the 4th Seaforths in A Subsection and the 1st Seaforths in B. Subsection. The 2nd Royal Scots Fusiliers will relieve the 6th Jats in C. Subsection.
   Details of relief to be arranged between Commanding Officers concerned.

3. The Indian Corps will be temporarily reorganised so that all British Infantry Units are grouped with the Lahore Division which remains in the line and Indian Units with the Meerut Division which will go into rest billets in area MERVILLE – CALONNE – ST FLORIS – HAVERSKERQUE.

4. Brigades are affiliated as under for the purpose of regrouping:—
   Dehra Dun Bde with Jullunder Bde
   Garhwal Bde with Sirhind Bde.

5. For march of relieved Units see march table attached.

6. Guides will meet relieving Units at Subsection Head Quarters at 9-30 pm on 10th July 15.

7. Completion of relief will be reported to WHITE HOUSE VIEILLE CHAPELLE.

B.L. Anderson Major
Bde Major Dehra Dun Bde

Copy 1 and 2 retained   Copy 7 to 2 Coy Train   13 to Jullunder Bde.
" 2 to 1st Seaforths   " 8 - Meerut Div   14 to Lahore Div.
" 3 " 4th "   " 9 - 4 Bde RFA
" 4 - 6th Jats   " 10 - 21st Bde
" 5 " 9th Gurkhas   " 11 - Garhwal Bde
" 6 - 2nd "   " 12 - 28th Bde.

Date	Unit	From	To	Route	Remarks
night 10th/11th July	1st Seaforths two Companies	KINGS ROAD	LA GORGUE and L'EPINETTE	RICHEBOURG ST VAAST — FOSSE BRIDGE	To march in small parties closing after passing RICHEBOURG. Last party to be clear of RICHEBOURG by 9-45 pm.
night 10th/11th July	1st Seaforths two Companies	Trenches	LA GORGUE L'EPINETTE	" " " "	To march in small parties closing after passing RICHEBOURG.
10th/11th July	,, ,, Seaforths	Trenches	" "	" " "	To march in small parties closing after passing RICHEBOURG.
10th/11th July	9th Gurkhas	KING GEORGES ROAD	CALONNE	RICHEBOURG ST VAAST — FOSSE BRIDGE — Road junction R.15.a.2.10 — L'EPINETTE.	To march in small parties closing after passing RICHEBOURG. Last party to be clear of RICHEBOURG by 8-45 pm.
10th/11th July	2nd Gurkhas	KINGS ROAD	CALONNE	" " " "	To march in small parties closing after passing RICHEBOURG; last party to be clear of RICHEBOURG by 9-15 pm.
10th/11th July	6th Jats	Trenches	CALONNE	" " " "	
10th/11th July	Machine Guns 107th Pioneers	Trenches	8 MAISONS	" " " "	To march in small parties closing after passing RICHEBOURG.
10th/11th July	Machine Guns 4th Cavalry	Trenches	CALONNE	RICHEBOURG ST VAAST.	To rejoin 107th Pioneers.
10th/11th July	Bomb Gun Section 4th Cavalry	KINGS ROAD	CALONNE	with 6th Jats.	
				with 2nd Gurkhas	To rejoin 4th Cavalry.

APPX. H

TEMPORARY COMPOSITION OF DEHRA DUN and JULLUNDER BRIGADES.

DEHRA DUN BRIGADE.

Brigadier General JACOB.

	B.M.	S.C.
Bde Head Quarters	ANDERSON	WYATT

6th Jats.

41st Dogras.

47th Sikhs.

58th Rifles.

2/2nd Gurkha Rifles.

1/9th Gurkha Rifles.

JULLUNDER BRIGADE.

Brigadier General STRICKLAND.

	B.M.	S.C.
Bde Head Quarters	ALEXANDER	SCOTT

1st Manchesters.

1st Seaforths.

4th Suffolks.

4th Seaforths.

Major.
Brigade Major Dehra Dun Bde.

OPERATION ORDER NO. 27.
By
Brigadier General E.P.Strickland,C.M.G.,D.S.O.
Commanding Jullundur Brigade.
13th July 1915.

Copy No. 3
Appx. "I"

1. The Brigade will take over the line from PORT ARTHUR to SIGN POST LANE, inclusive, from SIRHIND Brigade, on the night of the 14th/15th July.

RIGHT SUBSECTION. Lieut Colonel T.W.CUTHBERT D.S.O.
1st Seaforths and 4th Seaforths (less 2 Coys) from PORT ARTHUR inclusive to a point 100 yards S.W. of the SAP South of NEUVE CHAPELLE. Headquarters at North end of HUN Street.

LEFT SUBSECTION. Lieut Colonel H.W.CRUDDAS,D.S.O.,
4th Suffolks (less 2 Coys) and 1st Manchesters from left of 4th Seaforths to SIGN POST LANE, inclusive. Headquarters in a house on CHIMNEY CRESCENT about 500 yards South of CURZON POST.

Works   CHATEAU REDOUBT, CHURCH REDOUBT and HILL's REDOUBT will be
40 rifles in   garrisoned by 15th Lancers. (40 rifles in each)
each.   PORT ARTHUR KEEP by 1st Seaforths (50 rifles).

BRIGADE RESERVE.
To Right Sub Section -2 Coys 4th Seaforths at PONT LOGY.
To Left Sub Section - 2 Coys 4th Suffolks near CURZON POST.

2. Machine Guns and bomb guns in the line will be relieved under arrangements to be made by the Brigade Machine Gun Officer and Bomb Gun Officer respectively.

3. All details of reliefs will be arranged by Sub Sections Commanders in direct communication with the Officers Commanding the Units they are relieving.

4. 200 rounds S.A.A. per man will be taken into the line, with the exception of men carrying bombs who will carry 50 rounds.

5. O.C.Units will send to Brigade Headquarters a list of trench stores taken over by them from relieved units.

6. Units will pass PONT DU HEM cross roads as follows:-
1st Manchesters at 9.p.m.
4th Suffolks at 9.15.p.m.
1st Seaforths at 9.30.p.m.
4th Seaforths at 9.45.p.m.

7. 11th Bde R.F.A. are supporting Artillery Bde.

8. Progress of reliefs to be immediately reported to Sirhind Bde to whom all reports will be sent till 10a.m. on 15th

9. Brigade Headquarters will remain at present location till 10a.m. 15th instant when they will open at PONT DU HEM (M.14.D.10/9) where all reports should be sent.

Captain.
Brigade Major, Jullundur Brigade.

Issued to Signals at 4.p.m.

Copy No. 1. 1st Manchesters.
2. 4th Suffolks.
3. 1st Seaforths.
4. 4th Seaforths.
5. Bde Machine Gun Officer.
6. Bde Bomb Gun Officer.
7. Bde Signals.
8. Bde Supply Officer.
9. No. 3 Coy R.E.
10. Ferozepore Bde.
11. Sirhind Bde.
12. 11th Bde R.F.A.
13. 26th Coy S.& M.
14. 22nd Infantry Bde.
15. Lahore Division.
16. 15th Lancers.
17. Reht.15th Lancers (Thro' Sirhind Bde).
18.
19. Diary.
20.

Operation Order No. 29.   Copy No. 11

By

Brigadier General E.P.Strickland C.M.G.,D.S.O.
Commanding Jullundur Brigade.
30th June 1915.

Secret   Copy "J" APP
                                                              for W.D

Reference BETHUNE combined sheet 1/40000.

1. Ferozepore Brigade will relieve Jullundur Brigade on night 31st July / 1st August.

   4th King's Regiment will take over the line from LA BASSEE Road inclusive to OXFORD Street exclusive, including PORT ARTHUR.

   89th Punjabis and 100 Rifles 129th Baluchis will take over from OXFORD Street inclusive to CHURCH Street exclusive, including HILL's redoubt ((garrisoned by 15th Lancers who will remain).

   Connaught Rangers will take over from CHURCH Street inclusive to SIGN POST LANE exclusive, including CHURCH and CHATEAU Redoubts (garrisoned by 15th Lancers who will remain).

   57th Rifles will take over from SIGN POST LANE inclusive to COLVIN TRENCH inclusive, including LAFONE POST.

   4th Londons will take over PONT LOGY and CURZON POST.

   129th Baluchis will take over the Reserve Trenches at M.34.B.2/0.

   Guides and details of reliefs will be arranged mutually by Commanding Officers concerned.

2. A list of trench stores handed over will be given to relieving Commanding Officers and a duplicate sent to Brigade Headquarters on 1st August.

3. 200 rounds S.A.A. per man and 150 hand bombs per Regiment will be brought out of the Trenches.

4. Reliefs of Machine Guns will be arranged by Brigade Machine Gun Officer with Brigade Machine Gun Officer Ferozepore Brigade.

   Bomb Guns and 2 Guns of No.4.T.M.Battery at present in the line will come out with Battalions in whose areas they are located.

   The Section No.5.Motor M.G.Battery will be relieved separately under the orders of Ferozepore Brigade on the Night 31st July/1st August.

   Relieving Units will pass PONT DU HEM cross roads as follows:-

   4th King's Regt.....8.30.p.m.
   89th Punjabis.......8.45.p.m.
   Connaught Rangers...9.p.m.
   57th Rifles........9.15.p.m.
   129th Baluchis.....9.30.p.m.
   4th Londons........10.30.p.m.

   Ferozepore Brigade are posting officers to control traffic at EUSTON Post, ROUGE CROIX and PONT DU HEM.

   All Units will march to billets via LA BASSEE Road - PONT DU HEM cross roads. Billeting orders will issue separately.

   The detachment 4th Seaforths at CURZON POST will rejoin their Company at PONT LOGY at 7.p.m. 31st instant.

6. O.C.Units will wire progress of reliefs to Brigade Headquarters.

7. G.O.C.Jullundur Brigade will remain in Command of the line till 10.a.m. 1st August, at which hour Brigade Headquarters will move to White House, VIELLE CHAPELLE.Sq. R.34.A.3/6.

                                                          Captain.
                    Brigade Major, Jullundur Brigade...
Copy. No. 1.Lahore Division.   Issued to signals at 3.p.m.
         2.Ferozepore Bde.
         3.Sirhind Bde.
         4.5th Brigade R.F.A.   8. 4th Suffolks.
         5.11th Bde R.F.A.   9. 1st Seaforths.
         6. C.R.E.Lahore Lahore Divn 10. 4th Seaforths.
         7.1st Manchesters.   11. 47th Sikhs.
                                     12. 59th Rifles.
                                     13. Bde Machine Gun Officer.
        18.No.3.Coy.LDT.   14. Bde Bomb Gun Officer.
        19.Bde Supply Officer.   15. No.5.Motor M.G.Battery.
        20 - 24. Diary and spare.   16. No.4.T.M.Battery.
                                     17. Bde Signals.

Meerut Division
1st BN. Seaforth Highlanders
From 1st To 31 August 1915

Serial No 260

10.V.
Herbert

Confidential

121/6958

War Diary

of

1st Bn. Seaforth Highlanders.

FROM 1st August 1915. TO 31st August 1915.

A
September 1915.

Army Form C. 2118.

WAR DIARY
or
INTELLIGENCE SUMMARY.
(Erase heading not required.)

VOL XII PAGE 133

Instructions regarding War Diaries and Intelligence Summaries are contained in F.S. Regs., Part II. and the Staff Manual respectively. Title pages will be prepared in manuscript.

Place	Date	Hour	Summary of Events and Information	Remarks and references to Appendices
	1915			REF: BETHUNE SHEET. 1:40000
	1st August		In Billets at LA CLORGUE. Day spent in men getting cleaned up and clothes washed. BISHOP of NAGPUR held a divine service at 6.30 P.M.	
				Casualties nil
	2nd August		BRIGADIER GENERAL JACOB's C.B. Commanding DEHRA DUN Bde. visited the Commdg Officer at 9 A.M. Several Officers visited Baths were opened and allotted to the Bn. from 9 A.M. to 4 P.M. men being the time to bathe and change their clothes after their long spell in the trenches. We held in readiness at 8 P.M. every one equipped, although somewhat damped by a heavy shower. Brigadier and officers (and Major and officers) of the 4th Bn dined with the C.O. (Major Thomson) after the concert.	
				Casualties 2 sick
	3rd August		Some rain. 2nd Lt. CHRISTIE & Corpl. FORSYTH & unit 65 les 8 MAISONS for 9 P.M.	

T2134. Wt. W708—776. 500000. 4/15. Sir J. C. & S.

Army Form C. 2118.

VOL. VIII PAGE 134

WAR DIARY
or
INTELLIGENCE SUMMARY.
(Erase heading not required.)

Place	Date	Hour	Summary of Events and Information	Remarks and references to Appendices
	Continued 3rd August		instructions in the WEST, BOMB-THROWING CATAPULT. REV. J. H. MACNEILL brought to MEERUT DIVISION cavalry clearing station, CAPT. BRODIE, LIEUTS CULL and Kilgour went on leave. LIEUT WALKER, 3rd Gordons transferred to 1st Gordons.	REF. BETHUNE SHEET 40.N.W. Casualties 3 Sick
	4th August.	9 A.M.	Heavy rain in the morning. Holy Communion was held at 8 A.M. by REV. UNWIN. Battalion marched through LA GORGUE and Cinomatographed and a photo taken of S.M. SUTHERLAND, and 4 other N.C.O.'s men with distinguished service medals. 2 N.C.O's and 2 men were sent to the Divisional Magazine for instructions in firing BOMBS. Officers had a wicked match with the Officers of the 9th Seaforths in which the latter were the victors. Captain Cathill & members of the 2 Coy M.A.C. gave a concert in the evening which lerved out a great success, Lce Corpl Sanford 1st Seaforth being the Star performer.	Casualties 1 Sick

Army Form C. 2118.

135

WAR DIARY
or
INTELLIGENCE SUMMARY.
(Erase heading not required.)

Place	Date	Hour	Summary of Events and Information	Remarks and references to Appendices
	5th AUGUST		Warm wet in light breeze. Companies held parades for bathing Marching, Bayonet-fighting, Bomb throwing etc.	REF. BÉTHUNE SHEET 1/40,000
				Casualties 1 Sick
	6th AUGUST		Slight showers during the day. 3 Officers & 2 to 6 Hand rounds proceeded to LENGHEM for practice firing with Telescopic sights, night firing etc. In the afternoon a cricket match took place between the Officers of the 1st & 4th Bn³ Seaforths and the Officers of the 3/4 Bn 2nd Gurkhas & 1st Bn Gurkhas in which the latter were the Victors. Bn Crew Jacob played day played for the Officers of the Indian Battalions. Running Marching & bathing parades took place during the day	Appx L oxxx
				Casualties 1 Sick

Army Form C. 2118.

WAR DIARY
or
INTELLIGENCE SUMMARY.
(Erase heading not required.)

Instructions regarding War Diaries and Intelligence Summaries are contained in F. S. Regs., Part II. and the Staff Manual respectively. Title pages will be prepared in manuscript.

Place	Date	Hour	Summary of Events and Information	Remarks and references to Appendices
	7th August		Hot and sultry. Br. General Jacob CB & Major Thompson and Captain K.M. Anderson visited the 26th Bn. near A.R.R.A.S.	REF. 57/11114 SHEET 1/40,000 Arras
			Casualties 2 O.Rs	
	8th August		Dull and Damp. Divine service held at 11 A.M. in cricket field. Rev. McLeod 1/4 13th officiating. Battalion paraded at 8.30 p.m. and marched to PONT DU HEM where we relieved the 39th Bn. 9th M.R. CANADAS in Brigade reserve. Relief completed by 11 A.M.	
			Casualties 2 O.Rs	
	9th August		In Billets at PONT DU HEM. Officers then coy commander Parade for Marching, Bathing, clothing etc. evidenced when possible. C.O. and coy Commanders visited Hd. Qrs & companies of 7th & 1/9 Buckingham in Trenches finding out in doing so new routes by which they	

Army Form C. 2118.

134

WAR DIARY
or
INTELLIGENCE SUMMARY.
(Erase heading not required.)

Instructions regarding War Diaries and Intelligence Summaries are contained in F. S. Regs., Part II. and the Staff Manual respectively. Title pages will be prepared in manuscript.

Place	Date	Hour	Summary of Events and Information	Remarks and references to Appendices
Continued	9th August		Could reinforce the above mentioned units quickly required div H.Q.s & new recived from Auchens Gun class at MOLENGHEM M.E	REF. BETHUNE SHEET 1:40,000
				Casualties 2 sick
	10th August	Very Hot	20 men of 2nd Black Watch attached for 3 days reported their units at LAVENTIE. Boys near München the LA BASSEE Canal &/M Battery.	
				Casualties 2 Sick
	11th August		Hot — with a light Breeze. Parade for training continued. 2nd Lieut McNaughton joined from the Scots Greys in accordance Capt T. Brodie, Lieut Cobb and 2nd Lieut Kilgour rejoined from base to the B.W. United Kingdom. Fatigue party of 4 Officers & other and Rank	14.15 4.p.m ? 2M? P.K.W.M. Truth

Army Form C. 2118.

WAR DIARY
or
INTELLIGENCE SUMMARY.
(Erase heading not required.)

Instructions regarding War Diaries and Intelligence Summaries are contained in F. S. Regs., Part II. and the Staff Manual respectively. Title pages will be prepared in manuscript.

133

Place	Date	Hour	Summary of Events and Information	Remarks and references to Appendices
	11th August	Coy	Immediately behind the Gas Trench. 26 Posumee were killed by a Rifle Bullet traversing the night, and a Pte.B. 2 wounded.	REF BETHUNE SHEET KINZON
			Casualties	Return 1 wounded OR and 1 OR Total 3
	13th August	Day	Hot and Sultry. LIEUT MAXWELL & 2ND LIEUT BUCHANAN proceeded on leave to 10th U.K. Buchanan broke down at 9.30 PM and relieved the 1/9 Gurkhas on the front line. 3 Coys being in the firing line A, B & C. and are in support = D Coy. A Coy furnishing a garrison in LA FONE REDOUBT.(1 Officer + 53 Men), and "D" Coy furnishing a garrison of 1 Officer and 31 men in TILLELOY SOUTH POST. 2 N.C.O's were being unanimous during the relief by left five. A platoon of 8th Munster Fusiliers were attached to the Bn for instruction in the trench warfare. One man was wounded during relief. Casualties = 1 wounded 3 sick	

T2134. Wt. W708—776. 500000. 4/15. Sir J. C. & S.

Place	Date	Hour	Summary of Events and Information	Remarks and references to Appendices
	13th August		Dull and inclined to be wet. At 6.30 a.m. Enemy opened a Bombardment on our Trenches by MINENWERFERS followed immediately by a short burst from Field Guns. This lasted for about 50 yards completely demolishing, but luckily there first one burst in front of our own wire failing to reach into the Support Trench in rear with the result that we had no casualties. After a long delay their Howitzer Battery fired about 5 rounds, received no known reg. witness but on to this by a Rifle Breast and drew in hit. In following day Casualties 2 wounded 6.S. 3 left.	REF BETHUNE SHEET 1/40000
	14th August		Dins crisp morning, very quiet. Parapet keepers, repaired during the nights one man killed by machine guns fire during the repairing of the Breach. It was to form an iron netting to the top of 24 hours Trench loopholes, they received in the front line all night. Casualties 1 Killed 4 Sick	

Army Form C. 2118.

WAR DIARY
or
INTELLIGENCE SUMMARY.
(Erase heading not required.)

Instructions regarding War Diaries and Intelligence Summaries are contained in F. S. Regs., Part II. and the Staff Manual respectively. Title pages will be prepared in manuscript.

Place	Date	Hour	Summary of Events and Information	Remarks and references to Appendices
	15th August		Fine in Morning. Heavy Showers during the day. Lieut Turnsgitt Killed by a rifle bullet whilst out reconnoitring the wire in front of Parapet. Cadet Atkchen left for D.N. Headquarters. Casualties 1 Killed	REF SKETCH SHEET (N.W.F.) M. 45747 a the
	16th August		Dep. Line. Lieut Macleod proceeded on 2 weeks leave to the U.K. Reported by General Strickland that in front of BAREILLY BRIGADE on our left, we received word to stand to arms, opened a slow alarm so we stood down again and continued with our Trenches. Battalion relieved by the 1/9 Gurkha Rifles relief fairly delayed partly on account of the Relief of the North Staffords (R. Amy) attack an being completed until 2 A.M. by us. This dark relief was not completed until 2 A.M. when we marched to our previous Billets at PONT. NO HENI. Casualties 3 Lieut	

Army Form C. 2118.

WAR DIARY
or
INTELLIGENCE SUMMARY.
(Erase heading not required.)

Instructions regarding War Diaries and Intelligence Summaries are contained in F. S. Regs., Part II. and the Staff Manual respectively. Title pages will be prepared in manuscript.

Place	Date	Hour	Summary of Events and Information	Remarks and references to Appendices
	17th August		In Billets at PONT DU HEM. Hot and sultry, boys marched to the LA BASSEE CANAL for Bathing. 300 men detailed down to carry materials front line for use in Trenches. Casualties Nil	REF BETHUNE SHEET 1/40,000
	18th August		Day fine at LOMEau SOUTH TURNEY POSTS in preparation had to be approached by men being relieved and still discovered to be covered by sap, wire exchanged by Parties of "B" Company relieving on similar party of "D" Coy. Remainder of "B" Coy paraded at 8.15 P.M. and left for "B LINE" in Reserve to the 7th Reports. Carrying on and digging parties of 330 men with officers were on duties on communication Trenches one man being killed. Notification received that Lt. D. MacMahon would be permitted to a commission expiring in the East LANCASHIRE REGT. Casualties 1 killed 1 sick	

T2134. Wt. W708—776. 500000. 4/15. Sir J. C. & S.

WAR DIARY or INTELLIGENCE SUMMARY

Army Form C. 2118.

(Erase heading not required.)

Instructions regarding War Diaries and Intelligence Summaries are contained in F. S. Regs., Part II. and the Staff Manual respectively. Title pages will be prepared in manuscript.

Place	Date	Hour	Summary of Events and Information	Remarks and references to Appendices
	19th August		Morning quiet and sultry. Enemy fired about 60 shrapnel into our Billets at PONT DU HEM but doing no damage. They also shelled round about BDE HEADQUARTERS, at Rue de PARADIS and LAVENTIE. 220 men & 3 Officers working on a carrying & digging party with R.E. to Breast-work in Breast work and support Trenches. Casualties 2 NCR 1 Sick	Reference between 31st & 1st/1st.R.W.F (Shrapnel) GSW App O GSW
	20 AUGUST		In connection between our Company Commander, trouble in front line trenches brought to a large over Bridge. Cut her head at 11:15 P.M whilst leading the 1/4 Leaks to in the front line. Being completed by 10.45 P.M. very quiet during the time which were going on, but about 11 P.M. heavy fire opened away Heavy Rifle & Machine Gun fire on our front line. Only damage and three wounded slightly. Work on improving trenches carried out during the night. Casualties 1 Wounded & 1 Sick	MM

T2134. Wt. W708—776. 500000. 4/15. Sir J. C. & S.

Army Form C. 2118.

WAR DIARY
or
INTELLIGENCE SUMMARY.
(Erase heading not required.)

Instructions regarding War Diaries and Intelligence Summaries are contained in F. S. Regs., Part II. and the Staff Manual respectively. Title pages will be prepared in manuscript.

Place	Date	Hour	Summary of Events and Information	Remarks and references to Appendices
	21st August		Work on improving Trenches and communications continued. Hostile Rifle fire less than normal, pursued about Midnight and kept up until dawn. A great deal of shooting and digging went on in enemy's Trenches. Casualties Wounded 2 Ors.	REFERENCE BETWEEN LINES Instructions
	22nd August		G.O.C. Brigade visited the Trenches. Situation normal. Hostile Rifle fire heavy at times and then aeroplanes very active. 2nd Lieut STEVENSON 3rd ARGYLE and SUTHERLAND HIGHLANDERS attached was wounded by a Bomb on which he was experimenting. Casualties 1 Officer and 2 men Wounded, 1 Man killed, 2 Sick.	
	23rd August		O.C. 2nd BLACK WATCH R.H. visited Trenches with his transport commander preparatory to their delivering us Hostile Rifle and artillery fire about normal, Much noise in enemy's tient Continued	

Army Form C. 2118.

WAR DIARY
or
INTELLIGENCE SUMMARY.
(Erase heading not required.)

Instructions regarding War Diaries and Intelligence Summaries are contained in F. S. Regs., Part II. and the Staff Manual respectively. Title pages will be prepared in manuscript.

Place	Date	Hour	Summary of Events and Information	Remarks and references to Appendices
	23rd August Continued			REFERENCE BETHUNE SHEET 36A
			A small search light switched on from enemys lines about 1.30 A.M.	
			At 2 A.M. a great deal of flares were seen behind Ger lines followed immediately by heavy rifle fire as if they were practicing night-operations. 2nd Lieuts NORBURY, WYLIE, and DENNISTON joined the Battalion on first appointment and posted to companies.	MR 2/L MR
			2nd LIEUT CAMPBELL returned from leave.	
			Casualties nil.	
	24th August		About 4.30 A.M Enemy bombarded the left of our line with small Menenwerfer air bomb guns retaliated to such an extent that they were compelled to stop. Enemy who with short abusive language resort to which our men instantly retaliated. Remainder of day labour. 2nd LIEUT MACLEOD returned from leave and 2nd LIEUT STEWART proceeded on leave. 2nd Bn. R.H. BLACK WATCH relieved the Bn. relief completed by 10.40 P.M. without casualties. Bn. marched to Billets at LA GORGUE.	MR
			Casualties nil.	

Army Form C. 2118.

WAR DIARY
or
INTELLIGENCE SUMMARY.
(Erase heading not required.)

Instructions regarding War Diaries and Intelligence Summaries are contained in F. S. Regs., Part II. and the Staff Manual respectively. Title pages will be prepared in manuscript.

Place	Date	Hour	Summary of Events and Information	Remarks and references to Appendices
	25th August		In billets at LA GORGUE. 35 Rank and File Reinforcements joined and were posted to Companies. Day devoted to the men getting their Clothes Equipment etc clean, and Rifles inspected by Armourer Sgt.	SHEET 36.A. "A" SERIES
			Casualties Nil	
	26 August		The Meerut Divisional Bath was available to the Battalion and as to A.A.B. Bath were issued with a change of underclothing.	
			2nd Lieut. McNAUGHTON returned from leave.	
			Casualties 2 Sick.	
	27th August		Major LOWTH and Capt. BUTT sailed for ENGLAND	
			Adjutant received a different dress than Issued to PURITS. Orders issued to be observed by the Brigade and having to remain on the line, no fires when all night into sentrilies under RE. The following Decorations were granted by the Russian Government to S.M. McAdam Crew of the orders of St. George 3rd Class "Lce Sergt. McBride Sce Corp Pritchard Pte Harken whose name as it Class" Continued

T2134. Wt. W708—776. 500000. 4/15. Sir J. C. & S.

Army Form C. 2118.

WAR DIARY
or
INTELLIGENCE SUMMARY.
(Erase heading not required.)

Instructions regarding War Diaries and Intelligence Summaries are contained in F. S. Regs., Part II. and the Staff Manual respectively. Title pages will be prepared in manuscript.

Place	Date	Hour	Summary of Events and Information	Remarks and references to Appendices
	27th August	Continues	Sgt Brandin 3rd K.R.R. attached "Menin" Dr George, 3.5 Recon and 6 file reinforcements joined and were posted to Companies	SHEET 36A. FRANCE 73 SERIES
	28th August		Posts as usual occupied by the Battalion. Croix Barbée (East) Lieut. Cunliffe with 20 other Ranks. Rue du Puits Lieut. Brown with 25 other Ranks. Rouge Croix 2nd Lieut Neatby with 50 other Ranks. 100 Men working in trenches under R.E. Casualties Nil	
	29th August		Church Parade held during the morning. Key of the Bde consisting of the Welsh & the other half the L.F. moved into Pelerin to relieve the Munsters. 2nd Div Headquarters working in front line under R.E. Heavy rain during the evening and at night. Casualties 2 Sick	

Army Form C. 2118.

WAR DIARY
or
INTELLIGENCE SUMMARY.
(Erase heading not required.)

Instructions regarding War Diaries and Intelligence Summaries are contained in F.S. Regs., Part II. and the Staff Manual respectively. Title pages will be prepared in manuscript.

Place	Date	Hour	Summary of Events and Information	Remarks and references to Appendices
	30th August		Bombs examined. New Tube Respirators received 70 to 80 & test of these to search 2 officers and 2 N.C.Os of Platoon in Front Line under R.E.	REF. SHEET 36A (RANGE 'B') SERIES.
			Casualties Nil.	
	31st August		Three Officers proceeded to G.H.B. to inspect German captured Blockhouse with a view of gaining knowledge of all important army of the no man's land forward up to the enemy lines. Attack 3rd Sept. by a Court of Enquiry to enquire the killing in Action of 3 N.C.Os reference to Sgt KNIGHT & 2 Cause Instruction in Mortar Bombs. Lieut DAVIDSON admitted to Hospital Sick. Casualties 1 officer + 3 other ranks sick.	

Operation Order No 46
by
Brigadier General C W Jacob, C.B.
Commanding Dehra Dun Brigade
LA GORGUE 6-8-15

Appx L
3

Reference Sheets FRANCE 36a and BELGIUM & FRANCE 36. 1/40000.

1. The Brigade will relieve the GARHWAL Brigade in the trenches on night 8th/9th August.
2. 4th Seaforth Highlanders will relieve 2/3rd Gurkhas in A Subsection.
   9th Gurkhas will relieve 2nd Leicesters in B Subsection.
   6th Jats will relieve 2/8th Gurkhas in C Subsection.
   Brigade Reserve:-
      2nd Gurkhas on RUGBY Road in billets now occupied by 1/3rd Londons.
      1st Seaforths on LA BASSEE Road near PONT DU HEM in billets now occupied by Garhwal Rifles.
   Movements in accordance with attached movement table.
3. Maxim and Bomb Gun reliefs will be carried out on night 7th/8th Instant.
4. Troops of the 19th Division will be attached to the Brigade for instruction.
5. No 11 French Howitzer Battery will be attached to the Brigade.
6. Reports to RUE DE PARADIS.

Issued at 8 a.m.

B E Amberson Major
Bde Major Dehra Dun Bde

Copy 1 and 2 retained
Copy 3 to 1st Seaforths
Copy 4 to 4th Seaforths
Copy 5 to 6th Jats
Copy 6 to 9th Gurkhas
Copy 7 to 2nd Gurkhas
Copy 8 to Garhwal Bde

Copy 9 to 2 Coy Train
Copy 10 to Bde Bomb Gun
Copy 11 to Sig Officer
Copy 12 to Bde M.G.O.

Movement Table.

Unit	Point where junction with main.	Time	Route	Remarks
8th Gork.	Road junction on M.14.b.	8-15 p.m.	Road junction R.35.b. o/S. – LA BASSEE Road.	No movement of troops E & S of line PONT DU HEM – LA FLINQUE before 8-30 p.m.
9th Gurkhas	PONT DU HEM	8-30 p.m.	Road junction R.12.c. 6/3 – CHELTENHAM ROAD	"
4th Seaforths	ROUGE CROIX cross Roads	8-50 p.m.	Road junction R.35.b. o/S. – LA BASSEE ROAD.	"
2nd Gurkhas	RUGBY ROAD.	9 p.m.	LA BASSEE ROAD.	"
1st Seaforths	PONT DU HEM	9-15 p.m.	Road junction R.35.b. o/S. – LA BASSEE ROAD.	"

Operation Order No 47
by
Brigadier General C.W. Jacob C.B.
Commanding Dehra Dun Bde.

Appx 174

11th August 1915.

1. Reliefs will be carried out as under on night 12/13th August. Details of reliefs to be arranged between Comdg Officers concerned:—
   2nd Gurkhas to relieve "A" Subsection.
   1st Seaforths to relieve B Subsection.

2. MOATED GRANGE communicating trench will be at disposal of B Subsection until 11.p.m

3. 4 Platoons 8th North Staffords will be attached to 1st Seaforths in trenches for instruction and will join 1st Seaforths at PONT DU HEM at 7 pm on 12th Instant.

4. One Company 10th Warwicks (200 Rifles) will remain attached to the Brigade and will billet in CARTERS POST M.2.C.9/1.

5. Platoons of 10th Warwicks in trenches will on relief march to billets in ESTAIRES.

6. 8th North Staffords will relieve 10th Warwicks in billets on LA BASSEE ROAD on 12th Instant under arrangements to be made by 57th Brigade.

7. Reports to RUE DE PARADIS.

Issued at 5.30 pm.

B.G. Anderson Major
Bde. Major Dehra Dun Bde.

Copy 1 & 2 retained   Copy 9 to 10th Warwicks
Copy 3 to Meerut Div   Copy 10 to 8th N. Staffords
Copy 4 to 1st Seaforth   Copy 11 to 57th Bde
Copy 5 to 4th Seaforth   Copy 12 to Bareilly Bde
Copy 6 to 6th Jats   Copy 13 to Ferozepore Bde
Copy 7 to 9th Gurkhas   Copy 14 to 13th Bde R F A
Copy 8 to 2nd Gurkhas   Copy 15 to 2 Coy Train

Operation Order No 47.   App IV
by
Lieutenant Colonel G.T. Widdicombe C.B.
Commanding Dehra Dun Bde.   15th August 1915

Reference Map FRANCE 1/10000 36.S.W. B series 3rd Edition

1. From 6 pm on 16th Instant the front held by the Brigade will be divided as follows:—
   A. Subsection — SIGN POST LANE inclusive to COLVIN communication trench inclusive. Headquarters EBENEZER FARM.
   B. Subsection — COLVIN communication trench exclusive to WINCHESTER ROAD inclusive. Head Quarters temporarily — M.28.d.8/5.

2. The following reliefs will be carried out on the night 16th/17th August:—
   9th Gurkhas to relieve 2nd Gurkhas and 1st Seaforths in A Subsection.
   4th Seaforths to relieve 1st Seaforths in B Subsection.
   8 Platoons 8th N. Staffords now in trenches to rejoin Unit.
   4 Platoons N Staffords to join 4th Seaforths in trenches
   Details of reliefs to be arranged between Comdg Officers concerned.

3. Garrisons of Posts will be found as under:—
   LAFONE POST. 40 Rifles 1st Seaforths and 1 Machine gun 9th Gurkhas.
   TILLELOY SOUTH POST 30 Rifles 1st Seaforths
   TILLELOY NORTH POST 30 Rifles 2nd Gurkhas.

4. ROUGE CROIX POST EAST will be handed over to the BAREILLY Brigade at 6 pm on 16th Instant.

5. a. Machine Gun reliefs will be carried out before 7 pm on 16th Instant under arrangements of Brigade Machine Gun Officer.

6. Billets of relieved Units:—
   1st Seaforths :— PONT DU HEM
   2nd Gurkhas :— RUGBY ROAD.

6. Rockets with 1st Seaforths will be returned to Brigade Head Quarters.
All other trench stores will be handed over where they now are.
7. Reports to RUE DE PARADIS.

Issued at 9.30 pm   B E Anderson   Major
                     Bde Major Dehra Dun Brigade

Issued to Signal Section for distribution:—

Copy 1 and 2 retained
Copy 3. Meerut Division
Copy 4. 1st Seaforths
Copy 5. 4th Seaforths
Copy 6. 6th Jats
Copy 7. 9th Gurkhas
Copy 8. 2nd Gurkhas
Copy 9. 13th Bde RFA
Copy 10. 8th N. Staffords
Copy 11. Garhwal Bde
Copy 12. Bareilly Bde
Copy 13. Bde Machine Gun Officer
Copy 14. Bde Grenadier Officer
Copy 15. Bde Signalling Officer
Copy 16. 2 Coy Train
Copy 17. Ferozepore Bde.
Copy 18. Sirhind Brigade
Copy 19. 11 Trench Mortar Bty
Copy 20. Bde Bomb Gun Officer

WAR
DIARY

Operation Order No 48 App 3 'O'
by
Brigadier General C W Jacob CB.
Commanding Dehra Dun Brigade
19th August 1915.

Reference map FRANCE 1/20000 36. S.W.

1. The following reliefs will be carried out on night 20th/21st Inst:—
   2nd Gurkhas to relieve 3 Coys 9th Gurkhas in A. Subsection.
   1st Seaforths to relieve 4th Seaforths in B Subsection.
   2 Platoons 9th Welch to accompany 1st Seaforths to trenches in relief of 2 Platoons 9th Welch now with 4th Seaforths.

2. 1 Coy 9th Gurkhas will remain in B. line under orders of A Subsection Commander.

3. Garrisons of Posts will be found as under:—
   LAFONE POST :— 40 Rifles and 1 Machine Gun 9th Gurkhas
   TILLELOY. SOUTH POST :— 30 Rifles 9th Gurkhas.
   TILLELOY NORTH POST:— 30 Rifles 4th Seaforths.

4. Machine Gun reliefs will be carried out under arrangements to be made by Bde Machine Gun Officer before 7 pm on 20th Instant.

5. Billets of relieved Units:—
   4th Seaforths RUGBY ROAD.
   9th Gurkhas PONT DU HEM.

6. Reports to RUE DU PARADIS.

issued at 10 am

B E Anderson   Major
Bde Major Dehra Dun Bde

Copy 1 & 2 retained
Copy 3 to 1st Seaforths
Copy 4 to 4th Seaforths
Copy 5 to 9th Welch
Copy 6 to 9th Gurkhas
Copy 7 to 2nd Gurkhas
Copy 8 to Meerut Div
Copy 9 to Garhwal Bde
Copy 10 to Sirhind Bde

Copy 11 to 13th Bde RFA.
Copy 12 to B. M. G. O
Copy 13 to B. B G. O
Copy 14 to B. G. O.
Copy 15 to Signal Officer
Copy 16 to 2 Coy Train

Operation Orders No 49.
by
Brigadier General C. W. JACOB. C.B.
Commanding Dehra Dun Brigade
23rd August 1915.

Reference Sheets 36 and 36.A.

1. BAREILLY Brigade will relieve DEHRA DUN Brigade in IND. 3. Trenches on night 24th/25th Inst.
2. Reliefs and movements as per attached Table.
3. Machine and Bomb Gun reliefs will be carried out on the 23rd Inst.
4. Garrisons of Posts will be found as under at 7 p.m. on 24th Inst by the 9th Gurkhas:—
   MIN POST = 1. G.O and 25 Rifles
   RUGBY POST = 1. G.O and 25 Rifles.
   CROIX BARBEE EAST = 1. G.O and 38 Rifles.
5. No. 11 Trench Howitzer Battery and the 9th Welch Regiment will be attached to the BAREILLY Brigade.
6. Reports to RUE DU PARADIS until completion of relief.

Issued at 10 a.m.   [signed]   Major
                     Bde Major Dehra Dun Bde

Copy 1 and 2 retained   Copy 15. B.G.O
Copy 3.   1st Seaforths   Copy 16. B.M.G.O
Copy 4.   4th Seaforths   Copy 17. B.S.O
Copy 5.   9th Welch
Copy 6.   9th Gurkhas
Copy 7.   2nd Gurkhas
Copy 8.   Bareilly Bde
Copy 9.   Sirhind Bde
Copy 10. Garhwal Bde
Copy 11. Meerut Div
Copy 12. 13th Bde RFA
Copy 13. 11 Trench Bty
Copy 14. B.B.G.O

MOVEMENT TABLE.

Unit	Location	To be relieved by	Place where guides meet relieving Units	Time	Road	Destination	Remarks
2nd Gurkhas less One Coy of Gurkhas	IND. 3.A.	58th Rifles F.F. 1 Coy 2nd Black Watch. 1 Platoon 9th Welch 100 Rifles 69th Punjabis	ROUGE CROIX.	8-15 pm	SIGN POST LANE or next Communication trench — ROUGE CROIX-LA-BASSEE road.	Billets G.32.a+c.	Coy 9th Gurkhas to join battn at R-12 via Road junction M.20.a.4/4 and RIEZ BAILLEUL.
1st Seaforths 3 Platoons 9th Welch Regt.	IND. 3. B.	2nd Black Watch 3 Platoons 9th Welch Regt.	Junction WINCHESTER and BACQUEROT Roads	8-45 pm	MIN Communication trench — LA BASSEE road — Road junction G.32.a.0/0 — LA GORGUE.	Billets L.34.d	3 Platoons 9th Welch to rejoin Battn
4th Seaforths	Bde Reserve RUGBY ROAD.	1/4th Black Watch		8-30 pm	PONT DU HEM — LA BASSEE road — Road junction G.32.a.0/0 — LA GORGUE	Billets L.34.a+d.	
9th Gurkhas less One Coy.	Bde Reserve PONT DU HEM.	69th Punjabis		8-45 pm	Road junction M.20.a.4/4 — RIEZ BAILLEUL	R-12.	
		NOTE:- No movement EAST & SOUTH of line PONT DU HEM – LA FLINQUE before 8 p.m.					

Meerut Division
1st Seaforth Highlanders

From 1st To 30th Sept. 1915

Serial No. 260
D.D./Austral

11.VI
Lt/Herts

Confidential

printed

War Diary

with appendices

of

1st Seaforth Highlanders

FROM 1st September 1915. TO 30th September 1915.

Army Form C. 2118.

VOL. XIII

WAR DIARY
or
INTELLIGENCE SUMMARY.
(Erase heading not required.)

Instructions regarding War Diaries and Intelligence Summaries are contained in F. S. Regs., Part II. and the Staff Manual respectively. Title pages will be prepared in manuscript.

Place	Date	Hour	Summary of Events and Information	Remarks and references to Appendices
	1st SEPTEMBER 1915		Bn in Billets at LA CLOQUE. Brigadier Br-Genl. Guardier and Staff spoke to the B.C. on Battn and wishes to the officers and 2/o the men on fatigues. First trenches eight inspection duties.	REFERENCE SHEET 36A REVISED
				Casualties 3 sick
	2nd SEPTEMBER		Bomb throwing and bayonet fighting. Lieut FARRIER C.P.O. returned to Battn from leave. 2nd Lieut STONEY joined Battn from leave to the U.K.	
				Casualties 1 sick
	3rd SEPTEMBER		2nd Lieut ELLIOT and 25 other Ranks recently recovered sick from Casuals were posted to Companies in the same and 2/o all other ranks in front line all weight suffering went to trenches	App 'Q' Casualties 1 sick

WAR DIARY or INTELLIGENCE SUMMARY.

Army Form C. 2118.

Place	Date	Hour	Summary of Events and Information	Remarks and references to Appendices
	4th September 1915		MAJOR THOMSON and LIEUT ROSS returned from leave to U.K. on 3rd inst. At 6.45 C Coy relieved the 2nd Bn BLACK WATCH in RESERVE TRENCHES A.25.C (IND.S.7D) North of NEUVE CHAPELLE. Trenches were in a very filthy state. Casualties nil. Moving Billets completed by 8 P.M. Casualties nil	
	5th September		No.5414 Private A. Reid of "B" Coy accidentally shot and killed by Henry Mcrae. Pte of "A" Machine gun during the night. Casualties nil	
	6th September		Improving Communication Trenches and digging new ones approached running the day. Hostile artillery active. One gun at Tilley sent a few shells on Zillebeke and Gravenstafel. Casualties nil	

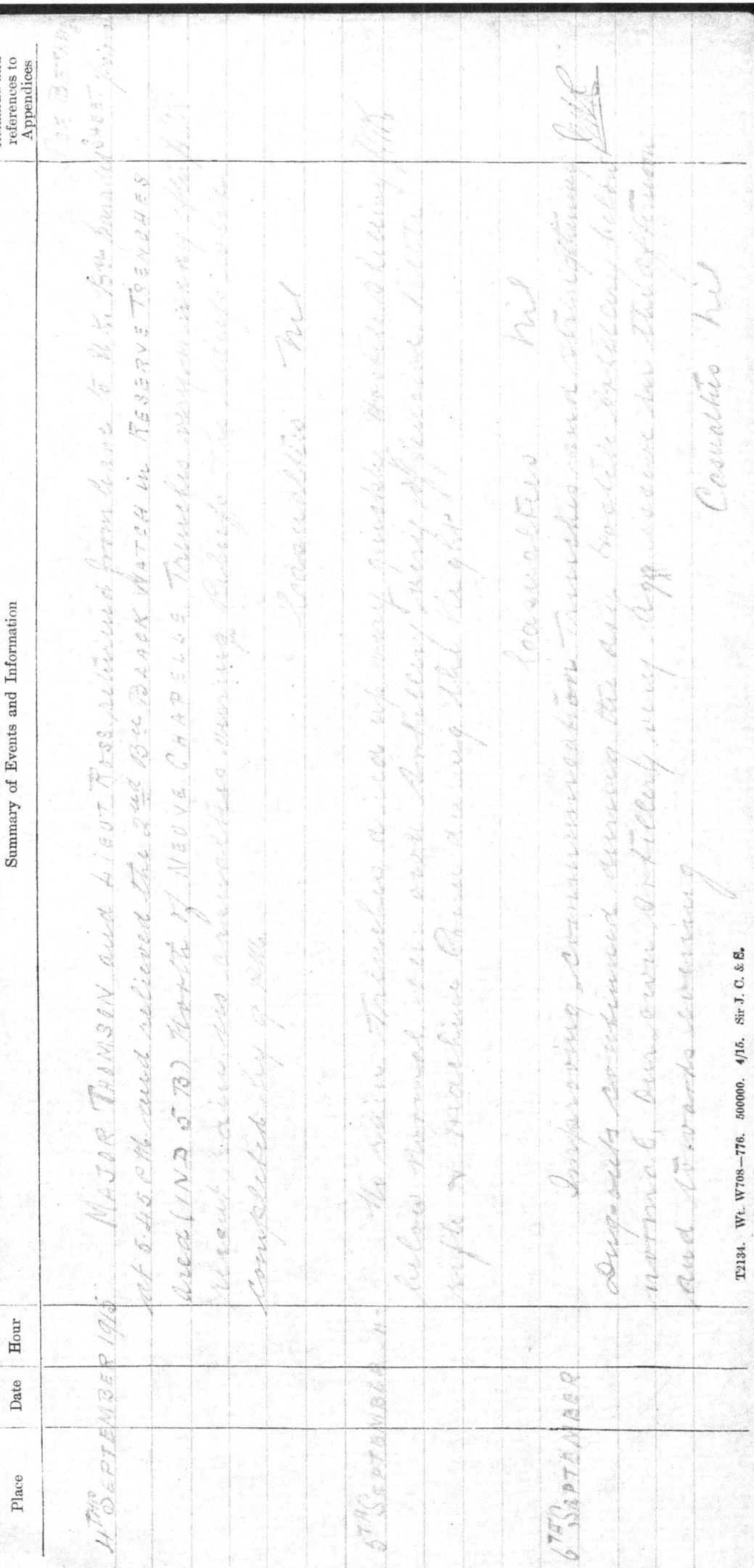

WAR DIARY or INTELLIGENCE SUMMARY.

Army Form C. 2118.

(Erase heading not required.)

Instructions regarding War Diaries and Intelligence Summaries are contained in F. S. Regs., Part II. and the Staff Manual respectively. Title pages will be prepared in manuscript.

Place	Date	Hour	Summary of Events and Information	Remarks and references to Appendices
	7th SEPTEMBER 1915		Hostile Artillery and Rifle fire usual. An addition to the enemy very active. In addition to the existing Captains THOMSON, BUCHANAN, CAPT WICKS, BAILLIE, BURN, ANSTRUTHER, MACKIE, LAING, LAING, VAIGNE, LINDSAY & Majors, Captain MACRAE to reinforced from EAST LANCASHIRE REGT. Second class of promotion. NORTH THEORY POST being held by platoons of 50 Lancashires & Lieut ERBUTHERS & 50 Bedfordshires. Capt KENT returned from HAVRE.	SEE BETHUNE SHEET 36
	8th SEPTEMBER		Battalion relieved by 1st Coldstreams on its right & left by 2nd Coldstreams. HQ CSM King hurt by R.E. Pyrotechnic Course from the Indians during the night. The casualties during the night were everything of Brownrigg W.	Appy 'R'
	9th SEPTEMBER		Wind changed from west to east over the tolerable limit. Work continued day and night improving existing Trenches and prepared 2nd LIEUT HADDON with a small patrol reconnoitred wire entanglement. MINE EXPLODED. Enemy mine exploded under the Tyburn & Noble Alleys at 3pm. Twenty during the night & which no casualties occurred [wounded]	

Army Form C. 2118.

WAR DIARY
or
INTELLIGENCE SUMMARY.
(Erase heading not required.)

Instructions regarding War Diaries and Intelligence Summaries are contained in F. S. Regs., Part II. and the Staff Manual respectively. Title pages will be prepared in manuscript.

Place	Date	Hour	Summary of Events and Information	Remarks and references to Appendices
	10TH SEPTEMBER 1915		Heavy shelling of our High Sap Coy. Our new bombing and sniping emplacements on Rampart Trenches unreported when engaged in Trench Mortar and rifle grenade fire by enemy during Relief.	10TH SEPTEMBER 3 A BEET /1/, 2, 3
			Casualties Nil	
	11TH SEPTEMBER		Work on Trenches continues. Situation normal. Artillery active on both sides fairly quiet.	Apx. 5
			Casualties 2 wounded 1 sick	
	12TH SEPTEMBER		Situation normal. B. & C. Coy Kings of Relieving with BORDER REGT. relieves Trenches at 10 AM Battalion relieved by the 22nd PUNJABIS, and Reliefs of the 6th BLACK WATCH, 1/4 BLACK WATCH, 4 / & 6th PUNJABIS. Relief completed by 8 PM & the 13th Marched to Billets at LA GORGUE.	Nil
			Casualties 1 wounded 2 sick	

WAR DIARY or INTELLIGENCE SUMMARY

Army Form C. 2118.

(Erase heading not required.)

Place	Date	Hour	Summary of Events and Information	Remarks and references to Appendices
	12th SEPTEMBER 1915		In Billets at LA GORGUE. Day mostly to visiting men in French cheval ups. Major Cuthbert 1st B.W. addressed all the Officers on the succession of his holding the command of the MEERUT DIVISION.	See Sheet 4 to Sept 1915 (inserted)
	14th SEPTEMBER		Company training for Trenches commenced early continued throughout the day. A conference was held by Major Cuthbert of the MAiR. Capt Brothers, Capt McAin & Capt W E Brothers & others in which splendid hints were given and were much appreciated by the junior officers. BUCHANAN rejoined from MACHINE GUN Corps at WISQUES. Casualties: 2 sick
	15th SEPTEMBER		Hot Baths were allotted to the 13th Coy in the morning. Marched and Change of Guard afterwards. Lieuts Ross and Matheson promoted Temporary Captains, and 2nd Lieuts Mailhead and Anderson promoted the former Lieut and the latter Temp Bigot. Lt Col HARVEY 2nd BLACK WATCH took over command of the BRIGADE (vice Col H.R.)	

Army Form C. 2118.

WAR DIARY
or
INTELLIGENCE SUMMARY.
(Erase heading not required.)

Instructions regarding War Diaries and Intelligence Summaries are contained in F. S. Regs., Part II. and the Staff Manual respectively. Title pages will be prepared in manuscript.

Place	Date	Hour	Summary of Events and Information	Remarks and references to Appendices
	16th September 1915		Training continued. BRIGADIER saw the officers in turn and expressed approval with what he had seen. 1st Essex & others in our Command. BRIGADE.	
			Casualties 2 sick	
	17th September		Work continued bringing in bay ones, sighting Machine Guns. 2 officers and 120 N.C.O. and other ranks on Ammunition fatigues in the front line.	
			Casualties 2 sick	
	18th September		2nd Lieut MALTBY Royal Scots Fusiliers was sent to Brigade with orders to report to the War Office in accordance with orders received at 2.15 a.m. the need which he is to fill in the Bn. Landed at 2.15. We need also the 2nd Rifles in the Reserve Line. The 4th Cheshires, the 10th and 9th Bn. Munsters sent up to Brigade. On receipt of the Battery of Canvas Engines in the Brigade, a Coy of Royal Welsh Disembark. Bty. prepared immediate to Bivouac Ridge completed by 7 P.M.	
			Casualties 1 sick	

WAR DIARY or INTELLIGENCE SUMMARY

Army Form C. 2118.

(Erase heading not required.)

Instructions regarding War Diaries and Intelligence Summaries are contained in F.S. Regs., Part II. and the Staff Manual respectively. Title pages will be prepared in manuscript.

Place	Date	Hour	Summary of Events and Information	Remarks and references to Appendices
	19th September	1915	Morning and forenoon quiet, but towards evening our Artillery were fairly active. A squadron of the ? run aeroplanes came over our lines flying very high. They were over for twenty minutes and though heavily bombarded by hostile fire kept their way and developed in a Westerly direction. A ? was sent up to support the ? but ?. Casualties wounded 3 Lieut ?	REFERENCE TRENCH MAP SHEET 36 SW 1 ?
	20th September		Hostile Artillery fairly active. Rifle + Machine Gun fire about normal. Enemy fired a few Rifle Grenades but a Coy's department line. Casualties 1 Killed 3 wounded	M.R.
	21st September		Slow bombardment on enemy trenches started about 2pm. App 54 "W" and continued all day. Enemy ? were ? during Heavy bombardment going on a few miles south of our position (at Map ref 27 British sect.) A few shells fell on our lines by enemy shrapnel that landed in ? behind ? of ? received ? attached. Casualties 1 killed, 5 wounded, 1 sick.	M.R.

Army Form C. 2118.

WAR DIARY
or
INTELLIGENCE SUMMARY.
(Erase heading not required.)

Instructions regarding War Diaries and Intelligence Summaries are contained in F. S. Regs., Part II. and the Staff Manual respectively. Title pages will be prepared in manuscript.

Place	Date	Hour	Summary of Events and Information	Remarks and references to Appendices
	1915			REF. MAP N.O 36 NE
	22nd SEPTEMBER		Bombardment continued and answered with vigor by enemy. Slight retaliation by enemy's guns. Our artillery bombarded Hun line opposite throughout last of the night. Bn came in from Reserve line, and Guards moved from Conduit Street into the Reserve line, and was attached in the Junction of N. Talbot Street and Reserve line. Operation orders 2. D. Brigade Received and Studied. Casualties 4 sick.	APP. 33, 34.1 FRASER 1,110.500 FRASER 24557-36 3 3x485 THIRD EDITION
	23rd SEPTEMBER		Bombardment still continued. Sent back army orders received from some Trench Mortars, behind our line afford in detail in the Shenton Order N.50 attached. A Coy of 2 Coys Loyal on reference APP. 'V' The 19 Cushions on the left of our line. Bn arrived by the APP. 'V' Battalion in our left. Bn K No3 and Bagsho 1st by that the ACH.A. W.X.Y. DUN BOE in the front line. Battalion remained in Reserve Lines. Casualties 1 Sick.	APP. 'V' 'W'. 'X'. 'Y'
	24th SEPTEMBER		Bombardment and enemy's lines still continued in (continued)	

WAR DIARY or INTELLIGENCE SUMMARY

Army Form C. 2118.

Place	Date	Hour	Summary of Events and Information	Remarks and references to Appendices
Contalmaison	24th September		accordance with 23rd Division order No. 56 paras 1 & 11 from Commanding, the Battalion concentrated in the RESERVE LINE, the DIVISIONAL RESERVE will move to [hutt?] forward of RUTHLEDY TRENCH immediately on the 25th inst. A meeting took place the following morning. Commanders completed by 4 p.m. The Assaulting Brigade & withdrew supports and Reserves being put in Position. See Operation order for the [Assault?] No 38. The following were received from Other Divl. HDE. To ALL UNITS. Fourth Army, Chief wishes troops to be informed that he feels confident they will nearly [?] our attack. He further wishes ["???"] reports on the situation wanted. Efforts of each Officer & Commander of this and charm He wishes this to be conveyed to these not fully and in such a manner as not to weaken our belief in the Enemy. Artillery Bombardment continues. Casualties Nil.	RE ENTRENCH MAP SHEET 56 SW 1:10,000 and MAP FRANCE SHEET 36 & Series 3RD EDITION Apx 2

T2134. Wt. W708—776. 500000. 4/15. Sir J. C. & S.

WAR DIARY
or
INTELLIGENCE SUMMARY.

(Erase heading not required.)

Army Form C. 2118.

Instructions regarding War Diaries and Intelligence Summaries are contained in F. S. Regs., Part II. and the Staff Manual respectively. Title pages will be prepared in manuscript.

Place	Date	Hour	Summary of Events and Information	Remarks and references to Appendices
	1915			
25TH SEPTEMBER			At 5.48 A.M. our Mine was so fired, & at 5.50 A.M. our return commenced and was carried out as per PROGRAMME 'A' attached, in accordance with instructions the 'B' Noted to RUE TILLELOY accordance with instructions the B' Noted 65 RUE TILLELOY the 58th Rifles having moved forward. Consecration of RUE TILLELOY completed by 7.30 AM. At 9.40 AM no further message received that the 58th had our front our posts so in accordance with the Previous instructions support were moved to hold their lines, enemy by this time has commenced a fairly heavy artillery fire on our line especially through support Reserve lines. At 10.40 A.M. Concentration order at B.M. 21 dated 25th Sept 1915 (attached) was received. B" Front and Support lines extending from SOUTH MOATED GRANGE STREET to NORTH TILLELOY STREET. During the movement for concentration operation order No.59 (attached) was received. Leaving the Adjutant to supervised the B" movement & Col The Major Commanding the B" forward the advance to our front line to see the order Progress.	(appendix) May 8 & 11 appendix 5, 6, 7 & 10 Frame 36 appendix 3 series 3rd Edition

T2134. Wt. W708—776. 500000. 4/15. Sir J. C. & S.

Army Form C. 2118.

WAR DIARY
or
INTELLIGENCE SUMMARY.
(Erase heading not required.)

Instructions regarding War Diaries and Intelligence Summaries are contained in F. S. Regs., Part II. and the Staff Manual respectively. Title pages will be prepared in manuscript.

Place	Date	Hour	Summary of Events and Information	Remarks and references to Appendices
CONTINUED 16/15				REF TRENCH MAP SHEET 36 SW 1/10000
	26th SEPTEMBER		Recieving verbal orders from G.O.C. that on account of the casualties O.C.s being hung up from an order 59 would be insufficient and that the MAUQUISSART-PIETRE road would be the objective and not the CITE. Our attack (one platoon in front attacking), during not: — the information received also stated in whom machines reported, and the fact that the division on our left had given way and had returned to their original trenches, having the left flank of the Barilly Bag been, and the Germans taking line advantage of this retirement, forced the Barilly Bag to abandon the trenches captured by them in the early morning. The situation now developed into trying to extricate the Barilly & Garhwal Brigade from their dangerous and difficult positions. Movement along the communicating trenches being nearly impossible, it was not until 8.30 P.M. that	WAR DIARY FRANCE SHEET 36 B SERIES 3rd EDITION

T2184. W. W708–776. 500000. 4/15. Sir J. C. & S.

WAR DIARY or INTELLIGENCE SUMMARY

Army Form C. 2118.

Place	Date	Hour	Summary of Events and Information	Remarks and references to Appendices
Continued 1915	25th SEPTEMBER		the Battalion could get even nearer our original line by that hour. Major MOUCHOPE Commanding 2nd BLACK WATCH confirmed the report of Major Crakaus 33rd Punjabis that the Germans had reoccupied their original front line, and that an attack was then necessary to recover it. The Brigade having got back, I was ordered to attempt another attack, but to help our own line on the event of no being counter attacked. In the meantime in order to help the Central Bde on the right, the 2nd Bn 2nd GURKHAS loaned a gun attack but it was unable to carry it out. The Germans having manned their original line with machine guns. During the advance through communicating trenches the Bn was subjected to a heavy Artillery Bombardment causing a good many casualties before reaching our front line, and very likely we were killed that we did not know where. Night was now closing	Appx A.6. C.O.D

WAR DIARY or INTELLIGENCE SUMMARY.

Army Form C. 2118.

Place	Date	Hour	Summary of Events and Information	Remarks and references to Appendices
Continued	1915			REF. TRENCH MAP SHEET 36 SW 1:- 1:10,000 and FRANCE SHEET 36 3 SERIES, 3RD EDITION
	25th September		in men in a disorganised state, which in a few minutes made any further movement impossible, the Battalion reached its original line, allowing the Black Watch to try and descend as the Royal Irish Rifles but nothing could be done until daylight except to improvise cover, when they were and made the best of an uncomfortable wet & miserable night.	
			Casualties 3 Killed 1 Missing 28 Wounded 2 Lieuts [?] Crossed	
	26th September		The BAREILLY and GARHWAL BRIGADES were ordered to Bieck at LA GORGE and eventually DEHRA DUN being ordered to hold the MEERUT DIVISION front, Disposition being as follows Right Sub Section 2nd & 9th GURKHAS with two Coys 3/3rd LONDON Infantry, Left Sub Section 1st Bn Seaforth Highlanders with two Coys Buenos Aires Infantry. (Mhowmere Bn newly arrived from Egypt.)	

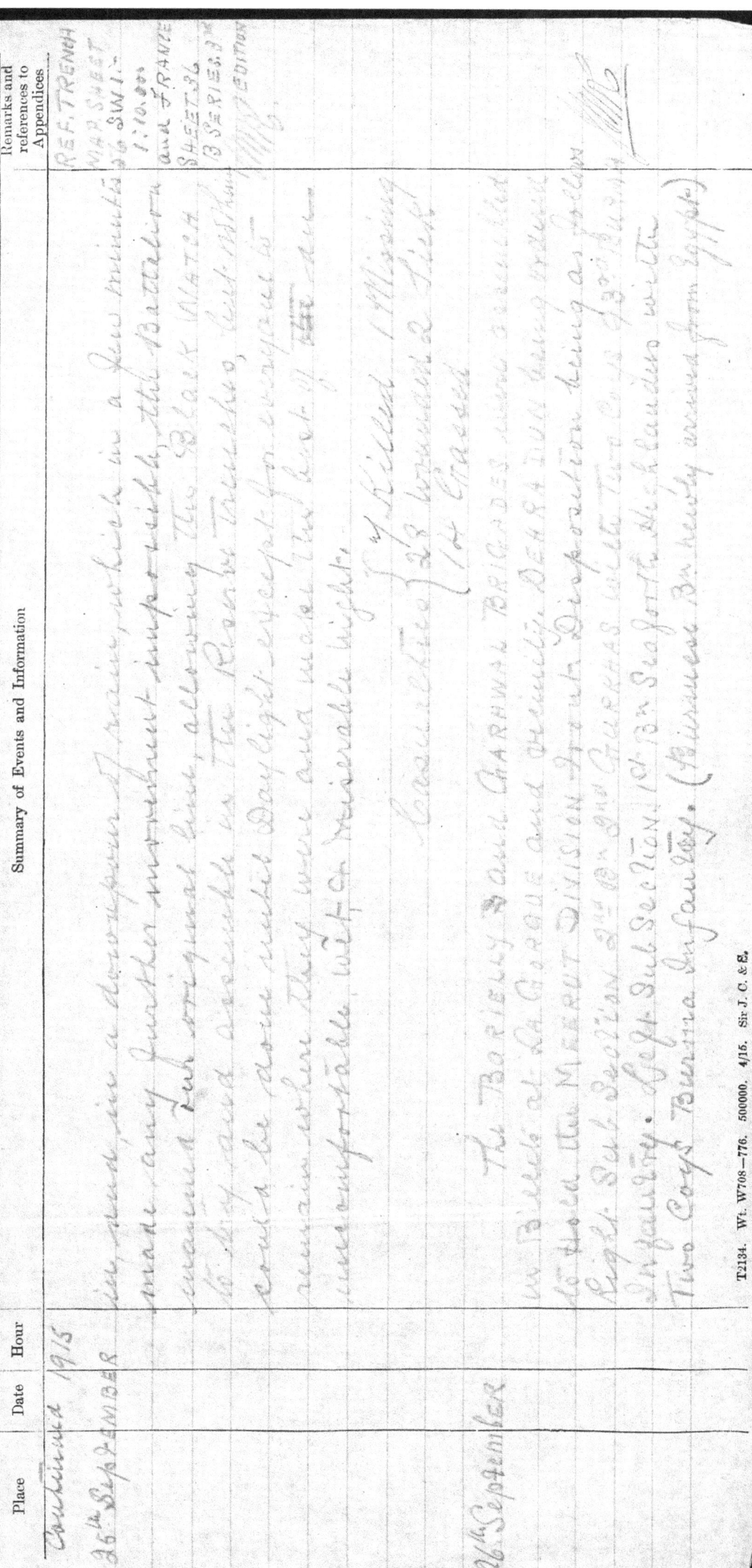

WAR DIARY or INTELLIGENCE SUMMARY

Army Form C. 2118.

Place	Date	Hour	Summary of Events and Information	Remarks and references to Appendices
Contined	1/9/15			
	26th SEPTEMBER		with the 1/4 SEAFORTHS and 1st/13th 9th GURKHAS in Brigade Reserve. Hostile Artillery normal throughout the day with ½ little Rifle or Machine Gun fire. Allowing the Bridge Damage caused by Shell fire to be carried out and completed.	See the MASTER 5 "SWL" 1/10,000 LARGE SHEETS 73 SERIES 3rd EDITION
			Casualties 1 Killed, 1 Wounded, 1 Sick.	
	27th SEPTEMBER		No Change in Dispositions. 80 Men sent to 1/9th Ly. R.E. for trenching purposes. At 4.30 am our position was heavily Shelled, until 8 am Average 1 round per 1 minute 9/6 Fire and Communicating Trenches carried out.	
			Casualties 2 Wounded 1 Sick	
	28th SEPTEMBER		At 9.45 AM Brigade Major Telephoned to the Commanding Officer that men to be withdrawn from the Left trenches, and at 11.20 AM Messengers were dispatched to evacuate the Section on Rugby Road on Receipt [?] 1 PM Orders were received for the Battalion to concentrate on LA BASSIE ESTAIRES Road North of PONT DU HEM	

T2134. Wt. W708—776. 500000. 4/15. Sir J. C. & E.

Army Form C. 2118.

WAR DIARY
or
INTELLIGENCE SUMMARY.
(Erase heading not required.)

Place	Date	Hour	Summary of Events and Information	Remarks and references to Appendices
Continued				REF: French MAP SHEET 36S.W.I 1:10,000 and French SHEET 36 1/8 SERIES 3rd EDITION
	28th SEPTEMBER 1915		and move by MOTOR LORRIES to GORRE (REF. BETHUNE SHEET 1:40,000) Concentration completed by 8 P.M. except 1 & Coy and Machine Gunners who were late in being relieved in Trenches. At 3.45 P.M. Bn. proceeded by MOTOR LORRIES, arriving at GORRE 10 night-fall. From there Bn. marched into the Trenches at GIVENCHY LES LABASSIE ridge relieving the 2nd Bn. 8 th TORKS & LIGHT INFANTRY and coming under the orders of the SIRHIND BRIGADE. Relief completed at 10 P.M. Bn. in 2 companies. Rain. Disposition B & C Coys in Firing Lines. A Coy in support and D Coy in Local Reserve. Casualties 5 Lieut	
	29th September		Still raining mud Trenches very wet and muddy. Day quiet only an exchange of hand Grenades occupying activity conducted to the North in direction of FOSSE 8 and HILL 70. Given up Bathing arrangements for Officers & Men in a few	

Army Form C. 2118.

WAR DIARY
or
INTELLIGENCE SUMMARY.
(Erase heading not required.)

Instructions regarding War Diaries and Intelligence Summaries are contained in F.S. Regs., Part II. and the Staff Manual respectively. Title pages will be prepared in manuscript.

Place	Date	Hour	Summary of Events and Information	Remarks and references to Appendices
Martinsart	1915			SEP. 1915 SEPT/45778
	29th SEPTEMBER		Skeleton dawn behind the Regt. last day looking turns over seven days in Reserve and were fitting & kitting themselves out of the trenches. The service has been as a great test the Regt being in the Front line since the 15th and for the last few days nearly knee deep in mud and water.	
			Casualties 1 Wounded 2 Sick	
	30th September		A.H.M. Enemy fired 50 (Pip Squeaks) Light Field One Shells at our Trenches. No Damage done. Our Artillery retaliated and they soon stopped. Weather fairly Sunshiny but wind was though Bombardier Wilson (right Section) was 29 Rank & File reinforcements joined which was posted to Companies.	
			Casualties 1 Wounded 3 Sick	

Operation Order No 52
by
Brigadier General C. W. Jacob C.B.
Commanding Dehra Dun Brigade

3rd September 1915.

Reference Sheet 36 and Trench Map.

1. DEHRA DUN BRIGADE will relieve BAREILLY BRIGADE in IND. 5 trenches on night 4th/5th September 1915.
2. Movements in accordance with attached Table. Details to be arranged between Commanding Officers concerned.
3. The following works will be handed over to BAREILLY Brigade by 12 noon on 4th Instant. Guards now in occupation will rejoin Units:—
   ETON POST.
   PONT DU HEM.
   CLIFTON POST.
4. No 11 Trench Mortar Battery will be attached to the Brigade.
5. Reports to LA BASSEE road M.8.d.

Issued at 5-30 P.M.   B E Anderson   Major
                       Bde Major Dehra Dun Bde.

Copy 1 & 2 retained
Copy 3. Meerut Div   Copy 13. B.B.G.O
Copy 4. Bareilly Bde   Copy 14. C.G.O.
Copy 5. 1st Seaforths   Copy 15. B.S.O.
Copy 6. 4th Seaforths
Copy 7. 9th Gurkhas
Copy 8. 2nd Gurkhas
Copy 9. 2 Coy Train
Copy 10. CRE
Copy 11. CRA
Copy 12. BMGO

NO MOVEMENT of troops except as detailed SOUTH of PONT DU HEM before 7-30 pm

MOVEMENT TABLE 4.9.15.

UNIT.	To Relieve.	LOCATION.	HEAD QUARTERS	Place where guides will meet.	Time	ROUTE.	REMARKS.
4th Seaforths	58th Rifles F.F. 2 coys 4th Black Watch	IND. 5. A	EBENEZER FARM.	EUSTON POST	8.45 P.M.	LA BASSEE ROAD.	C.O.s + Coy Comdrs to be at new Head Quarters to visit line at 10 a.m. on 4-9-15.
9th Gurkhas	69th Punjabis	IND. 5. B.	S. of junction SUNKEN TRENCH and RUE TILLELOY.	Junction of MIN + SUNKEN trenches with RUE DU BACQUEROT.	8.45 P.M.	RUGBY and BACQUEROT roads	" " " "
1st Seaforths	2nd Black Watch	B. line North of MOATED GRANGE trench.	Off MIN trench 80 yards East of N.TILLELOY POST.	Junction of MIN trench + RUE DU BACQUEROT.	7.45 P.M.	PONT ROCHON – RIEZ BAILLEUL – PONT DU HEM.	" " " "
2nd Gurkhas	1/4th Black Watch	B. line SOUTH of MOATED GRANGE trench.	B. line to junction of LAFONE trench + B. line.	EUSTON POST	7.45 pm	RIEZ BAILLEUL – PONT DU HEM – LA BASSEE ROAD.	" " " "
Brigade Bomb Company.		CARTERS POST. M.8.a.			6 am	Road junction 4.22.a.2/1.– LA BASSEE ROAD.	" " " "
Garrison LAFONE POST 40 men 2nd Gurkhas.		LAFONE POST M.35. b.0/3.		Junction RUGBY and BACQUEROT ROADS.	12 noon	RIEZ BAILLEUL – PONT DU HEM – RUE DU BACQUEROT.	" " " "
Garrison COLVIN POST 40 men 2nd Gurkhas.		COLVIN POST M.29.a.5/1.			12 noon	" " " "	" " " "
Machine Guns.	Relief to be carried out on 3rd					arrangements of Brigade	M.G.O
Bomb Guns.	Relief to be carried out by 12 noon on 4th September					arrangements of	B.B.G.O.

for Diary

'R'

1. ...

2. ...MOATED GRANGE up to COLYN STREET. C & D to ...of MOATED GRANGE up to WINCHESTER ROAD —...

3. D Coy will move at 5.30 pm (by platoons) ...Coys at 6 pm (by platoons.)

4. A Coy will use MOATED GRANGE trench.
   B.   MIN.
   C.   MIN

5. BIRDCAGE STREET will be left entirely for 9th Ghurkas.

Secret.   Operation Order No 53
              by
        Lieutenant-Colonel G.T. WIDDICOMBE.
        Commanding Dehra Dun Brigade.

Copy No......

11-9-15

Sheets 36 and 36a and Trench Map.

1. GARHWAL and BAREILLY Bdes will relieve DEHRA DUN Bde in IND. 5 trenches tomorrow 12th Inst. GARHWAL Bde will take over the line from SIGN POST LANE exclusive to SOUTH MOATED GRANGE STREET inclusive. BAREILLY Bd will take over the line from SOUTH MOATED GRANGE STREET exclusive to WINCHESTER ROAD inclusive.

2. 2nd Gurkhas will take over the front and Support line trenches to SOUTH MOATED GRANGE STREET inclusive by 10 a.m on 12th Instant.

3. Reliefs and movements in accordance with attached Table. Details to be arranged between Commanding Officers concerned.

4. No 11 Trench Mortar Battery will be attached to Bareilly Bde.

5. Reports to LA BASSEE ROAD. M.8.d

Issued at 11-30 pm   B.G. Anderson   Major
                       Bde. Major Dehra Dun Bde

Copy 1 & 2 retained
Copy 3. 1st Seaforths
Copy 4. 4th Seaforths
Copy 5. 9th Gurkhas
Copy 6. 2nd Gurkhas
Copy 7. Meerut Div
Copy 8. Bareilly Bde
Copy 9. Garhwal Bde
Copy 10. 4th Bde RFA
Copy 11. 13th Bde RFA
Copy 12. 2 Coy Train
Copy 13. 11 Trench Battery
Copy 14. C.R.E
Copy 15. C.R.A
Copy 16. B.B.G.O
Copy 17. B.M.G.O
Copy 18. B.S.O.
Copy 19. B.G.O.
Copy 20. Jullunder Bde

MOVEMENT TABLE 12-9-15

Unit	Location	To be relieved by	Time of arrival of relief	Destination	Route	Remarks
4th Seaforths	B. Line.	2/8th Gurkhas.	7-20 to 7-40 pm at RUE BACQUEROT.	Billets LA GORGUE	Road junction M.23.a.0/7 – LA FLINQUE – LE DRUMEZ	To move by platoon at suitable distance as far as LE DRUMEZ. Last platoon to be clear of communicating trenches by 7 pm.
9th Gurkhas	B. Line.	58th Rifles	7-10 pm at RUE BACQUEROT.	Billets = L.27.b.	Road junction M.23.a.0/7 – LA FLINQUE – LE DRUMEZ – ESTAIRES.	To move by platoon at suitable distance as far as LE DRUMEZ. Last platoon to be clear of communicating trenches by 6.45 pm
1st Seaforths	IND. 5. B.	33rd Punjabis. 1 Coy 2nd Black Watch. 2 Coys 4th Black Watch. 1 Coy 69th Punjabis.	6-45 pm at RUE BACQUEROT.	Billets LA GORGUE.	LA BASSEE road – road junction – G.32.a.2/1.	Guides will meet relieving Units at Support Line
2nd Gurkhas	IND. 5. A.	3rd Londons Garhwal Rifles	7-15 pm at RUE BACQUEROT.	Billets – L.26.d.	LA BASSEE road road junction G.32.a.2/1.	Guides will meet relieving Units at Support line.
Bde Grenade Company. Machine & Bomb Guns	M.8.d	Under arrangements of Machine & Bomb Gun Officers concerned		School Room LA GORGUE.	LA BASSEE road ESTAIRES.	To arrive at new billets at 6 pm.
1st Line All Units	LA BASSEE Road.			Billets of Units.	Shortest.	To leave present billets at 2-45 pm.

Secret

Operation Order 54. Copy No. 3
by
Lieut Colonel W. J. St. J. HARVEY.
Commanding Dehra Dun Brigade.
16th September 1915.

Reference Sheets 36 and 36a and Trench Map.

1. DEHRA DUN Brigade will relieve GARHWAL and BAREILLY Brigades in IND. 5. trenches on 18th September 1915.

2. Movements in accordance with attached Table. Details to be arranged between Comdg Officers concerned.

3. The following works will be handed over to BAREILLY Brigade by 1.p.m on 18th Instant. Guards now in occupation will rejoin Units:— HARROW, ETON, CHELTENHAM, PONT DU HEM, BOUT DEVILLE, CLIFTON WORKS and LA GORGUE CEMETRY.

4. Numbers 5, 11 and 13 Trench Batteries will be attached to the Brigade.

5. Reports to M.8.d.

Issued at 8 pm.   Major
                     Bde Major Dehra Dun Bde

Copies 1 and 2 retained   Copy 15. Bde S.O.
Copy 3 to 1st Seaforths   Copy 16. Bde G.O.
Copy 4 to 4th Seaforths   Copy 17. 5 Trench Bty
Copy 5 to 9th Gurkhas   Copy 18. 11 Trench Bty
Copy 6 to 2nd Gurkhas   Copy 19. 13 Trench Bty
Copy 7 to Meerut Div   Copy 20. 4th Cavalry
Copy 8 to C.R.A   Copy 21. Jullunder Bde
Copy 9 to C.R.E
Copy 10 to Garhwal Bde
Copy 11 to Bareilly Bde
Copy 12 to 2 Coy Meerut Train
Copy 13 to Bde M.G.O
Copy 14 to Bde B.G.O

MOVEMENT TABLE 18-9-15

Unit	To relieve	Location	Time of arrival at junction of communicating trench and RUE BACQUEROT	ROUTE	REMARKS
4th Seaforths	3rd Londons Garhwal Rifles	IND.5.A (SUNKEN ROAD exclusive but including DUCKS BILL to SOUTH MOATED GRANGE STREET inclusive).	7-15 p.m.	Road junction G.32.a.2/1 - LA BASSEE ROAD - RUE BACQUEROT - SOUTH TILLELOY STREET.	C.Os will leave next H.Q at 10am on 17th Instant.
1 Coy 2nd Gurkhas	3rd Londons	IND.5.A- SIGN POST LANE exclusive to SUNKEN ROAD (DUCKS BILL exclusive).	7-15 p.m.	ESTAIRES - LA BASSEE Road - RUE BACQUEROT - SUNKEN STREET.	" " " " "
9th Gurkhas	33rd Punjabis 269-4th Blackwatch 1Coy 69th Punjabis 1Coy 2nd Black Watch.	IND.5.B- SOUTH MOATED GRANGE STREET exclusive to WINCHESTER ROAD inclusive	7. pm.	ESTAIRES - LA BASSEE ROAD - RUGBY ROAD - NORTH TILLELOY and BIRD CAGE STREETS.	" " " " "
2nd Gurkhas (two Coy)	2/8th Gurkhas	B. lines South of MOATED GRANGE STREET.	7-30 pm.	ESTAIRES - LA BASSEE ROAD - RUE BACQUEROT - SUNKEN STREET.	" " " " "
1st Seaforths	58th Rifles.	B. lines North of MOATED GRANGE STREET.	7-30 pm	Road junction G.32.a.2/1- LA BASSEE ROAD.	" " " " "
Grenadier Company		Billets M.B.L.	6 pm at M.B.L.		
Machine Guns.	Relief to be completed by 1.pm on 18th September under arrangements of Bde machine gun officer.				
Bent Guns.	Relief to be completed by 1.pm on 18 th September under arrangements of Bde Bomb Gun officer.				
40 men 2nd Gurkhas 1.m.gun.	4 th Cavalry.	LAFONE POST.	10-45 am.	ESTAIRES - LA BASSEE ROAD - RUE BACQUEROT - SUNKEN STREET.	
40 men 1st Seaforths 1.m.Gun.	4th Cavalry.	COLVIN POST	11 am.	Road Junction G.32.a.2/1 - LA BASSEE ROAD - RUE BACQUEROT - S.TILLELOY STREET - COLVIN STREET	
40 men 1st Seaforths.	58th Rifles.	NORTH TILLELOY POST.	11-15 am	Road Junction G.32.a.2/1 - LA BASSEE Road - RUGBY ROAD - MAIN STREET	
30 men 2nd Gurkhas.	2/8th Gurkhas	SOUTH TILLELOY POST	11-30 am.	ESTAIRES - LA BASSEE Road - RUGBY ROAD - SOUTH TILLELOY STREET	

Secret   B.M. 6   21.9.15

Instructions to Battalions of Dehra Dun Brigade on the day of assault.

1- As the assaulting troops go forward & vacate their assembly positions the Brigade will move forward & concentrate as shown on attached table.

2- 1st Seaforths will maintain touch with 58th Rifles & 2nd Gurkhas will maintain touch with 39th Garhwalis & will keep G.O.C. informed as these troops leave their assembly places.

3- In the event of all troops of both advanced brigades moving forward from our fire trenches picquets of 1 N.C.O. & 9 men will be posted every 100 yards in the fire trench. 2nd Gurkhas will find these picquets in IND. 5. A & 1st Seaforths in IND. 5. B. In the event of a further advance these picquets will rejoin their units.

Wyndham Major
Bde. Major Dehra Dun Brigade

Operation order 55
by
Brigadier General W.J. St J. HARVEY
Commanding Dehra Dun Bde

Secret

3

REFERENCE: TRENCH MAP and MAP
of FRANCE 1:40000

22nd September 1915

1. Information

The 1st Army is resuming the offensive in the Southern part of the line. The Indian and other Corps not engaged in the Main offensive are carrying out local operations all along the 1st Army front.

The Indian Corps will:—

(a) attack the enemy's line between SUNKEN ROAD and WINCHESTER ROAD and establish our line along the road running through MAUQUISSART to the DUCKS BILL.

(b) Press on with its left in front, till its left gains the high ground between HAUT POMMEREAU and LA CLIQUETERIE FERME.

(c) Continue its advance from there in a South Easterly direction.

The Meerut Division will make the attack to be delivered by the Indian Corps. Lahore and 20th Divisions will co-operate in the attack and advance and maintain touch when the Meerut Division advances beyond the enemy's first and second line trenches.

2. Intention

The Garhwal and Bareilly Brigades will make the assault.

The Dehra Dun Brigade will be in Divisional Reserve.

3. Trench Mortar Batteries

After the assault No 5 Trench Mortar Battery will be attached to the Brigade.

4. Machine Guns

Two Machine guns will remain with each Battalion at disposal of Battalion Commander.

Remaining machine guns will be Brigaded under orders of Brigade Machine Gun Officer.

5. Fire on Enemy's Trenches.

During the deliberate bombardment the Brigade will maintain rifle, rifle grenade and Machine Gun fire by day and night in accordance with instructions already issued.

6. Positions of Assembly.

The boundary line between Garhwal and Bareilly Brigades will run from M.30.c.0/4 parallel to COLVIN STREET till it cuts MOATED GRANGE STREET thence parallel to SOUTH TILLELOY STREET to "B" LINE.

On relief Dehra Dun Brigade will occupy positions of assembly as follows:-

1st Seaforths - B.LINE North of ~~MOATED GRANGE~~ SOUTH TILLELOY STREET ST.
2nd Gurkhas - B.LINE South of SOUTH TILLELOY ST.
4th Seaforths - ROUGE CROIX EAST POST and G.H.Q. line North east of it.
9th Gurkhas - MIN and RUGBY POSTS and BACQUEROT STREET.
Grenadier Coy - BACQUEROT STREET.
Bde Machine Guns - BACQUEROT STREET.

7. Advanced Depots of S.A.A. & grenades.

The following advanced Depots of S.A.A. and hand grenades have been formed:-

LAFONE POST } 100 boxes S.A.A. and
COLVIN POST } 500 hand grenades in each.

In rear of BIRD CAGE - 1000 hand grenades
near BIRD CAGE - 100 boxes S.A.A.

Junction LAFONE STREET } 250 boxes S.A.A
and RUE TILLELOY } 300 rounds VERY pistol ammunition.

M.29.C.0/6 where Tram } 1000 Hand
line crosses RUE TILLELOY } Grenades

The trench ammunition of "B" LINE has been assembled by the assaulting Bdes in Depots in the front line. The above Depots have been marked by notice boards and direction arrows have been ~~have been~~ erected in the front line to point out the way to the nearest ammunition

ammunition at hand grenade Depot.
The positions of these Depots are to be explained to all ranks.

8. R.E. Stores.

Advanced Depots of R.E. Stores have been formed at:—
DUCKS BILL.
NECK of DUCKS BILL
M.30.c.0/4.
HEAD of COLVIN STREET.
In rear of the BIRD CAGE.

9. Medical.

Collecting Stations are established in Dug outs as follows:—
(i) M.28.d.8/4 near the junction of LAFONE STREET and RUE TILLELOY.
(ii) M.28.d.6/2.
(iii) M.34.b.5/9. EBENEZER FARM.

Wounded will reach the collecting Stations by LAFONE STREET or by NORTH or SOUTH MOATED GRANGE STREETS and MOATED GRANGE STREET or by TRAM STREET and TILLELOY TRENCH TRAM LINE. Advanced Dressing Station is at M.14.c.3/1, and the route from Collecting Stations by the tram lines or by EBENEZER STREET to M.21.d.7/1 and thence by the tram line. Only the above communication trenches are specially adopted to take stretchers.

10. Traffic

Traffic in the long communication trenches must move in accordance with the direction arrows. The following have been marked for traffic moving from our rear to our front:—
SUNKEN STREET — COLVIN STREET.
SOUTH TILLELOY STREET
NORTH TILLELOY STREET
BIRD CAGE STREET

The following have been marked for traffic moving from our front to our rear:—
EBENEZER STREET.
MOATED GRANGE STREET
MIN STREET
LAFONE STREET
SOUTH MOATED GRANGE STREET
NORTH MOATED GRANGE STREET
TRAM STREET.
These traffic rules may be broken for urgent tactical reasons only.

11
French Police. Traffic control posts will be posted by the Staff Captain at 5 pm on the day preceding assault as follows:—
Junction MOATED GRANGE STREET and SOUTH TILLELOY STREET.
Junction MOATED GRANGE STREET and SUNKEN STREET.
Junction MIN STREET and RUE DU BACQUEROT.
Junction EBENEZER STREET & RUE DU BACQUEROT.
Each post will consist of one British and one Indian soldier.

12.
Distinguishing flags. The following distinguishing flags will be carried to assist in showing the localities reached by our troops:— Garhwal Bde BLUE with RED bar
Bareilly Bde BLACK with YELLOW bar
Dehra Dun Bde plain YELLOW.

The flags are 2' square and bars are 8" broad.
Distinguishing flags of Divisions on right and left are:—
LAHORE DIV—YELLOW with black stripe in centre—
Flag 2'-6" square.
20th DIV — Top half GREEN bottom half PINK
Flag 2' square.

A coloured diagram of these flags has been issued.

13. Daylight Rockets	Daylight rockets to inform the Artillery that the Infantry is making a further advance will be carried. These rockets will be used in bunches of several fired simultaneously. This signal should be used only if the ordinary communications are interrupted. After the assault has been launched no other signal will be made by daylight. Rockets of Garhwal Brigade are RED. Those of Bareilly and Dehra Dun Bdes are BLUE.
14 Prisoners	Prisoners will be sent to Brigade Head Quarters under escort. They are to be searched for documents and other articles as soon as possible after being captured. These must accompany the prisoners and be handed over from one escort to another.
15 Sandbags.	Each man will carry two sandbags.
16 Packs	Packs will not be carried. Arrangements will be made to stack packs during the night preceding assault or on morning of assault as follows:— 1st Seaforths — Close to WINCHESTER ROAD 2nd Gurkhas — Close to RUE TILLELOY 4th Seaforths — Close to RUE BACQUEROT 9th Gurkhas — Close to RUE BACQUEROT.
17 Transport.	From 6 pm on 24th instant all baggage wagons and 1st line transport will be kept loaded up.
18 Entrenching tools.	20 shovels per company will be carried. Remaining entrenching tools will be loaded on tool limbers on the night 23rd/24th under Battalion arrangements.

19 Secret documents		Secret documents, plans, sketches showing our line will not be taken beyond present battalion Head Quarters.

| 20 General Instructions | | The importance of advancing at all costs must be impressed on all ranks. If one portion of the line is held up there is no necessity for other portions to check.

It is most important that communication is kept up. |

21 Reports.   Report Centre is at M.22.C.4/5.

Issued at ..4 p.m..
                             Bde. Major Dehra Dun Brigade   Major

To Signal Section for distribution.

Copy 1 and 2 retained
Copy 3 to 1st Seaforths
Copy 4 to 4th Seaforths
Copy 5 to 9th Gurkhas
Copy 6 to 2nd Gurkhas
Copy 7 to 93rd B. Infy
Copy 8 to Meerut Div
Copy 9 to Bareilly Bde
Copy 10 to Garhwal Bde
Copy 11 to 2 Coy Train
Copy 12 to 4th Bde RFA
Copy 13 to 13th Bde RFA.
Copy 14 to 5th French Battery
Copy 15 to Bde M.G.O
Copy 16 to Bde G.O
Copy 17 to Bde S.O.
Copy 18 to Bde B.G.O

OPERATION ORDER No 56

By

Brigadier General W. J. St. J. HARVEY,

Commanding Dehra Dun Brigade.

Copy 3

22nd September 1915.

1. During the night 23rd/24th September the line now held by the DEHRA DUN BRIGADE will be adjusted as follows:-

   JULLUNDER BRIGADE will extend its front to SUNKEN ROAD exclusive. DEHRA DUN BRIGADE will extend its front to WINCHESTER STREET exclusive.
   Dividing line between Subsections will be H.30.c.0/4.

2. JULLUNDER BRIGADE will relieve Company 2nd Gurkhas between SIGN POST LANE and SUNKEN ROAD. Relieved Company will rejoin Battalion in "B" LINE.

   4th Seaforths will extend left to H.30.c.0/4.

   9th Gurkhas will extend left to take over from 60th Brigade, front and support line trenches up to WINCHESTER STREET.

   Details of reliefs will be arranged between Commanding Officers concerned.

3. Subsection Commander IND.5.B. may draw a Company 1st Seaforths in support to strengthen his line if necessary.

Issued at 4.40 p.m.

Major
Brigade Major Dehra Dun Brigade.

Issued to Signal Section for distribution.

Copy 1 and 2 retained.
Copy 3. 1st Seaforths.
Copy 4 4th Seaforths.
Copy 5 9th Gurkhas
Copy 6 2nd Gurkhas.
Copy 7. Meerut Division
Copy 8 Bareilly Bde.
Copy 9 to Garhwal Brigade.
Copy 10 to 4th Barigade R.D.A.
Copy 11 to 13th Brigade R.F.A.
Copy 12 to 2 Coy Train.
Copy 13 to Bde Machine Gun Officer
Copy 14 to Brigade Grenadier Officer
Copy 15 to Brigade Signalling Officer
Copy 16. to Brigade Bomb Gun Officer
Copy 17 to 60th Bde

War Diary

UNIT.	PLACE.	HEAD QUARTERS.	ROUTE.
2nd Gurkhas.	HOME COUNTIES TRENCH, SOUTH of COLVIN STREET.	Near COLVIN STREET.	SUNKEN STREET and SOUTH TILLELOY STREET
1st Seaforths	Trench along N Edge of RUE TILLELOY.	Near Junction RUE STREET and RUE TILLELOY.	NORTH TILLELOY and BIRDCAGE STREETS.
4th Seaforths	"B" LINE. South of SOUTH TILLELOY STREET.	Junction LAHORE STREET and "B" LINE.	SUNKEN STREET.
9th Gurkhas	"B" LINE. North of MOATED GRANGE STREET.	Junction NORTH TILLELOY STREET and "B" LINE.	1 Coy via SOUTH TILLELOY STREET (To follow Bde Machine Guns) 2 Coys via NORTH TILLELOY STREET. 1 Coy via BIRD CAGE STREET
Grenadier Company.	HOME COUNTIES TRENCH, NORTH OF COLVIN STREET.	Junction COLVIN & HOME COUNTIES TRENCH.	SOUTH TILLELOY STREET.
Bde Machine Guns.	HOME COUNTIES Trench North of COLVIN STREET.	Junction COLVIN & HOME COUNTIES TRENCH.	SOUTH TILLELOY STREET (To follow Grenadier Company).
Bde Head Quarters.	BAREILLY BRIGADE Advanced Report Centre.	Junction COLVIN STREET and HOME COUNTIES TRENCH.	SOUTH TILLELOY STREET

OPERATION ORDER NO 57.

by

Brigadier General W. J. ST. J. HARVEY.
Commanding   Dehra   Dun   Brigade.

23rd September 1915.

Secret

Reference Trench Map.

1. The GARHWAL and BAREILLY BRIGADES will relieve DEHRA DUN BRIGADE in IND.5. trenches.

2. Reliefs will be carried out in accordance with attached movement table and special instructions already issued.

3. Garrisons of NORTH and SOUTH TILLELOY POSTS will rejoin their Units in "B" LINE at 6-30.p.m. on 24th Instant.

4. From 6.p.m. on 24th Instant no troops except sentries are to be in the bays utilized for a special purpose.

5. Reports to M.22.c.4/5.

issued at 10-15 p.m.　　　　　　　　　　Major
　　　　　　　　　　　　　　Brigade Major Dehra Dun Brigade

Copy No 1 and 2 retained.
Copy No 3 to 1st Seaforths.
Copy No 4 to 4th Seaforths,
Copy No 5 to 9th Gurkhas.
Copy No 6 to 2nd Gurkhas
Copy No 7 to 93rd Burmah Infantry
Copy No 8 to Meerut Division
Copy No 9 to Bareilly Brigade.
Copy No 10 to Garhwal Brigade.
Copy No 11 to 2 Coy Meerut Train.
Copy No 12 to 4th Brigade R.F.A.
Copy No 13 to 13th Brigade R.F.A.
Copy No 14 to 5th Trench Mortar Battery
Copy No 15 to Bde Machine Gun Officer
Copy No 16 to Brigade Grenadier Officer
Copy No 17 to Brigade Bomb Gun Officer
Copy No 18 to Brigade Signalling Officer.
Copy No 19 to Jullunder Bde
Copy No 20 to 60th Brigade.

MOVEMENT TABLE.

UNIT	Location	To be relieved by.	Destination	Route	Headquarters	Remarks
4th Seaforths	IND.5.A	Garhwal Bde	ROUGE CROIX EAST POST on G.H.Q. Line.	INSPECTION TRENCH —LAFONE STREET —EBENEZER ST.	M.28.a.5/8.	
9th Gurkhas	IND.5.B.	Bareilly Brigade	RUGBY. POST. MIN POST BACQUEROT STREET.	Inspection Trench BIRDCAGE STREET.	M.22.c.8/7.	
Grenadier Coy	M.8.d and IND.5.A.	—	BACQUEROT ST from SOUTH TILLELOY STREET to 100 yards west.	RUGBY ROAD	M.22.c.8/7 4/13.	To be in position by 6-30 pm
Bde Machine Guns	IND 5	Garhwal and Bareilly Machine Guns	BACQUEROT ST from Grenadier Coy to 60 yards west of SUNKEN ROAD.	M.22.c.4/5	M.22.c.4/5.	Relief by day under orders of Bde M.G.O
Bde Bomb-Guns	IND.5.		Dug outs M.23.a.3/9.		M.22.c.4/5	Relief by day under orders of Bde Bomb Gun Officer
93rd Infantry	BEAUPRE FARM.		CARTERS POST M.8.a.9/10.	LA GORGUE— Road Junction G.32.a.2/1.—LA BASSEE ROAD	CARTERS POST	

N.B. ALL TIMES WILL BE NOTIFIED LATER BY WIRE OR MOTOR CYCLIST.

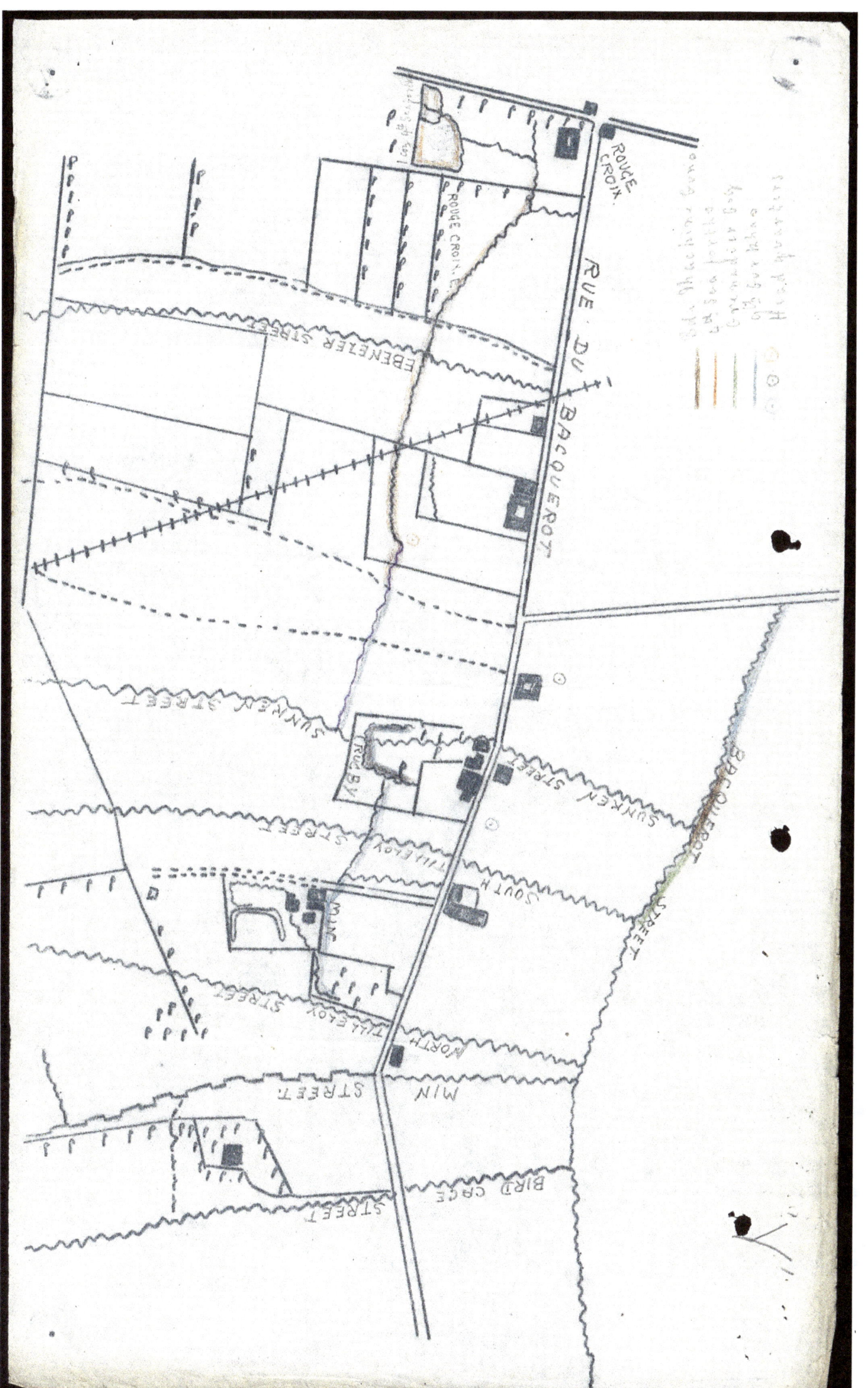

24.9.18. 4 pm

1. The Battalion will remain concentrated at ... but in a state of constant readiness.

2. Nothing will be taken forward from the line except ... equipment, ...

3. ...

4. ...

OPERATION ORDER No 52.

by

Brigadier General W.J.St.J. HARVEY.

Commanding Dehra Dun Brigade.

24th September 1915

1. The GARHWAL and BAREILLY BRIGADES will assault at C.O. in accordance with programme issued. Value of Zero will be communicated by wire.

2. As the assaulting Infantry go forward and vacate their assembly positions the DEHRA DUN BRIGADE will move forward and concentrate as shown on attached table.

3. 1st Seaforths will maintain touch with 58th Rifles and 2nd Gurkhas will maintain touch with 39th Garhwalis and will keep G.O.C. informed as these troops leave their assembly positions.

4. In the event of all troops of both advanced Brigades moving forward from our fire trenches, picquets of one N.C.O. and Nine men will posted every 100 yards in the fire trench. 2nd Gurkhas will find these picquets in IND. 5.A. and 1st Seaforths in IND. 5.B. In the event of the Brigade making a further advance these picquets will rejoin Units.

5. Reports to N.32.c.4/5 up to time of forward concentration. Afterwards to junction COLVIN STREET and HOME COUNTIES TRENCH.

Issued at 11.55 a.m.

Major.
Bde Major Dehra Dun Brigade.

Copy 1 and 2 retained.		Copy 11.	Jullunder Bde.
Copy 3	1st Seaforths	Copy 12	2 Coy Train.
Copy 4	4th Seaforths.	Copy 13.	5 Trench Mortar Bty
Copy 5	9th Gurkhas.	Copy 14	C.R.A. Meerut Div
Copy 6	2nd Gurkhas	Copy 15.	Bde M.G.O.
Copy 7	53rd Infantry	Copy 16.	Bde. B.G.O.
Copy 8	Meerut Division	Copy 17.	Bde Sig O.
Copy 9	Bareilly Bde.	Copy 18.	Bde Grenadier O.
Copy 10	Garhwal Bde.	Copy 19.	4th Bde R.F.A.
		Copy 20.	13th Bde R.F.A.

UNIT.	PLACE.	HeadQuarters	ROUTE.
2nd Gurkhas.	HOME COUNTIES TRENCH, SOUTH of COLVIN STREET.	Near COLVIN STREET.	SUNKEN STREET and SOUTH TILLELOY ST.
1st Seaforths	Trench along N edge of RUE TILLELOY.	Near Junction MIN STREET & RUE TILLELOY.	NORTH TILLELOY and BIRDCAGE STREETS.
4th Seaforths	SOUTH "B" LINE. North of SOUTH TILLELOY STREET.	Junction LAFONE STREET and "B" LINE	SUNKEN STREET.
9th Gurkhas.	"B" LINE. North of MOATED GRANGE STREET.	Junction NORTH TILLELOY STREET and "B" LINE.	1 Coy via SOUTH TILLELOY ST (To follow Bde Machine Guns). 2 Coys via NORTH TILLELOY STREET. 1 Coy via BIRDCAGE STREET.
Grenadier Company.	HOME COUNTIES TRENCH, NORTH of COLVIN ST.	Junction COLVIN and HOME COUNTIES TRENCH	SOUTH TILLELOY STREET.
Bde Machine Guns.	HOME COUNTIES TRENCH North of COLVIN STREET	Junction COLVIN & HOME COUNTIES TRENCH	SOUTH TILLELOY ST (To follow Grenadier Company).
Bde Head Quarters	BAREILLY BDE Advanced Report Centre	Junction COLVIN STREET and HOME COUNTIES TRENCH	SOUTH TILLELOY STREET
Bde Bomb Guns.	Trench along N edge of RUE Tilleloy.	Near Junction MIN STREET and RUE TILLELOY	BIRD CAGE STREET (To follow 9th Gurkhas).

Copy.

Report on Operations &c &c

1. Move to RUE TILLELOY at 6.15 am in accordance with instructions, 58th Rifles having moved forward. Battalion concentrated on RUE TILLELOY by 7.30 am.

2. Received BM 31 at 10.40 am.

3. Received Operation Order N° 39 at 11 am.

4. Received verbal orders from GOC on arrival on fixed line about 12 noon that owing to the GARHWAL BRIGADE being hung up, Operation Order N° 39 was modified in that the MARQUISSART PIETRE road would now be the right and not the centre of attack. This order entailed a move to the left of 50 yards on debouching from the communication trenches, a difficult operation made worse by the Brigade Machine Guns raking N. TILLELOY STREET for over 1 hour.

A'

5. On leaving GOC it became evident from

2

numbers of men of BAREILLY BRIGADE
in the trenches and his conviction that
things were not going well in front.
The BMSO of Bareilly Brigade confirmed
this news & directed him to report at
once to Brigadier. Subsequently met
Bareilly Brigade Signalling officer who
gave information which caused me
to accompany him to Brigadier. The
G.O.C. on hearing report cancelled
attack orders but directed that, if
GERMAN front line was still occupied
by our troops, one Company should at
once be pushed across from vicinity of
BIRDCAGE followed if possible by rest of
battalion. By this time, 2pm, movement
along trench was very difficult & prospect
of launching Company one left effectively
remote. At 2.30pm about, I found Major
Wauchope Commanding 2nd Black
Watch who confirmed information of

on a reconnoissance —

Two Officers & about four troopers came to Reg.t this day with messages for BARELLY BRIGADE. Sepoys Nam[...]pa[...] informed me that 3 out 4 of the have [...] never delivered messages of the utmost importance —

7/2/[..]   Sigd. [...] Pearson Lt Col
            Commdg Hyfield [...]

Operation Order 59
by Brig Genl W.J. St.J. HARVEY
Comdg Dehra Dun Bde
25-9-15

Ref trench map.

1. Garhwal + Bareilly Bdes have taken enemys 1st + 2nd line trenches.
   The advanced troops of Bareilly Bde are reported to have reached the River LAYES about 400ˣ north of the MAUQUISSART – PIETRE road

2. The Dehra Dun Bde will attack through the Garhwal and Bareilly Bdes and advance towards PIETRE.
   The MAUQUISSART – PIETRE road gives the line of direction for the centre.
   When PIETRE is reached the attack will be continued towards HAUT POMMEREAU and LA CLIQUETERIE.

3. The 1st Seaforths on the left and 2nd Gurkhas on the right will carry out the attack each battalion on a one company front.
   The 9th Gurkhas will be in Brigade Reserve behind the 1st Seaforths and 4th Seaforths in Brigade reserve behind the 2nd Gurkhas

4. Seaforths in Brigade Reserve

Major
BM Dehra Dun Bde

S E C R E T.

NOT TO BE CARRIED FORWARD BEYOND OUR FRONT PARAPET UNDER ANY CIRCUMSTANCES.

P R O G R A M M E   "A"

TIME TABLE if GAS and SMOKE are EMPLOYED.

- 0.2 (i.e., 2 minutes before ZERO) Mine fired.
- 0.0 Daylight rocket signal sent up from Bareilly Brigade Hdqrs (near junction of COLVIN St and HOME COUNTIES TRENCH.).
- 0.0 Commencement of GAS.
- 0.0 Artillery, except guns in our parapet, open shrapnel fire on the enemy's front trenches, and H.E. fire on enemy's defences further in rear.
- 0.4 Two field guns and Hotchkiss gun in our front parapet open fire.
- 0.5 Smoke screens on flanks commence.
- 0.5 Smoke commences along entire front concurrently with the Gas.
- 0.8 Gas to be cut off.
- 0.8 Infantry fill up all bays of the fire trench and get into pos--ition to cross our parapet.
- 0.9 Infantry cross our parapet and form up.
- 0.9 Artillery lifts 100 yards.
- 0.9 Field gun in our front trench near the BIRDCAGE ceases fire.
- 0.10 Assault commences.
- 0.10 Field gun in our front trench near DUCKS BILL ceases fire.
- 0.11 Artillery lifts another 100 yards.
- 0.14 Artillery lifts to German 2nd position about 500 yards in rear of their front trench.
- 0.15 Smoke screens on flanks stop, but the smoke has still to disperse.
- 0.20 Hotchkiss gun in our front parapet ceases fire.

P R O G R A M M E   "B"

TIME TABLE if GAS and SMOKE are N O T EMPLOYED.

- 4.20 A.M. By this time the assaulting infantry are to be lying in position outside our parapet.
- 4.25 A.M. Artillery bombardment commences including guns in our front parapet.
- 4.27 A.M. MINE exploded.
- 4.30 A.M. Assault.
- 4.30 A.M. Artillery lifts 100 yards.
- 4.30 A.M. Field guns in our front trenches cease fire, but Hotchkiss gun continues to fire.
- 4.31 A.M. Artillery lifts another 100 yards.
- 4.34 A.M. Artillery lifts to German 2nd position about 500 yards in rear of their front line.

Copy

R16 71   (25)/5.)

1st Seaforths & 11th Seaforths Brigade will consolidate its advance as under aaa. 5th Gordons front & support line from SOUTH MOATED GRANGE Street to COLVIN STREET aaa. 1st Seaforths front & support line from SOUTH MOATED GRANGE STREET to NORTH TILLELOY STREET aaa. 4th Seaforths front & support line from COLVIN STREET to SOUTH TILLELOY STREET aaa. 9th Gordons front & support line from NORTH TILLELOY STREET to NORTH MOATED GRANGE STREET.

4p   D D Brigade.

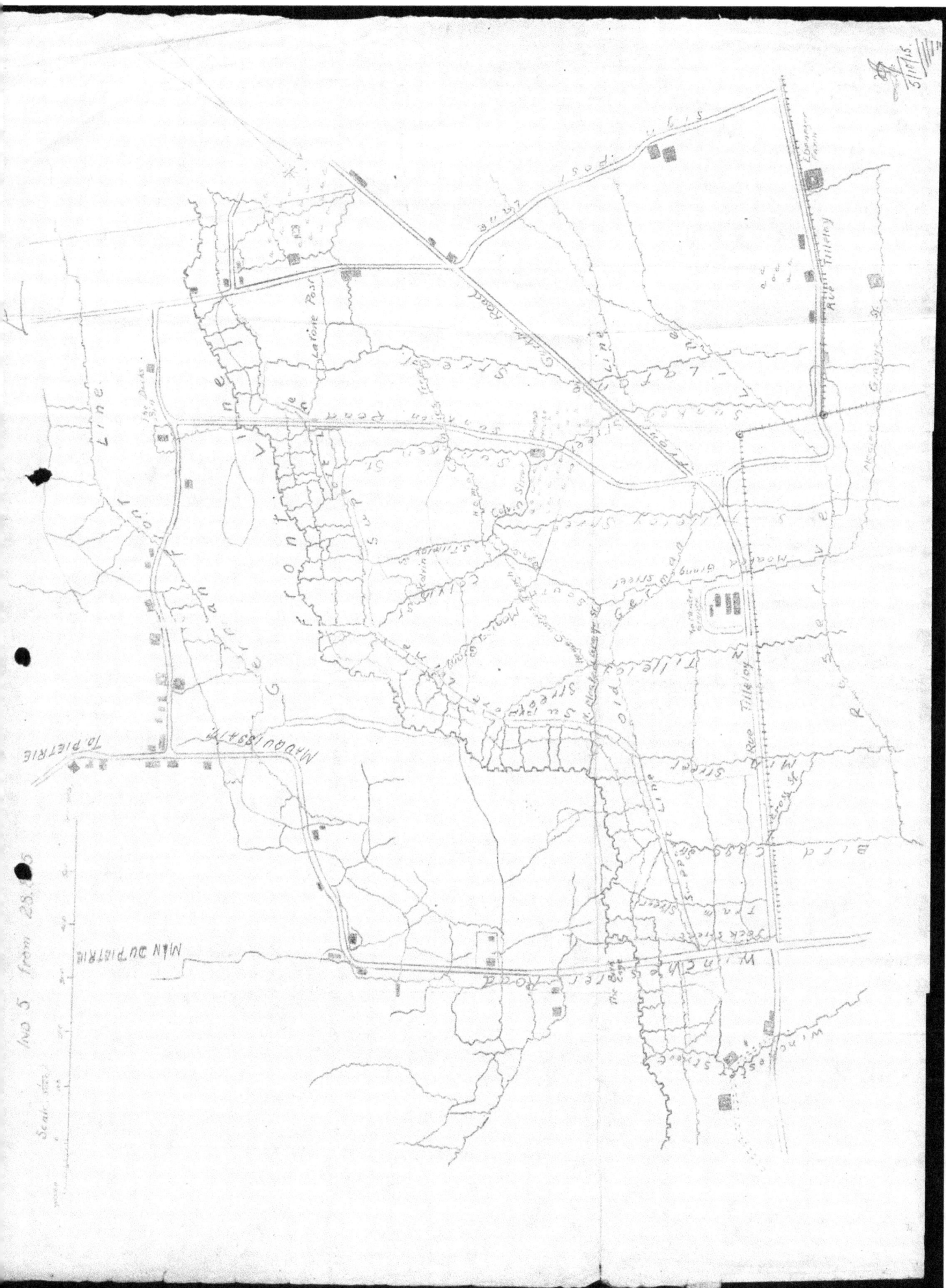

Meerut Division.
Seaforth Highlanders.
From 1st To 31st October 1915

Serial No. 260

12.V.
33 sheets.

Confidential

121/7601

War Diary

with appendices

of

Seaforth Highlanders.

FROM 1st October 1915. TO 31st October 1915.

Army Form C. 2118.

VOL XIV

WAR DIARY
or
INTELLIGENCE SUMMARY.
(Erase heading not required.)

Instructions regarding War Diaries and Intelligence Summaries are contained in F. S. Regs., Part II. and the Staff Manual respectively. Title pages will be prepared in manuscript.

Place	Date	Hour	Summary of Events and Information	Remarks and references to Appendices
				REFERENCE BETHUNE SHEET 1/40,000
	1st OCTOBER 1915.		The 10th Btln in the trench line holding GIVENCHY-LES-LA BASSEE. 2nd Brigade relieved by the 3rd Essex Brigade, who in turn the Btln was relieved. Then attached to Army. Being bombarded all interned on my right. Fairly quiet in our own sector. 3/1 Engineers joined and posted to Coys	App. F attd
			Casualties 1 Lieut	
	2nd October "		Lines held by the Lahore Corps. Adjacent Meerut Division holding the Line LA BASSEE CANAL inclusive to junction S.W. Rue de Bois inclusive. Battalion still by the Army Res. in the village, installed in billets less than usual.	
			Casualties 6 Lieut	
	3rd October "		Everything very quiet. Moved Division will be relieved by the A.C.B.Bkb. Casualties Wounded 10 Died.	

Army Form C. 2118.

WAR DIARY
or
INTELLIGENCE SUMMARY.
(Erase heading not required.)

Instructions regarding War Diaries and Intelligence Summaries are contained in F. S. Regs., Part II. and the Staff Manual respectively. Title pages will be prepared in manuscript.

Place	Date	Hour	Summary of Events and Information	Remarks and references to Appendices
	4th OCTOBER 1915		At 12.30 A.M. Greh. MUSTAIN Escorte returned with Touch of 2nd Leicesters and Rifle Grenades fired on our Trenches, we retaliated with Grenades & Trench Mortars & Lead Guns. own Rifle Grenades & Trench Mortars & Lead Guns. Casualties 1 Officer 2 men died	SEE BATHING SHEET
				1 40772
				Apx H
	5th OCTOBER "		Enemy shelled our Trenches with MINENWERFERS and Trench Guns. We retaliated with Howitzers, Lead Guns, and Trench Mortars.	
			Fire was kept up by Trench and Heavy Artillery and musketry.	Apx H
			Message from HIS MAJESTY THE KING to SIR JOHN FRENCH attached.	alle
			Casualties 1 killed 2 wounded & sick	
	6th OCTOBER "		Artillery shelling Enemy's lines during the day. Strong Artillery Fire by guns of 1st Corps Divisions 6th & over Command of Givenchy Flare Entanglements, and Bonnet. 1st Battalion and the 2nd Bn BLACK WATCH holding the subsection, Bn Head Quarters in a cellar in GIVENCHY near	
			Casualties 1 wounded & sick	

WAR DIARY or INTELLIGENCE SUMMARY.

Army Form C. 2118.

(Erase heading not required.)

Instructions regarding War Diaries and Intelligence Summaries are contained in F. S. Regs., Part II. and the Staff Manual respectively. Title pages will be prepared in manuscript.

Place	Date	Hour	Summary of Events and Information	Remarks and references to Appendices
	7th October 1915		Germans almost continuously shelled our BOMBED position & the enemy Blowing up the trenches west of Black Watch Redoubt. Artillery active on both sides all day.	REFERENCE BETHUNE SHEET 1/40,000
	8th October	—	Casualties 2 wounded. Lt Col [?]	
		4.30 AM	Enemy opened a heavy bombardment of BLACK WATCH REDOUBT followed by violent shelling of all our trenches and bombardment of reserve areas. Our guns replied. Followed by violent shelling of all trenches & bombardment of reserve. Attacked with Bombs from our Front trench Bn Counter attacked & retook the lost ground. Casualties in Bn were B Wells 2nd Lt Beaumont & Lt Dunlop. Ranks 3 killed. 2 killed 2 wounded [?]	
	9th October		Quiet day. Artillery and rifle fire on both sides.	

Army Form C. 2118.

WAR DIARY
or
INTELLIGENCE SUMMARY.
(Erase heading not required.)

Instructions regarding War Diaries and Intelligence Summaries are contained in F. S. Regs., Part II. and the Staff Manual respectively. Title pages will be prepared in manuscript.

Place	Date	Hour	Summary of Events and Information	Remarks and references to Appendices
Contined	9th October 1915		Lively exchange of Rifle and Machine Gunnadier day. Hostile shelling increased towards evening to which we returned. 1 killed, 2 wounded. Casualties 2 Sick.	See Routine Orbit AAQMG
	10th October 1915		Morning fairly quiet. At 12.15 our 24th Howitzer Battery in German line opened fire from Heavy Bombardment from our Railway Triangle to the front North of La Bassée canal. Men returned throughout the night. Exchange of Rifle grenades at intervals during the day. 1 wounded. Casualties 2 Sick.	App I attd
	11th October		Fairly quiet in the morning, his Battery of 4 inch guns was shaving, to which H.Q. was successfully replied by firing by the vicinity of Head Quarters from 6.30 pm to 11.30 pm doing, however no damage. Garibaldi Brigade were relieved by the Garhwal Brigade the 3rd Garhwalis taking the place of	AMB AMB

T2134. Wt. W708—776. 500000. 4/15. Sir J. C. & S.

WAR DIARY or INTELLIGENCE SUMMARY.

Army Form C. 2118.

(Erase heading not required.)

Instructions regarding War Diaries and Intelligence Summaries are contained in F. S. Regs., Part II. and the Staff Manual respectively. Title pages will be prepared in manuscript.

Place	Date	Hour	Summary of Events and Information	Remarks and references to Appendices
Continued	11th October 1915		The 2nd BLACK WATCH in our Inlustin. In the evening a large fire was observed to the South. Cork bombardment was opened. News that there is no LOOS on fire.	REF BETHUNE & WESTERHAM N76
			Casualties 8 Killed	
	12th October		Heavy Bombardment on our right extensities. Enemy Artillery Railway Triangle near LA BASSÉE and also the Western of HOHENZOLLERN REDOUBT. Afternoon bombardment more violent	12th Afternoon
			Casualties 2 Wounded, 1 Sick	
	13th October	At 12.30	Rifle fire which was attended by our troops.	
		at 1 P.M.	Heavy commencing which the LAHORE DIVISION attack hour, followed by the MEERUT DIVISION from the whole our line from MAQUISSART to LA BASSÉE CANAL. Attack was in the form of Smoke Bomb thrown but our troops to draw the enemy attention from...	

Army Form C. 2118.

WAR DIARY
or
INTELLIGENCE SUMMARY.
(Erase heading not required.)

Instructions regarding War Diaries and Intelligence Summaries are contained in F.S. Regs., Part II. and the Staff Manual respectively. Title pages will be prepared in manuscript.

Place	Date	Hour	Summary of Events and Information	Remarks and references to Appendices
Courcelles	13th October 1915		from the real attack further South. Enemy replied immediately with very Rifle, Machine Gun & fire followed by Howitzers + Field Guns. Bombardment on our trenches morning 14/15. However very little damage. Near Loos of 14 October 2nd Lieuts HADOW and BUCHANAN led a strong patrol into the Enemy's Trenches, gaining some useful information.	REABETH ½ SHEET
				Casualties 1 Wounded
"	14th October		Fighting still continues at Railway Triangle and further South. On our own front lively exchanges of Rifle and Bomb Grenades continued all day. At 6.45 PM enemy fired a MINENWERFER [?] which damaged in good deal of our parapet, we retaliated at once with Salvos of Howitzer Field and Trench MORTARS, doing considerable damage to their trenches. 3 wounded	
				Casualties 2 killed

T2134. Wt. W708—776. 500000. 4/15. Sir J. C. & S.

WAR DIARY
or
INTELLIGENCE SUMMARY.

Army Form C. 2118.

(Erase heading not required.)

Instructions regarding War Diaries and Intelligence Summaries are contained in F. S. Regs., Part II. and the Staff Manual respectively. Title pages will be prepared in manuscript.

Place	Date	Hour	Summary of Events and Information	Remarks and references to Appendices
	15th OCTOBER 1915		Hostile field gun and rifle fire exchanged throughout the day. Artillery attempting to hit the T/M. By Authority Instructions all the Brigade French Colonels who either knew Capt RANDERSON proceed to HAVRE for two months duty on the Central Training Depot. Informed. Casualties nil.	REF BETHUNE SHEET 36B. 36.2
	16th OCTOBER 1915		Very quiet with the exception of an exchange of Hand Grenades occasionally. Capt RANNY and Coy CMS completed reconnaissance for the Former 3rd Class "Legion d'Honneur" and the later MEDAILLE MILITAIRE. Casualties 2 slight	
	17th OCTOBER		Morning and forenoon very quiet. Artillery on both sides remained in action been very actively employed from 3-30 to 4-30 in Retaliation to Enemy firing a few Rifle grenades & a MINENWERFER. Casualties 1 Killed 2 slight	

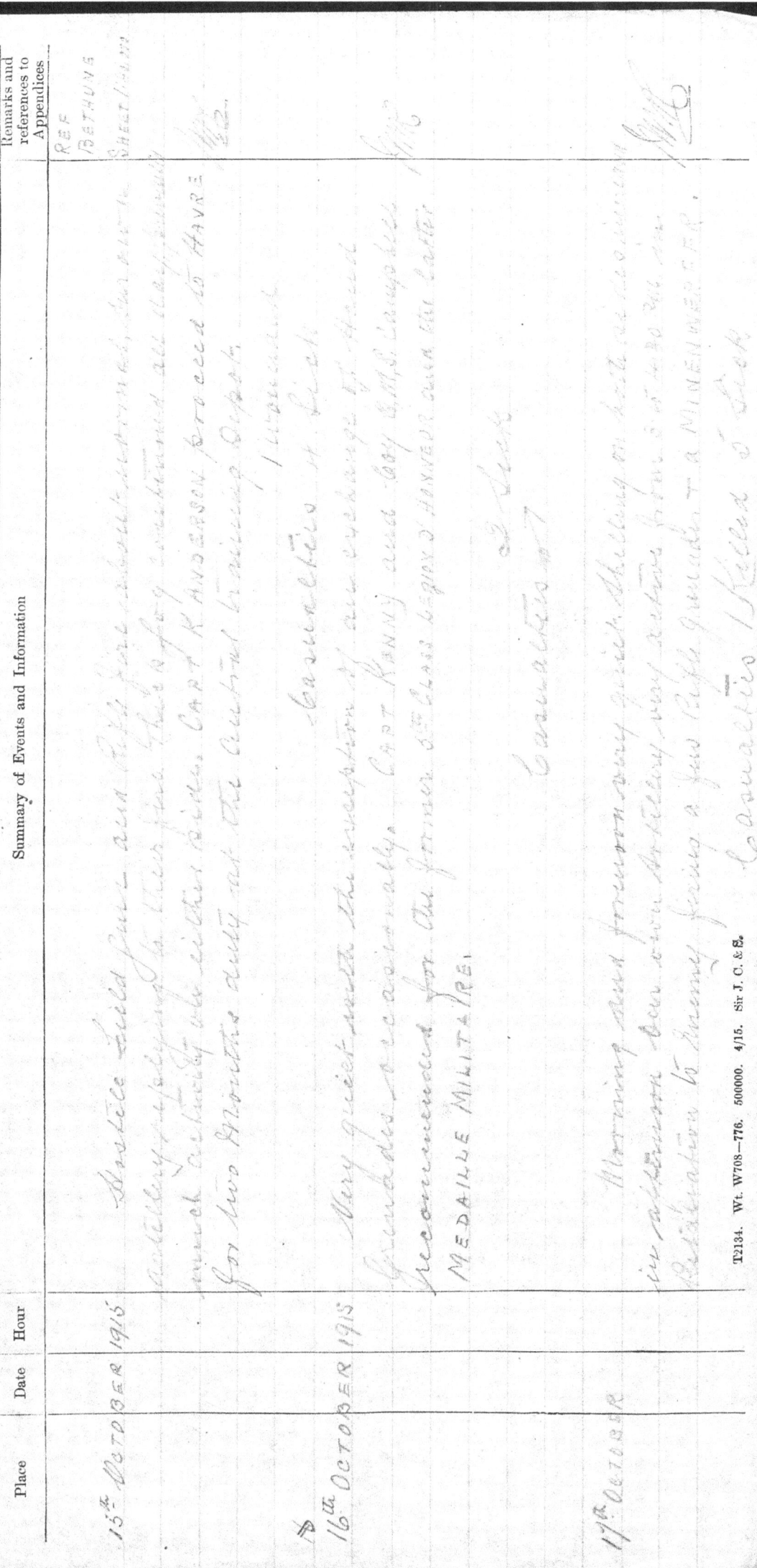

Army Form C. 2118.

WAR DIARY
or
INTELLIGENCE SUMMARY.
(Erase heading not required.)

Instructions regarding War Diaries and Intelligence Summaries are contained in F. S. Regs., Part II. and the Staff Manual respectively. Title pages will be prepared in manuscript.

Place	Date	Hour	Summary of Events and Information	Remarks and references to Appendices
	18th October 1915		Usual exchange of Rifle and hand grenades. About 11 A.D. A.M. fire from 2 Minenwerfers to which we retaliated with 4 rounds from Hawiljes field Guns & Trench Mortar Batteries. Remainder of the day fairly quiet. 2nd Lieut Hadow Recommended for the Military Cross and Sergt N Macleod for the Distinguished Conduct Medal.	REF. BETHUNE SHEET PHOTO WR Maps K & L arld.
	19th October	11.30 A.M.	March 19 11.30 A.M. Enemy bombarded our trenches with Minenwerfers and field guns. This was replied to by our Howitzers Field Guns and Trench Mortar Batteries. Remainder of the day quiet. The Bn was Relieved by the 86th Brigade The Bn being relieved by the 3rd Bn Royal Fusiliers Relief finished at 11.30 P.M., when we marched to Lepinette about 8 miles from the Trenches, arriving there about 4 P.M. after doing 31 days in the front line.	

Casualties 1 Wounded 1 Sick

Army Form C. 2118.

WAR DIARY
or
INTELLIGENCE SUMMARY.
(Erase heading not required.)

Instructions regarding War Diaries and Intelligence Summaries are contained in F. S. Regs., Part II. and the Staff Manual respectively. Title pages will be prepared in manuscript.

Place	Date	Hour	Summary of Events and Information	Remarks and references to Appendices
	20th October 1915		Lt Hildebrand LEPINETTE. Both Batts relieved to the B/n where everyone had a bath and a change of underclothing. Both of which were greatly needed. The Bn having been in the trenches for 31 days without change of clothes	Ref. Osturne Sheet 57.c.D.10
	21st October		2 ratio shields for Lewis Drill musketry Drawing general tidying and making general fit	Casualties Nil
			and visiting church set	Casualties 5 wds.
	22nd October 1915		Training continued especially in general training 2nd Lieuts HADON MILNER and CURISTIE proceed on leave to the United Kingdom.	Casualties two N.C.ols Wounded
	23rd October		Training as above with Bombing and running continued	App 4 N 2nd
			Casualties 2 O.rks	

T2134. Wt. W708—776. 500000. 4/15. Sir J. C. & E.

Army Form C. 2118.

WAR DIARY
or
INTELLIGENCE SUMMARY.
(Erase heading not required.)

Instructions regarding War Diaries and Intelligence Summaries are contained in F. S. Regs., Part II. and the Staff Manual respectively. Title pages will be prepared in manuscript.

Place	Date	Hour	Summary of Events and Information	Remarks and references to Appendices
	24th October 1915		Divine service was held at 10.30 a.m. REV J Markson 4th Regiment officiating	SEE BETHUNE SHEET (1143 ord)
	25th October 1915		Usual Sunday parades, accompanying Officer visited 2nd Bn at VAR DE ENNES. Casualties 2 sick	
	26th October 1915		Training continued. Nothing of importance to relate. Casualties 1 sick	
	27th October 1915		Rained all day preventing training being carried on. Casualties nil	Maj "O" attd
	28th October 1915		At 10 AM the Battalion paraded and marched to point B.34.d.3.1 near HINGES for inspection by His Majesty THE KING. No sooner had the Bn paraded than it rained.	

WAR DIARY or INTELLIGENCE SUMMARY

Army Form C. 2118.

Place	Date	Hour	Summary of Events and Information	Remarks and references to Appendices
Corbie	26th Mar 1915		Arriving at shed recently about 4:30 AM the 2nd Bn Durham L.I. Brigade was formed up in line of Battalion Columns on their R. flank. After waiting 40 minutes in the rain for over an hour we were visited by HM King George V His Majesty could not review us. We afterwards learnt that he had with him assent of those wounded him from inspecting 11 Brigade. The 28th Jubilee having been announced by Brigadier coming into action in Flanders in charge of the number of officers who had been in France with the Br and who are still extant. Received word at 1 pm that Rn 249 Princess Pat's 1914 officers 23 PtO Rank 249 Following no 1 having been away officers 3, other ranks 151. Rejoined wounded died sick officers 2, other ranks 158 during that period the Bn Observed as being present	REF BETHUNE SHEET

WAR DIARY
or
INTELLIGENCE SUMMARY.
(Erase heading not required.)

Army Form C. 2118.

Place	Date	Hour	Summary of Events and Information	Remarks and references to Appendices
Chocques	28th October 1915		Officers & 11 M other Ranks left 4th about 20.30 to 2.21 Cloths never left them. On arrival, proceeded to billets in the trenches Nos. 100 on Transports, Grooms, servants, etc. Lieut. J. ANDERSON proceeded on leave to the UK in his car. Casualties = 1 Wounded 2 Sick	Ref BEF returns 81-35
"	29th October "		Training continued nothing of importance to relate. Casualties — Nil	
"	30th October "		No. for 29th. Casualties = 1 Wound (accidental) 1 sick	
"	31st October "		Rained all day. Divine service held in field between showers. Rev. J. Applebee in Service. Mainly RB. Casualties = 1 sick	

OPERATION ORDER No 60.
by
Brigadier General W.J.St.J. HARVEY.
Commanding Dehra Dun Brigade.

Copy No. 3

1st October 1915.

Reference Map FRANCE-BETHUNE 1/40000 (Combined sheet) and 1/10000 trench map.

1. The front held by the Indian Corps will be re-adjusted and the MEERUT Division will hold from the LA BASSEE CANAL to ORKNEY ROAD inclusive.

2. The DEHRA DUN BRIGADE will hold from GIVENCHY RIDGE to ORKNEY ROAD inclusive (1st Seaforths on GIVENCHY RIDGE).

3. The Brigade will march to LE HAMEL tomorrow in accordance with attached march table. Subsequent movements and reliefs in accordance with attached relief table.

4. A Section of the Grenadier Company will be attached to each Subsection.

5. Reports to A.1.d.6/8.

Issued at 6.30 p.m.

Major.
Brigade Major Dehra Dun Brigade.

Copy No 1 and 2 Retained.   Copy 12 Bde M.G.O.
Copy No 3 to 1st Seaforths.   Copy No 13 Bde G.O.
Copy No 4 to 4th Seaforths   Copy 14 to Bde S.O.
Copy No 5 to 93rd Infantry   Copy No 16 to Bde B.G.O.
Copy No 6 to 9th Gurkhas   Copy 17 Bareilly Bde
Copy No 7 to 2nd Gurkhas   Copy 18 57th Bde.
Copy No 8 to Meerut Division.   Copy 19 19th Division
Copy No 9 to 107th Pioneers   Copy 20 to C.R.A.
Copy No 10 to 3rd Coy S and M   Copy 21 to C.R.E.

Copy.

The Secretary of State for War has received the following message from His Majesty the King:-

To—

 Field Marshal Sir John French,
  Commander-in-Chief,
   British Expeditionary Force.
     30th September 1915

I heartily congratulate you and all ranks of my Army under your command upon the successes which have attended their gallant efforts since the commencement of the combined attack.

I recognise that this strenuous and determined fighting is but the prelude to greater deeds and further victories. I trust the sick and wounded are doing well.

 Sgd. George R.I.

    cont.

UNIT	LOCATION	To be relieved by	Place where guides met relieving Units	Time	Date	Destination	Route	Remarks
2nd Gurkhas	IND.2.C.	57th Bde	FESTUBERT CHURCH S.25.d.3/3.	5·30 pm	20th Inst	Billets VIEILLE CHAPELLE and LA COUTURE	Road junction F.5.a.2/5.	
9th Gurkhas	IND.2.B.	57th Bde.	LE PLANTIN A.2.c.1/3.	5 pm	20th Inst	" " "	" " "	
93rd Infy	IND.2.A North of FIFE ROAD.	57th Bde.	LE PLANTIN A.2.c.1/3.	5·15 pm	20th Inst	Local Reserve SOUTH of FIFE ROAD.		
93rd Infy	IND.2.9. South of FIFE ROAD.	84th Bde	LE PLANTIN A.2.c.1/3.	5 pm	21st Inst	Billets VIEILLE CHAPELLE and LA COUTURE	Road junction F.5.a.2/5.	
4th Seaforths	F.6.C.	57th Bde	ESTAMINET CORNER.F.6.c.3/8.	4 pm	21st Inst	" " "	" " "	
1st Seaforths	IND.1.&B	85th Bde			19th Inst	Billets L'EPINETTE		under orders of GARHWAL Brigade
66 Punj Bty	IND.1.&B				19th Inst	Billets GORRE		" " " "
Bde Machine Guns	IND.2.	57th + 84th Bde M.Guns			20th and 21st Inst	Billets GORRE		under orders of B.M.G.O
Grenadiers under instruction	GORRE				19th Inst	LE HAMEL		Join with Gren of Units to which they belong

MARCH TABLE 2-10-18

Unit	Starting point	Time	Destination	Route
2nd Gurkhas	ZELOBES	10 a.m.	vicinity of LE HAMEL	LOCON - Bridge X.13.d
4th Seaforths	ZELOBES	10.5 a.m.	" "	LOCON - Bridge X.13.d
93rd Infantry	ZELOBES	10-10 a.m.	" "	LOCON - Bridge X.13.d
9th Gurkhas	ZELOBES	10-15 a.m.	" "	LOCON - Bridge X.13.d
Bde Bomb Guns & No 5 Trench Mortar Battery	ZELOBES	10-20 a.m.	" "	LOCON - Bridge X.13.d
Bde machine guns	ZELOBES	10-25 a.m.	" "	LOCON - Bridge X.13.d
Grenadier Coy.	ZELOBES	10-30 a.m.	" "	LOCON - Bridge X.13.d
107th Pioneers	ZELOBES	10-32 a.m.	" "	LOCON - Bridge X.13.d
3 Company Sappers and Miners	ZELOBES	10-40 a.m.	" "	LOCON - Bridge X.13.d

RELIEF TABLE 2-10-15

Unit	Destination	To relieve	Place where guides will met	Time	Route	Remarks
2nd Gurkhas	IND. II. A	8th Gloucesters	ESTAMINET CORNER - F.5.b.6/6.	6-30 p.m.	GORRE	
4th Seaforths & Coy 9th Gurkhas	IND. II. B	8th North Staffords	ESTAMINET CORNER F.5.b.6/6	6 p.m.	GORRE.	
9th Gurkhas less Coy 93rd Infantry	IND. II. C.	10th Worcesters	Junction RUE DE L'EPINETTE and RUE DE CAILLOUX	6 p.m.	RUE DU BOIS - RUE DE L'EPINETTE.	
93rd Infantry less 1 Company	INTERMEDIATE LINE and POSTS	10th Warwicks	ESTAMINET CORNER F.5.b.6/6.	5-30 p.m.	GORRE	Relief of posts to be carried out by day.
Bde machine guns	Relief to be carried out by		day under arrangements of		B.M.G.O	
Bde Bomb guns No 5 Trench Mortar Battery	Relief to be carried out by		day under arrangements of		Bde Bomb gun officer.	
Grenadier Company	Billets LE HAMEL					
Signals	Relief to be completed		by 5 p.m.			

SECRET.   Copy No 2

OPERATION ORDER NO 65
by
Br.-General W.G.Walker V.C.,C.B.   App. 'G'
Commanding Sirhind Brigade.

Reference Map BETHUNE Sheet 1/40,000.   dated 1st October 1915.

1. BAREILLY Bde. will relieve SIRHIND Bde. in trenches today.
   1/Seaforth Highlanders will remain in IND:1 C and will come under
   orders of G.O.C. BAREILLY Bde.
   IND:1 A will be taken over by 69th Punjabis and 33rd Punjabis.
   IND:1 B will be taken over by 2nd Black Watch and 4th Black Watch.
   58th Rifles relieve 27th Punjabis at GORRE.
   Details of relief as already arranged in this office No. 96 B.M.
   of 30/9/15.

2. Depots and 1st line transport, less such carts as are required by
   units with them, will march as soon as possible to new billets.
   The billeting area is not yet known but will be communicated as soon
   as received.

3. Ingoing units will use S. bank of CANAL and outgoing units the
   N. bank.

4. Units will march independently.
   Route for all units:-

       GORRE - LE HAMEL - LES GLATIGNIES - Rd. jn. X 13 a 2.8 -
       LOCON - LESTREM - level crossing R 4 a 8.6 - LA GORGUE.

   4/King's will start from LE HAMEL at 5-50 p.m.
   27th Punjabis will start from GORRE at 4-15 p.m.

5. G.O.C. SIRHIND Bde. will command the line until completion of
   reliefs. After that Bde. H.Q. at LA GORGUE - position not yet
   known.

                                          E.G. Hamilton
                                                Captain.
                                          B.M. Sirhind Brigade.

Copy 1 1/H.L.I.
  "   2 1/Seaforths. ✓
  "   3 4/King's.
  "   4 1/1 G.R.
  "   5 27th Punjabis.
  "   6 19th Division.
  "   7 Bareilly Bde.
  "   8 Lahore Division.
  "   9 Depot 1/H.L.I.
  " 10   "   1/1 G.R.
 11. Staff Captain.
 Copy 12 Bde. M.G.O.
  " 13 Bde. Signals.
  " 14)
  " 15) War Diary.
  " 16)   Issued to Signals at 11-30 a.m.

OPERATION ORDER No 61.

by

Brigadier General   W.J.ST.J. HARVEY.

Commanding   DEHRA   DUN   Brigade.

5th October 1915.

Reference Trench Map.

1. Subsection limits will be as under from 5.p.m. tomorrow:-

   IND.1.C.- THE SHRINE A.9.a.7/5 to GRENADIER ROAD exclusive A.3.c.1/2.

   IND.2.A. GRENADIER ROAD inclusive A.3.c.1/2 to STUART ROAD exclusive. A.3.a.3/35.

   IND.2.B.- STUART ROAD inclusive A.3.a.3/35 to STAFFORD ROAD exclusive S.27.c.3/2.

   IND.2.C.- STAFFORD ROAD inclusive S.27.c.3/2 to ORKNEY ROAD inclusive S.27.c.2/2.

2. One Company 9th Gurkhas will be transferred from IND.2.B. to IND.2.C. Details of re-adjustment will be arranged between Subsection Commanders.

3. 93rd Burmah Infantry will relieve 2nd Gurkhas in IND 2.A. tomorrow.

   Details of relief will be arranged between Commanding Officers concerned.

4. 2nd Gurkhas on relief become Brigade Reserve at F.6.c.

5. Reports to BREWERY, GORRE. F.3.c.5/4.

Issued at 7-15 p.m.

                                                Major.
                            Brigade Major Dehra Dun Brigade.

To Signal Section for distribution.

Copy 1 and 2 retained.
Copy 3 to Meerut Div
Copy No 4 to 1st Seaforths
Copy No 5 to 4th Seaforths.
Copy No 6 to 93rd Infantry
Copy No 7 to 9th Gurkhas.
Copy No 8 to 2nd Gurkhas.
Copy No 9 to B.M.G.O.
Copy No 10 to B.G.O.
Copy No 11 to B.B.G.O.

Copy 12 to B.Sig O.
Copy 13 to C.R.A.
Copy 14 to C.R.E.
Copy 15 13th Bde R.F.A.
Copy 16 to Bareilly Bde.
Copy 17 to 56th Bde.

Secret   Operation Order No.   Copy No 16
                    by
      Brigadier General C.G. Blackader, D.S.O.   I
          Commanding Garhwal Brigade.

Reference Maps:-   9th October 1915.
1/40000 BETHUNE (Combined) Sheet.
1/10000. Trench Map, 36c N.W.1.

Intention   1. The Garhwal Brigade will relieve the Bareilly Brigade
             in IND.1. on the 11th October.
Reliefs   2. Reliefs will be carried out as per accompanying march table.
             Details to be arranged by Os.C. concerned.
1st Seaforths. 3. 1st Seaforths remain in their present position, and O.C.
             retains command of "B" Subsection.
Posts   4. Garrisons for Posts :-

             SPOIL BANK   40 rifles   4th Cavalry   & 1 M.G.
             ORCHARD FARM   30   "   do   & 1 M.G.
             MAIRIE   40   "   2nd Leicrs.   & 1 M.G.
             HILDER   25   "   do   & 1 M.G.
             GIVENCHY   50   "   do   & 2 M.Gs.
             MOATED FARM.   15   "   1st Seaforths & 1 M.G.
             POPPY   15   "   do   & 1 M.G.
             PONT FIXE   20   "   2/8 Gurkhas
             HERTS   30   "   do

Trench and Post Stores. 5. Subsection Commanders will forward to Staff Captain
             list of trench and post stores taken over and of those
             actually in possession where no relief takes place.
Baggage Waggons. 6. Baggage waggons will come up to Units at 7a.m. on the
             11th October.

2

Rations   7. Ration Carts will be marshalled daily and marched by the senior Quarter Master in the following order:-

Head to pass GORRE Church at 5 p.m.

- 2nd Leicesters
- 1/3rd Londons.
- No 5 Trench Mortar Battery
- 2/8th Gurkhas

} ROUTE. WATERLOO Bridge - South of Canal - WESTMINSTER Bridge and Road. Transport to halt 50 yards West of WINDY CORNER.

- Garhwal Rifles.
- 2/3rd Gurkhas

} WATERLOO Bridge - South of Canal - VAUXHALL Bridge and road. Transport to halt 50 yards West of road junction A.8.c.5.1.

Command.   8. G.O.C. Garhwal Brigade will assume command of IND.1. on completion of reliefs.

Reports   9. Reports to LOISNE Chateau until 3.30 p.m. 11th. after that to F.11.c.6.6.

                                       Major.
                           Brigade Major, Garhwal Brigade.

Issued to Signal Section at 6 am. 10-10-15

Copy No 1 to 2nd Leicesters
    "   2   1/3rd Londons
          3   2/3rd Gurkhas
          4   Garhwal Rifles
          5   2/8th Gurkhas
          6.   Bde. M.G.O.
          7.   Bde. Bomb Gun Officer
          8.   Bde. Grenade Coy
          9.   Meerut Division
         10.   Bareilly Bde.
         11.   Dehra Dun Bde
         12.   9th Bde R.F.A.
         13.   No 5. Trench Mortar Battery.
         14.   Bde. Signals.
         15.   No 3 Coy Train.
         16.   1st Seaforths
         17.   War Diary
         18 } File.
         19 }

Arm	March Table to accompany 94th Bde. Operation Order No. 9.2	Route		Remarks
	To retire	Guides will meet units at		1st line depots to remain
Garhwal Rifles 39th Regt, 33rd Punjabis IND.1.A		HAZARA Bridge 12 noon	LES GLATIGNIES – Rd junct K.27.c. – GORRE – Bridge K.3.c. – C...and South Bank	F.4.b-8.0
2nd Leicesters, Black Watch IND.1.B	2nd + 4th	2nd B.W. Hd Qrs A.6.c.4.2 1.30 p.m.	do do and VAUXHALL Bridge road	F.4.a.10.2
1/3 Gurkhas, 2/8 Gurkhas 1 Coy 3rd Londons	Bde Reserve	A.6.C.5.1	LES FACONS Rd junct A.27.c, Rieux as above	F.4.a.4.1 F.3.b.5.2	Coy 3/Londons join Brigade at GORRE Chalien
Bde Grenade Coy, Bde machine gun dett, Bde Bomb gun dett, No 5 French Mortar Battery		Details to complete by 12 noon under arrangements to be made by Os.C. concerned	Follow Garhwal Rifles to GORRE	F.3.b.6.3 F.4.c.4.5
Bde Signals		Signal to be complete by 3 p.m.		F.3.b.4.1

Note:– 1st Divis march will reach units to GORRE.

Secret 12.10.15   'J' Copy No 6
                   BM 524/3

In continuation of BMS 24/2 which has been issued to all concerned :-

There will be a smoke feint attack by the Lahore Division from 12.30pm to 2pm and by the remainder of the Indian Corps from 1pm to 2pm tomorrow.
As gas will be used in certain parts of the line at the above time all ranks are to have their smoke helmets by them ready to put on at a moment's notice, in case of a change of wind.
The Brigade Reserve will stand to arms at 12.30 pm. The Brigade Machine Guns in reserve coming up to Brigade Grenade Coy. From that hour until "dismiss" is given there will be no movement between the canal & our front except for tactical reasons.
At 1.55 pm. 3 strong reconnoitering patrols and mining parties are proceeding to Aq 7.7, Aq a 8.4 and Aq d 5.7, to obtain information regarding the enemy's line.
Artillery are firing from 1 to 2pm on the enemy's line in front of ours.
Machine and Bomb gun Detachments are co-operating under special instructions.
Units in the front line are to take advantage of any opportunity which may offer for bringing fire to bear on the enemy should he show himself.
Should the wind be unsuitable the above will not take place. Special instructions are being issued to those concerned.
Reports to Brigade Report Centre at A14a2.8 from 10.0 am tomorrow.

OC 1st Seaforths   D H Cameron
                               Major
12.10.15.   Brigade Major Dehra Dun Bde

Copy No....3....

DEHRA DUN BRIGADE OPERATION ORDER No 62.

'K'

GORRE.   18th October 1915

Reference:- Map FRANCE-BETHUNE, 1/40000 (Combined Sheet) and trench Map 1/10000.

1. DEHRA DUN BRIGADE (less 1st Seaforths) will hand over IND.2. front from LOOP Northwards to 57th Brigade, 19th Division on night 20th/21st Instant and the remainder of IND.2. front from LOOP inclusive to GRENADIER ROAD to 84th Brigade, 28th Division on night 21st/22nd Instant

2. Movements in accordance with attached table.

    Details of reliefs will be arranged between Commanding Officers concerned.

3. DEHRA DUN BRIGADE will take over front from VINE STREET exclusive to ESTAIRES-LA BASSEE ROAD exclusive on 22nd instant under orders to be issued later.

4. Reports to BREWERY, GORRE.

Issued at 9-45 p.m.

Major.
Brigade Major Dehra Dun Brigade.

Copies No 1 and 2 retained.
Copy No 3 to 1st Seaforths.
Copy No 4 to 4th Seaforths.
Copy No 5 to 93rd Infantry
Copy No 6 to 9th Gurkhas.
Copy No 7 to 2nd Gurkhas.
Copy No 8 to Meerut Division.
Copy No 9 to 13th Brigade R.F.A.
Copy No 10 to 2 Coy Train.
Copy No 11. to 57th Brigade.
Copy No 12. to 84th Brigade.
Copy No 13 to Garhwal Brigade.
Copy No 14 to 56th Brigade.
Copy No 15 to B.M.G.O.
Copy No 16 to 66 Trench Battery
Copy No 17 to B.G.?.
Copy No 18 to Bde Sig O.

Copy No 20. C.R.A. Meerut
Copy No 21 to C.R.E. Meerut
Copy No 22 to B.E.G.O.

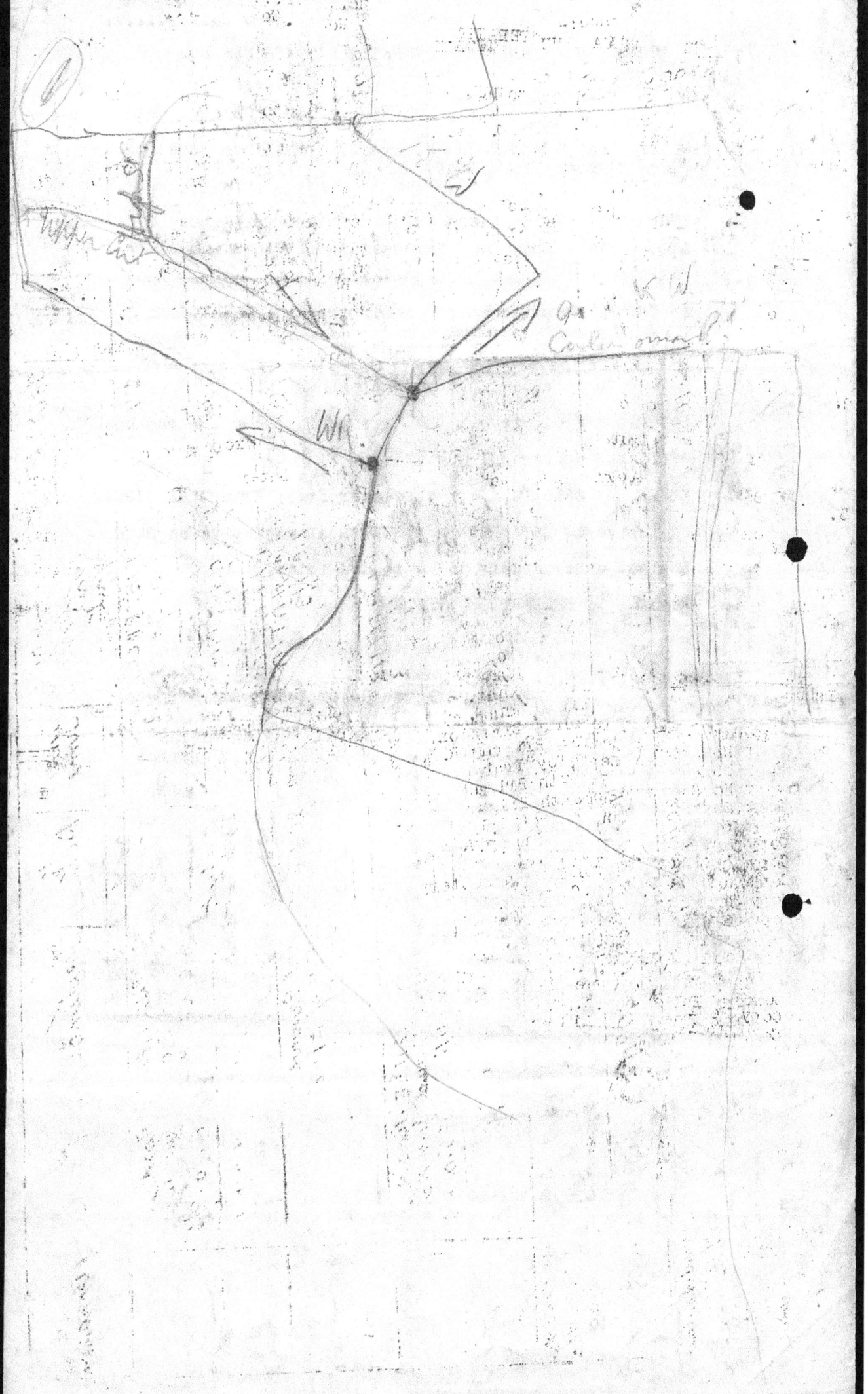

MOVEMENT TABLE

UNIT	TO RELIEVE	DESTINATION	Guides meet relieving units at	ROUTE	REMARKS
4th Seaforths	1st Gurkhas and H.L.I.	HAZARA TRENCH (inclusive) to CRESCENT TRENCH (exclusive)	WINDY CORNER at 6 pm	RICHEBOURG ST VAAST.	C.O.s and 2nd Cmdrs to be at WINDY CORNER at 10 am to visit line.
9th Gurkhas	H.L.I. from HAZARA TRENCH to VINE STREET. 1st Gurkhas from VINE STREET to CINDER TRACK	CINDER TRACK (inclusive) to HAZARA TRENCH (exclusive)	WINDY CORNER at 6-15 pm	RICHEBOURG ST VAAST.	" " " " "
2nd Gurkhas	29th Punjabis	LANSDOWNE POST.	RAILHEAD ST VAAST at 6 pm	N of RICHEBOURG ST VAAST. Track from ST VAAST to LANSDOWNE POST.	
Bde machine guns	Bde machine guns				By day under arrangement of B.M.G.O.
Bde Bomb guns		EDWARDS 15 mm KEEP. 16 mm LANSDOWNE 50 mm			By day under arrangement of Bde 13.9.0
Garrisons of Posts	H.L.I. and 29th Punjabis.				
Garrisons of keeps	H.L.I. and 1st Gurkhas	COPSE KEEP 15 mm and 1 machine gun ORCHARD. 40 mm and 1 machine gun MOLE HILL 15 mm and 1 machine gun	WINDY CORNER at 11 am		By day under arrangements of O.C. 2 Gurkhas
1st Seaforths		LA COUTURE.			Will move on 22nd not until orders to be issued later

Operation Order No. 94   Copy No. 1
              by
Brigadier General C. G. Blackader, D.S.O.
        Commanding Garhwal Brigade.
                                18th October 1915.

Reference Maps:-
1/10,000 Trench & 1/40,000 BETHUNE.

1. The Garhwal Bde and 1st Seaforths will be relieved by the 55th Brigade on the 19th October.

2. Reliefs will be carried out under the orders of the G.O.C Garhwal Brigade in accordance with the accompanying table. Details to be arranged by Commanding Officers concerned.

3. Garrisons of forts will be relieved under the orders of the Subsection Commanders concerned.

4. Units and 1st line depots of Garhwal Bde will move to the billets occupied on the 10th October — 1st line will move at 10 a.m.

5. Divisional Trench stores will be removed by units.

6. Transport for units must be brought up the South bank of the canal and be halted on the North bank, West, and clear of VAUXHALL and WESTMINSTER Bridges.

7. Rations will be delivered in billets in LOCON and LOISNE on the 19th and 20th October.

8. During the period at LOISNE units will be prepared to assemble as laid down in Operation Order No 91.

9. Reports of reliefs to be handed in at Brigade Head Quarters at F.11.c.6.6 as units pass.

10. On completion of reliefs reports to LOISNE CHATEAU.

                                            Major
                                Brigade Major Garhwal Brigade

Issued by Signals at 8 p.m.

Copy No 1 to 2nd Leicester
       2 to 3/Londons
       3 to 2/3 Gurkhas
       4 to Garhwal Rifles
       5 to 2/8 Gurkhas
       6 to 1st Seaforths ✓
       7 to Bde Signals
       8 to Bde Grenade Coy
       9 to Bde Bomb Gun Dett.
      10 to No 5 T.M. Bty
      11 to Bde Machine Gun Sect.
      12 to No 3 Coy Train
      13 to Dehra Dun Bde
      14 to 85th Infy Bde
      15 to Meerut Divn
      16 to 9th Bde R.F.A.
      17 to War Diary
      18 to File

Unit	Location	Troops to accompany Battalion	Brigade Operation Order 94. Place and hour guides west-relieving unit	Route	Remarks
Garhwal Rifles 1st Seaforth	IND.1. A		The Buffs	VAUXHALL Bridge 9 A.M.	Proceed to billets L'EPINETTE
	IND.1. B		Royal Fusiliers	WESTMINSTER BRIDGE 9-30. A.M.	
2nd Leicesters	#3.1. B.		Middlesex Regt.	WESTMINSTER BRIDGE 10. A.M.	via CORRE
1/3 Gurkhas 2/8 Gurkhas	Bde Reserve		E. Surrey Regt.	VAUXHALL BRIDGE 10-30. A.M.	West CORRE

Brigade Machine Guns and No 5 Trench Mortar Battery will complete relief by 10 A.M. under arrangements to be made by Bn HQrs
No 5 French Mortar Battery and Brigade Bomb Gun detachment will follow Leicesters out of line
Brigade Grenade Company will march 12 noon.
No 66 Trench Mortar Battery will accompany 1st Seaforths, as far as CORRE.

DEHRA DUN BRIGADE OPERATION ORDER No. 63.

30th October 1915.

Reference Map 1/40000 BETHUNE Combined Sheet and
    Trench Map 1/10000.

1. The DEHRA DUN BRIGADE will take over front from CINDER TRACK inclusive to CRESCENT TRENCH exclusive from GARHWAL BRIGADE and SIRHIND BRIGADE, LAHORE DIVISION on night 21st/22nd October 1915.

2. 4th Seaforths will take over front from CRESCENT TRENCH exclusive to HAZARA TRENCH inclusive.
9th Gurkhas will take over front from HAZARA TRENCH exclusive to CINDER TRACK inclusive.
2nd Gurkhas will be in Brigade Reserve at LANSDOWNE POST
93rd Infantry will be in Brigade Reserve in RICHEBOURG ST VAAST.
1st Seaforths will be in Brigade Reserve at LA COUTURE.

3. Movements in accordance with attached table. Details to be arranged between Commanding Officers concerned.

4. Garrisons of Posts will be found by 2nd Gurkhas, Garrisons of Keeps by the Battalion holding Subsection in which they are situated.

5. Reports to RED HOUSE, LA COUTURE from completion of reliefs of IND.2. to 4.p.m. on 21st Instant, after that to WELLINGTON ROAD, R.3C.c.1/9.

Issued at a.m. to Signal
Section for distribution.

                                            Major.
            Brigade Major Dehra Dun Brigade.

Copy 1 and 2 retained.   Copy 13 to C.R.A. Meerut
Copy 3 to Meerut Div   Copy 14 to C.R.E. Meerut
Copy 4 to 1st Seaforths.   Copy 15 to 2 Coy Train.
Copy 5 to 4th Seaforths.   Copy 16. B.M.G.O.
Copy 6 to 93rd Infantry   Copy 17 to B.G.O.
Copy 7 to 9th Gurkhas.   Copy 18 to B.S.O.
Copy 8 to 2nd Gurkhas.   Copy 19 to B.P.G.O.
Copy 9 to Garhwal Bde.   Copy 20 to 66th Trench Bty.
Copy 10 to Sirhind Bde.
Copy 11 to 13th Bde R.F.A.
Copy 12 to 18th Bde R.F.A.

DEHRA DUN BRIGADE.
OPERATION ORDER   No 64.

23rd October 1915.

Reference Map FRANCE BETHUNE 1/40000 and Trench
  Map 1/10000.

1. BAREILLY BRIGADE will relieve DEHRA DUN BRIGADE

   in IND.4. on 24th Instant.

2. Movements in accordance with attached table.

   Details to be arranged between Commanding Officers

   concerned.

3. Units will report location of Head Quarter Billets.

4. Relief Reports to WELLINGTON ROAD. R.30.c.1/8.

Issued at.....p.m. to
Signal Company for
Distribution.
                                              Major.
                        Brigade Major Dehra Dun Brigade.

Copy No 1 and 2 retained.
 "   No 3 to Meerut Div
 "   No 4 to 1st Seaforths.
 "   No 5 to 4th Seaforths.
 "   No 6 to 23rd Infantry
 "   No 7 to 9th Gurkhas.
 "   No 8 to 2nd Gurkhas.
 "   No 9 to Garhwal Bde.
 "   No 10 to Ferozepore Bde
 "   No 11 to Bareilly Bde.
 "   No 12 to 13th Bde R.F.A.
 "   No 13 to 2 Coy Train.
 "   No 14 to C.R.E. Meerut Div
 "   No 15 to C.R.A. Meerut Div.
 "   No 16 to B.M.G.O.
 "   No 17 to B.G.O.
 "   No 18 to B.B.G.O.
 "   No 19 to B.S.O.
 "   No 20. to 66th Trench Bty
 "   No 21 to 18th Bde R.F.A.

MOVEMENT TABLE – 24-10-15

UNIT	To be relieved by	Place and time where guides meet relieving Unit	Destination	Route	Remarks
9th Gurkhas	69th Punjabis	WINDY CORNER. 5-30 pm	Billets R.19 and 6	RICHEBOURG ST VAAST- FOSSE.	Guides will meet C.O. and Adv. party London at WINDY CORNER at 11-30 am
4th Seaforths	Black Watch	WINDY CORNER- 5-30 pm	Billets R.11.6 and R.15.a & c	RICHEBOURG ST VAAST- PONT LEVIS- VIEILLE CHAPELLE-CROIX MARMUSE	" "
93rd Infy	58th Rifles F.F.		Billets CALONNE Q.9.a.	LA COUTURE-PONT LEVIS- VIEILLE CHAPELLE- Road Junction R.20.c.8/2- CORNET MALO- Road Junction Q.14.c.3/6.	" "
2nd Gurkhas	Black Watch		Billets QUENTIN Q.16.d and Q.22.b.	ST YAAST-LACOUTURE- PONT LEVIS- VIEILLE CHAPELLE- Road Junction R.20.c.8/2.	Move off at 5-30 pm
Bde Machine Guns	Bareilly Machine Guns		Billets R.13.c.	RICHEBOURG ST VAAST- FOSSE.	Relief by day
Bde Bomb Guns	Bareilly Bomb Guns		Billets R.13.c.	" "	" "
Bde Grenade Coy			Billets R.13.c.	" "	" "
COPSE KEEP	15 men 69th Punjabis				
ORCHARD KEEP	40 men 13th Black Watch				
MOLE HILL KEEP	15 men Black Watch				
EDWARD POST	15 men 58th Rifles F.F.				
MEN'S POST	15 men 58th Rifles F.F.				
RAE'S POST	1 and 3. 33rd Punjabis				
BONES POST	1 and 3. " "				Rejoin Unit.
ST YAAST	1 and 3. " "				
GROTTO	1 and 3. " "				
ANGLE	1 and 3. " "				
PENIN. MARIRE	1 and 3. " "				
LANSDOWNE	50 Black Watch				

SECRET   No. S.C. 105/1.

                                    Headquarters Dehra Dun Brigade.
                                    27th October 1915.

Memorandum.

   The Brigade will parade at Sq.Q.34.d.3.1., at 11-30 a.m., tomorrow 28th instant, for inspection by His Majesty the King.

2. DRESS:- MARCHING ORDER without packs or smoke helmets.

3. The Brigade will be drawn up in line of battalions in column of companies at 6 paces distance.

   Machine Gun Sections without transport will fall in 10 paces in rear of the right flank of their battalions.

   The Grenade Company will fall in 10 paces in rear of the right of the centre battalion.

4. Units will march by the following routes.

1st Seaforths.)	
4th Seaforths.)	PARADIS, PACAUT.
Grenade Company.)	
Machine Guns.)	
93rd Burmas.)	QUENTIN,- Road through Q.22.d.
2nd Gurkhas.)	
9th Gurkhas.	Road junction Q.30.b., road through Q.29.b.

5. Parade states will be handed to the Staff Captain on the Parade ground at 11-15 a.m.

                                    C M Tomkeith Captain
                                    Staff Captain Dehra Dun Brigade,
To,
   The Officer Commanding,
       1st Bn Seaforth Highlanders.
       1/4th Bn Seaforth Highlanders.
       93rd Burma Infantry.
       9th Gurkha Rifles.
       2nd Gurkha Rifles.
       Brigade Grenade Coy.
       Brigade Machine Gun Coy.

Headquarters Dehra Dun Brigade.

27th October 1915.

The following will be the procedure:-

The Brigade will be drawn up with bayonets fixed and troops standing at ease to await the Divisional Commander.

On the Divisional Commander's arrival the Brigade Commander will call the troops to attention and give the order to "Slope Arms" (Rifle battalions acting according to custom.)

The Divisional Commander will then order the troops to stand easy, the executive word being given by the Brigade Commander.

On the arrival of the Corps Commander the Divisional Commander will himself call the troops to attention and give the order to "Slope Arms".

As His Majesty approaches, the Divisional Commander will call the troops to attention and will give the order "Royal Salute, Present Arms", and again after an interval "Slope Arms".

His Majesty will then ride along the front and as soon as he has got well clear of the line the Brigade Commander will give the order "Order Arms" and will call for three cheers for His Majesty.

Meerut Division

1st Seaforth Highlanders

From 1st To 30 November 1915

CONFIDENTIAL

WAR DIARY

OF

The Officer Commanding, 1st Seaforth Highlanders

FROM   November 1st 1915   TO   November 30th 1915.

(VOLUME XV.)

Army Form C. 2118.

Vol XV

WAR DIARY
or
INTELLIGENCE SUMMARY.
(Erase heading not required.)

Instructions regarding War Diaries and Intelligence Summaries are contained in F. S. Regs., Part II. and the Staff Manual respectively. Title pages will be prepared in manuscript.

Place	Date	Hour	Summary of Events and Information	Remarks and references to Appendices
	1st November 1915		Rain prevented any work being carried out in billets. Corpl MACRAE and RIGBY, Lieut LINDON-BENN and 2nd Lieuts WILSON, WYLIE & DENNISTON were granted a weeks leave to the United Kingdom. Lieuts HADOW and CHRISTIE, 2nd Lieut MILLER returned from leave. Casualties Nil	See attd sheet K100,000 Apps Q atta.
	2nd November		Batt. marched from billets at LEPINETTE and took over the trenches on the front line from 2nd LEICESTERS, one Coy of the Pic. de FAIS. between EDWARD ROAD and ALBERT ROAD. Relief was completed by 9.30 pm. The trenches were in a very bad state being knee deep in water and bankets falling in. Position 1 Kili Hill by Bn. from Square 9.15 D 9/6 to Square S.15 D.10/10. The 93rd BURMESE INFANTRY on our right and the 1/9 Ghurkha Rifles on our Left Flank.	
			Casualties 2 sick	

WAR DIARY
or
INTELLIGENCE SUMMARY.
(Erase heading not required.)

Army Form C. 2118.

Place	Date	Hour	Summary of Events and Information	Remarks and references to Appendices
	3rd November 1915		Rained almost all day. Hostile snipers were rather active. A few shells were fired at our Reserve Trenches doing however no damage. Casualties 2 Wounded 2 Sick	SEE BATHING SHEET 2 Sick
	4th November		Rain ceased and weather got less misty, at stand to, owing to scale of trenches Battalion was redistributed so as to hold every line with Regges own Machine Guns only. Rearrangement completed by 3.30 am 60 snipers "B"Coy and Machine Guns in strong line with 4th Ox & Bucks Post. D Coy in Reserve in Old British Lines. C Coy astride RUE DE BOIS in breastworks. A Coy with Bn Head Qrs in RU DE BEREAUX. At 2.30 P.M. 13 was relieved by 1/4 OxBucks but leaving A & C Coys in position as above. B & D Coys and H.Qrs proceeding to Billets between LACOUTURE and VIEILLE CHAPELLE arriving about 4 P.M. with many cases of sore feet. Capt. KENNEY proceeded on leave to United Kingdom. Casualties 2 Killed 1 Wounded	
	5th November 1915		The SEHRA DUN B.E. (now less 4 OxBucks) were relieved by the 139th Bde 46th DIVISION during the morning. The Bn marching to Crois home South of LESTREM and at 4 P.M. proceeded by Motor Buses to STEENBECQUE. Capt. MAXWELL proceeded on leave to U.K. in Ce D.M. Casualties 2 Sick	SEE REF SHEET TRAIN 2LA

Army Form C. 2118.

WAR DIARY
or
INTELLIGENCE SUMMARY.
(Erase heading not required.)

Instructions regarding War Diaries and Intelligence Summaries are contained in F.S. Regs., Part II. and the Staff Manual respectively. Title pages will be prepared in manuscript.

Place	Date	Hour	Summary of Events and Information	Remarks and references to Appendices
	6th November 1915		In Billets at STEEN BECQUE where the day was devoted to drying clothes and getting the men's feet in order with "Anti Oil" and "Anti Frost Grease". Casualties Nil	REFERENCE SHEET 36A SHEET 11/16
	7th November 1915		Men's feet in fairly good condition, as Coys were practised in Short Marches and Drill. Casualties 2 Sick	JMR
	8th November 1915		Training continued as for the 7th. Capt RIGBY returned off leave. No otherwise to record. Casualties Nil	JMR
	9th November 1915		Training of Coys as above. Capts MAORAE KENNEY and MAXWELL, 2nd Lieuts WYLLIE and DENNISTON returned of leave. Lt LYNDEN-BELL for some unknown reason failed to return. Capt McKAY-SCOBIE joined Bn and took over command of C Coy. Casualties Nil	JMR
	10th November 1915		Entered A.B. RITCHIE our late commanding officer now in	JMR

Army Form C. 2118.

WAR DIARY
or
INTELLIGENCE SUMMARY.
(Erase heading not required.)

Instructions regarding War Diaries and Intelligence Summaries are contained in F. S. Regs., Part II. and the Staff Manual respectively. Title pages will be prepared in manuscript.

Place	Date	Hour	Summary of Events and Information	Remarks and references to Appendices
Continued	10th November 1915		command of the 26th B.DE 9th Division visited the Battalion and was entertained to lunch by Lt-Col Thomson and Officers. our own G.O.C. B.Gr General HARVEY was also present. Capt CADDELL MOTOR AMBULANCE CONVOY very kindly provided a number of ZINC BATHS which enabled the whole of the Battalion to have a bath, this was much appreciated by the men. 2nd Lieut J. McNAUGHTON was appointed Transport Officer vice Lieut KINDER-BALL. Casualties Nil	REFERENCE SHEET. FRANCE 51
	11th November 1915		Still in Billets at STEENBECQUE day training continues. Rained heavily towards evening and continued all night. Casualties 1 sick.	
	12th November "		Still raining and continued to do so until midday. twenty officers went from being carried out. Casualties Nil	
	13th November "		The MEERUT DIVISION having been ordered to vacate their billeting area the 8th DEHRA DUN BRIGADE handed ready to move off at	

Army Form C. 2118.

WAR DIARY
or
INTELLIGENCE SUMMARY.
(Erase heading not required.)

Instructions regarding War Diaries and Intelligence Summaries are contained in F. S. Regs, Part II. and the Staff Manual respectively. Title pages will be prepared in manuscript.

Place	Date	Hour	Summary of Events and Information	Remarks and references to Appendices
Continued	13 November 1915	8.30 A.M.	with the Batt⁴ leading and marched about 12 miles, the Bn. billeting at ECQUEDECQUES about 13 miles west of LISLIERS, arriving there about 12.55 P.M. The march was started in a downpour of rain and very high wind, the rain stopped about 9.15 A.M. although it continued to be very cold all day. Rev. J.A. McNEILL joined from Meerut Cavalry leaving Captain LIEUT LYNDEN-BELL returned from leave having been retained by the Imbarkation Authorities in England. Casualties Nil	REFERENCE SHEET 57C FRAME 635
	14ᵗʰ November		Being Sunday the Bn paraded for Divine Service at 11 A.M. Brig General HARVEY, commanding the Brigade was present and inspected Capt KENNY, with the CROIX DE CHEVALIER (5ᵗʰ class LEGION OF HONOUR) awarded to him by the FRENCH GOVERNMENT. Casualties 1 sick	
	15ᵗʰ November		The Bn paraded under the Adjt at 10.30 A.M. for close order movements. The boys carried out platoon & coy Drill in the afternoon. Casualties 2 sick	

Army Form C. 2118.

WAR DIARY
or
INTELLIGENCE SUMMARY.
(Erase heading not required.)

Instructions regarding War Diaries and Intelligence Summaries are contained in F. S. Regs., Part II. and the Staff Manual respectively. Title pages will be prepared in manuscript.

Place	Date	Hour	Summary of Events and Information	Remarks and references to Appendices
				REFERENCE FRANCE SHEET 36A
	16th November 1915		The Bn carried out training in the usual drill and extended order movements.	
			A football match between the Officers of the 1st & 13th 9th Gurkha Rifles in the afternoon, resulting in a win for the 1st Sea High'rs Officers by 3 goals to 2.	
			2nd Lieut G.M. Macario joined on being commissioned from the 1st/13th 4th Seaforth Highlanders.	
			Casualties Nil	
	17th November 1915		Bn parade for Route Marching under Capt. Jacobs at 10 A.M. Heavy showers of rain continued throughout the day.	
			Major General Jacob Commanding Meerut Division visited the Officers and bid us all Good Bye on his leaving this Division to take over command of the 21st Division B.E.F.	
			Casualties Nil	

Army Form C. 2118.

WAR DIARY
or
INTELLIGENCE SUMMARY.
(Erase heading not required.)

Instructions regarding War Diaries and Intelligence Summaries are contained in F. S. Regs., Part II. and the Staff Manual respectively. Title pages will be prepared in manuscript.

Place	Date	Hour	Summary of Events and Information	Remarks and references to Appendices
				REFERENCE
	18th November 1915		Bn paraded at 9.15 A.M. and moved to WESTREHEM, distance about 10 miles, where we Billeted. D/ Col THOMSON, CAPT ROSS and LIEUT MACLEOD proceeded on leave to the United Kingdom. Casualties Nil	FRANCE SHEET 36 A
	19th November 1915		Batt⁰ paraded at 10 A.M. under the Adjt for Route Marching combined with Field Movements. 2nd Lieut ST KILGOUR proceeded on leave to the United Kingdom. Casualties 3 sick	
	20th November 1915		Training in Platoon and Company in extended order carried out under Company Commanders. Casualties 1 sick	
	21st November 1915		Divine service was held at 10.30 A.M. and Evening Service at 6.30 P.M. in the Village School. Officers and men newly from Leave. Casualties 2 sick	
	22nd November 1915		Training under Company arrangements continued. CAPTAIN	

Army Form C. 2118.

WAR DIARY
or
INTELLIGENCE SUMMARY.
(Erase heading not required.)

Instructions regarding War Diaries and Intelligence Summaries are contained in F.S. Regs., Part II. and the Staff Manual respectively. Title pages will be prepared in manuscript.

Place	Date	Hour	Summary of Events and Information	Remarks and references to Appendices
Continued	22nd November 1915		L. Anderson joined on return from the 3rd Battalion. At 3 PM orders were received for the Battalion with all transport vehicles (but no transport personal or animals) and one company of the 2nd BLACK WATCH attached would entrain at LILLIERS at 11.51AM the following day, destination not known. CAPT Ross and LIEUT MACLEOD rejoined from leave.	REFERENCE FRANCE SHEET 36 A
			Casualties NIL	
	23rd November 1915		The Battalion paraded at 6AM (having previously sent off an advance party at 4AM) and marched to LILLIERS STATION arriving there at 8.35 AM. The train was then loaded up with Rations for 4 days, Stores Baggage etc, and by 11.30 was ready to move off, destination proved them to be MARSAILLES. LIEUT & M.M. N. REID joined us at the Railway Station on his being posted from the 3rd Battalion. Our TRAIN left the Station punctually at 11.50 AM.	
			Casualties NIL	

Army Form C. 2118.

WAR DIARY
or
INTELLIGENCE SUMMARY.
(Erase heading not required.)

Instructions regarding War Diaries and Intelligence Summaries are contained in F. S. Regs., Part II. and the Staff Manual respectively. Title pages will be prepared in manuscript.

Place	Date	Hour	Summary of Events and Information	Remarks and references to Appendices
	24th November 1915		On the train enroute to MARSAILLES. Lt Col THOMSON and 2nd LIEUT KILGOUR rejoined at ABBEYVILLE Station from leave. Casualties 1 accidentally burnt during train journey.	REFERENCE FRANCE SHEET 56A
	25th November 1915		Arriving at MARSAILLES at about 4 PM. marched to the Docks and and at 9.15 PM embarked on board H.M.T. LAKE MANITOBA. 2nd LIEUT SULLIVAN joined on board the Ship on being posted from the 3rd Bn. Casualties Nil	
	26th November 1915		On board ship at MARSAILLES. A draft of 56 N.C.O's & Men joined and were posted to Companies. Casualties Nil	
	27th November 1915		The Ship moved from the Docks and anchored in the the Harbour. Emergency stations and Boat stations to the troops on board, and emergency Lowering practised. Casualties Nil	

T2134. Wt. W708-776. 500000. 4/15. Sir J.C.&S.

Army Form C. 2118.

WAR DIARY
or
INTELLIGENCE SUMMARY.
(Erase heading not required.)

Instructions regarding War Diaries and Intelligence Summaries are contained in F. S. Regs., Part II. and the Staff Manual respectively. Title pages will be prepared in manuscript.

Place	Date	Hour	Summary of Events and Information	Remarks and references to Appendices
	28th November 1915		Divine Service was held at 10.30 am and evening service at 6.15 pm. At 12.45 PM we sailed out of MARSEILLES arriving in TOULON harbour at 6.30 PM with all lights out and no previous warning submarine attack. Casualties Nil	
	29th November 1915		Sailed from TOULON at 1 AM destination unknown. Life belts previously issued being kept constantly with each man all day. All lights & being much reduced and screened, old Iron being slung over the sea to stop about thirty eight lifebelts on board. Casualties Nil	
	30th November 1915		At sea. Physical training carried out by companies on deck. Aw much warmer. Steam quite suddenly fell below what was required. Lifebelts were kept on. The afternoon was being spent helping greatly to pass the time away. A rumour was kicked of those embarking at MARSEILLES.	

WAR DIARY
or
INTELLIGENCE SUMMARY
(Erase heading not required.)

Army Form C. 2118.

Place	Date	Hour	Summary of Events and Information	Remarks and references to Appendices
Continued	30th November 1915		*Continued* — on the 26th November 1915 who with the Battalion at that port on the 11th of October 1914 with the following result. He disembarked at Marseilles with 12th on 11.10.14. 23 Officers & 43 other Ranks of that number 3 Officers and 226 other Ranks remained to embark on the 28.11.15. The 3 Officers were Lt Col Worthington who landed in France as a Captain [illegible] was wounded, sent home to England for 6 Months, Capt. & Adjt T. Massie, landed as Transport Officer, invalided home in the 2nd of the whole period, Captain B Kenny, landed in France as 2nd Lt, and was with the Bn in the field the whole period except being a Month at HAVRE for a rest. Of the 226 other Ranks 108 had not been away from the Bn during the whole period. Being the anniversary the event was celebrated in the customary manner, and although pieces de résistance being on board ships, the Haggis was well in evidence at Dinner. Invitations Atl. Brock and other ladies printed to the occasion.	J Massie Carnallio N.L.

Army Form C. 2118.

WAR DIARY
or
INTELLIGENCE SUMMARY.
(Erase heading not required.)

Instructions regarding War Diaries and Intelligence Summaries are contained in F. S. Regs., Part II. and the Staff Manual respectively. Title pages will be prepared in manuscript.

Place	Date	Hour	Summary of Events and Information	Remarks and references to Appendices
Continued				
	31st November 1915		Referring again to the Census mentioned overleaf it was found that out of the 108 other ranks mentioned as not having left the By. 29 N.C.O.s men only continued in the trenches the whole the whole period, the others being at various periods employed as servants, Grooms, Transport Drivers, and Clerks behind the actual trenches line. Conditions	

SECRET   Copy No. 3

DEHRA DUN BRIGADE OPERATION ORDER NO 65.

                                          1st November 1915.

Reference map FRAME BETHUNE 1/40000 and Trench map 1/10000.

1. DEHRA DUN BRIGADE will take over IND.3. trenches from the GARHWAL BRIGADE on the 2nd Instant.

2. The 93rd Infantry will take over from PIPE TRENCH exclusive to S.15.d.9/6 and the 1st Seaforths will take over from S.15.d.9/6 to the CINDER TRACK exclusive.

3. Movements in accordance with attached table. Details to be arranged between Commanding Officers concerned.

4. Reports to WHITE HOUSE, VIEILLE CHAPELLE.

                                          Major.
                        Brigade Major Dehra Dun Brigade.

Issued to Signal Section for distribution at 5.15 p.m.

Copy 1 and 2 Retained.
Copy 3 to 1st Seaforths.
Copy 4 to 4th Seaforths.
Copy 5 to 93rd Infantry
Copy 6 to 9th Gurkhas.
Copy 7 to 2nd Gurkhas.
Copy 8 to Meerut Division.
Copy 9 to C.R.A. Meerut
Copy 10 to C.R.E. Meerut
Copy 11 to Bareilly Bde.
Copy No 12 to Garhwal Bde
Copy 13 to Jullunder Bde.
Copy 14 to 2 Coy Meerut Train.
Copy 15 to Bde Sig Officer
Copy 16 to Bde M.G.O.
Copy 17 to Bde B.G.O.
Copy 18 to Bde G.O.
Copy 19 to 66th Trench Bty

POSTS TO BE TAKEN OVER FROM GARHWAL BRIGADE.

POST.	Location.	Garrison.	Unit.
WATERS.	S.15.d.3/3	15 and 1.M.G.	93rd Infantry
FALLEN TREE	S.15.d.5/8	15 and 1.M.G.	93rd Infantry
PALL MALL	S.15.b.5/4.	15 and 1.M.G.	1st Seaforths.
FACTORY	S.9.d.4/5.	15 and 1.M.G.	1st Seaforths.
CATS.	S.15.a.6/6.	15.	9th Gurkhas.
CHOCOLATE	S.14.b.8/8	15.	9th Gurkhas.
DEAD COW	S.14.d.9/2	15.	9th Gurkhas.
HAYSTACK.	S.14.d.3/9.	4.	9th Gurkhas.
PATH	S.14.b.1/3.	4.	9th Gurkhas.
Z. ORCHARD.	S.14.b.5/7.	4.	9th Gurkhas.
ALBERT	S.8.d.5/3.	4.	9th Gurkhas.
DOGS.	S.9.c.3/7.	15.	9th Gurkhas.
SCOTT.	S.8.a.0/1.	4.	9th Gurkhas.
HUNTER	S.8.a.9/9	4.	9th Gurkhas.
RICHEBOURG	S.8.c.5/1.	30.	9th Gurkhas.

MOVEMENT TABLE 2-11-15

UNIT	To relieve	LOCATION	Place where guides will meet	Time of arrival	ROUTE	REMARKS
3rd Infantry	2/8th Gurkhas	IND.3.A	CHOCOLAT MENIER CORNER	5-15 pm	QUENTIN-PACAUT-ZELOBES-LA COUTURE	
1st Seaforths	2nd Leicesters	IND.3.B	WINDY CORNER	5-15 pm	FOSSE-RICHEBOURG ST VAAST	
2nd Gurkhas	2/3rd Gurkhas	2 Coys in Breastworks between ALBERT & EDWARD Roads. 2 Coys at S.B.6.3/3		5-30 pm	ZELOBES-LA COUTURE	
9th Gurkhas	3/Londons	Billets		1 pm	ZELOBES	By platoons after passing VIEILLE CHAPELLE.
	Garhwal Rifles	Billets X.11.6		12 noon	ZELOBES	" " " "
Bde Gurkha Company.	Bde Gurkha Coy Garhwal Bde.	Billets X.5.d		12-30 pm	ZELOBES	" " " "
Bde Machine Guns	Bde M.G. Garhwal Bde	Billets at X.4.6.4/6.				under arrangements of B.M.G.O. By day
Bde Bomb Guns	Bde Bomb Guns Garhwal Bde	Billets at X.5.d.6/0.				under arrangements of B.B.G.O. By day.
Garrisons of Posts (See Table of Posts)	Present Garrisons		S.7.d.7/7.	2 pm		

DEHRA DUN BRIGADE OPERATION ORDER NO 66.

12th November 1915.

Reference Map FRANCE 1/40000, Sheet 36.a.

1. DEHRA DUN BRIGADE with 19th B.F.A. and 128th and 129th I.F.A.'s will move to a new area tomorrow in accordance with attached March Table.

2. Baggage wagons will march with Units to new billets rejoining train Companies after completion of moves.

3. Supply wagons will refill as at present on the 13th Instant and march under orders of O.C. Train to deliver Supplies to Units in new billets; thence rejoining their train Companies in new billets. Refilling Point on 14th Instant will be notified later.

4. Reports to Head of Column.

                                          Major
                      Brigade Major Dehra Dun Brigade.

Issued at........p.m. to Signal Section for Distribution

Copy No 1 and 2 retained.
Copy No 3 to 1st Seaforths.
Copy No 4 to 2/3rd Infantry
Copy No 5 to 9th Gurkhas.
Copy No 6 to 19th B.F.A.
Copy No 7 to 128th I.F.A.
Copy No 8 to 129th I.F.A.
Copy No 9 to Meerut Division.
Copy No 10 to C.R.A.
Copy No 11 to C.R.E.
Copy No 12 to O.C. 2 Coy Train.
Copy No 13 to Signal Officer.

MARCH TABLE

UNIT	Starting Point	Time	ROUTE	Destination	Remarks
1st Seaforths	Road crossing D.25.d.6/7.	8-30 a.m.	ST VENANT-BUSNES-LILLERS	AVROINNES-LIERES-ECQUEDECQUES	
9th Gurkhas	" " " " "	8-36 a.m.	" " "	"	
93rd Infantry	" " " " "	8-42 a.m.	" " "	"	
19th R.F.A.	" " " " "	8-48 a.m.	ST VENANT-BUSNES	BUSNES	
128th I.F.A.	" " " " "	8-52 a.m.	ST VENANT-BUSNES	Area CANTRAINE-L'ECLEME.	
129th I.F.A.	" " " " "	8-56 a.m.	ST. VENANT-BUSNES	Area CANTRAINE-L'ECLEME.	
Baggage Wagons	" " " " "	9 a.m.	Same as Units		In order of Units. Not to pass road junction D.25.b.2/9 before 8-50 a.m.

Copy No...7....

DEHRA DUN BRIGADE OPERATION ORDER NO 67.

17th November 1915. 'S'

Reference Map FRANCE 1/40000 36.a and
Map BELGIUM 1/100000 Sheet HAZEBROUCK, 5.a.

1. The DEHRA DUN BRIGADE will move to a new area tomorrow in accordance with attached March Table.

2. Baggage wagons will rejoin Units on completion of move.

3. Reports to Head of Column during March and afterwards to FONTAINE-LES-HERMANS.

                                            Major
               Brigade Major Dehra Dun Brigade.

Issued at 5.15 p.m. to Signal Section for Distribution.

Copy No 1 and 2 Retained,
Copy No 3 to 1st Seaforths,
Copy No 4 to 3rd Infantry
Copy No 5 to 6th Gurkhas.
Copy No 6 to 128th I.F.A.
Copy No 7 to 129 I.F.A.
Copy No 8 to 2 Coy Meerut Train.
Copy No 9 to Meerut Division.
Copy No10 to Bareilly Brigade.

MARCH TABLE.

UNIT	Starting Point	TIME	Destination	Route	Remarks
1st Seaforths	AMES. T.30.a.3/9	10 a.m.	WESTREHEM.	AMETTES — NEDONCHELLE	
9th Gurkhas	" " "	10-6 a.m.	NEDONCHELLE	AMETTES	
93rd Infantry	" " "	10-12 a.m.	AMETTES.		
Baggage Wagons of Units of Dehra Dun Brigade.	" " "	—	Same as units.	Same as units	In order of Units.
128 I.F.A.	" " "	10-30 a.m.	NEDON.	AMETTES.	
129 I.F.A.	" " "	10.40 a.m.	NEDON	AMETTES	

WAR DIARY
1ST BATTN SEAFORTH HIGHLANDERS
7TH (MEERUT) INDIAN DIVISION
DECEMBER
1915.

CONFIDENTIAL

WAR DIARY

OF

The Officer Commanding 1/Seaforth Highlanders

FROM December 1st 1915 TO December 31st 1915.

(Volume XVI)

Army Form C. 2118.

Vol. XVI

WAR DIARY
or
INTELLIGENCE SUMMARY.
(Erase heading not required.)

Instructions regarding War Diaries and Intelligence Summaries are contained in F. S. Regs., Part II. and the Staff Manual respectively. Title pages will be prepared in manuscript.

Place	Date	Hour	Summary of Events and Information	Remarks and references to Appendices
	1st December 1915		At Sea. Generally getting warmer. Rigged training courses on all lights, extinguished at 5.30 p.m. as a precaution against submarine attack.	
			Casualties Nil	
	2nd December		Sickness cried. The Carried Sir. Leve MALTA at 8 a.m. Officers and warrant officers were allowed leave to go on shore. 6 Officers and 100 other ranks disembarked of reinforcement and embarked on boats for Egypt.	
			Casualties Nil	
	3rd December		Left MALTA at 6 a.m. in company with a Transport and British Transport, and escorted by a French Destroyer. Submarine Boats were rigged up for the Troops.	
			Casualties Nil	
	4th December		At Sea. Weather warmer, and as a Caution, everything of importance to record.	
			Casualties Nil	

WAR DIARY
or
INTELLIGENCE SUMMARY.
(Erase heading not required.)

Army Form C. 2118.

Place	Date	Hour	Summary of Events and Information	Remarks and references to Appendices
	5th December 1915		Sunday. Divine service held at 10.30 A.M. and a Voluntary service at 3.30 P.M. Practised emergency parade and calls. Behaved and issued to the Troops. Casualties NIL	
	6th December		Dickover in Alexandria Harbour at 2.30 P.M., no one was allowed on shore. A concert was given on board at 8 P.M. Casualties 1 sick	
	7th December		At 6.30 A.M. the Ship was Berthed alongside the Quay where we landed the details taken on board at MALTA at 10.30 A.M. Left the Quay and anchored in the outer harbour. Some Officers who were ashore on shore rejoined here. At 5.30 P.M. left ALEXANDRIA for PORT SAID. Casualties 4 sick	
	8th December		Arrived at PORT SAID and at 9 A.M. anchored in the Stream. Ship coaling. Officers & warrant officers allowed on shore. Received orders to proceed direct to BASRA in MESOPOTAMIA. Casualties	

WAR DIARY
or
INTELLIGENCE SUMMARY.
(Erase heading not required.)

Army Form C. 2118.

Instructions regarding War Diaries and Intelligence Summaries are contained in F. S. Regs., Part II. and the Staff Manual respectively. Title pages will be prepared in manuscript.

Place	Date	Hour	Summary of Events and Information	Remarks and references to Appendices
	9th DECEMBER 1915		Left PORT SAID at 3.15 P.M. COL THOMAS 9th BHOPAL'S the 14th Indian Officers and 61 other Naval Ratings embarked before and availed. Casualties 1 sick	
	10th DECEMBER 1915		Arrived at SUEZ at 1 P.M. One Officer & 1 I.A.J.T. and two Officers and 36 other Ranks Royal Flying Corps embarked who were sent ashore with the M.L.O. Left SUEZ at 8 P.M. Casualties 1 sick	
	11th DECEMBER 1915		In the RED SEA. Musketry, Semaphore, and Machine Gun instructions went on and out of duty in addition to other Training. Lieut MacLeod observed Br Signalling Officer. Officers N.C.O. and men are being exercised when available as considered necessary	

T2134. Wt. W708—776. 500000. 4/15. Sir J. C. & S.

Army Form C. 2118.

WAR DIARY
or
INTELLIGENCE SUMMARY.
(Erase heading not required.)

Instructions regarding War Diaries and Intelligence Summaries are contained in F. S. Regs., Part II. and the Staff Manual respectively. Title pages will be prepared in manuscript.

Place	Date	Hour	Summary of Events and Information	Remarks and references to Appendices
	12th DECEMBER 1915		Sunday. Divine service at 10.30 A.M. and voluntary service at 6.45 P.M. The sun is now getting hot, and Helmets were taken into wear for the 1st time. Casualties 1 Sick.	
	13th DECEMBER "		In RED SEA. Heavy showers of rain accompanied by lightening came on and lasted from 10 P.M. to 12 Noon; cool and great wind for the remainder of the day. Concert held at 9.15 P.M. Casualties Nil	
	14th DECEMBER "		Still in the RED SEA. Cool strong breeze blowing, but hot & stuffy below decks. Casualties Nil	
	15th DECEMBER 1915		In RED SEA. Strong wind blowing. Wireless operator CRUIKSHANKS, Royal Navy, tried by G.C.M. for not complying with orders issued. Passed PERIM Island about 9 P.M., all lights on Port side extinguished after dark. Weather fine with cool breeze. Casualties Nil	

T2134. Wt. W708—776. 500000. 4/15. Sir J. C. & S.

Army Form C. 2118.

WAR DIARY
or
INTELLIGENCE SUMMARY.
(Erase heading not required.)

Instructions regarding War Diaries and Intelligence Summaries are contained in F. S. Regs., Part II. and the Staff Manual respectively. Title pages will be prepared in manuscript.

Place	Date	Hour	Summary of Events and Information	Remarks and references to Appendices
	16th DECEMBER 1915		Arrived at ADEN at 9 A.M. and took about 30 tons of Water on Board. Received Parcels of Kopjes etc. from 13th Major Return to be delivered to Commandant BASRAH also Books and some maps of MESOPOTAMIA for the Commanding Officer. Left ADEN at 5. P.M.	Casualties Nil
	17th DECEMBER 1915		In Arabian Sea, coast quite near on Port side Rocky Mountainous, weather fine with cool Breeze.	Casualties Nil
	18th DECEMBER "		At Sea, running up the Arabian Coast, Wind keen Wind blowing but quite warm. Nothing to report.	Casualties Nil
	19th DECEMBER "		At Sea Divine Service at 10.30 A.M. and at 6. P.M Emergency Parade and stations practised. Very strong beam winds but otherwise weather quite warm.	Casualties Nil

Army Form C. 2118.

WAR DIARY
or
INTELLIGENCE SUMMARY.
(Erase heading not required.)

Instructions regarding War Diaries and Intelligence Summaries are contained in F. S. Regs., Part II. and the Staff Manual respectively. Title pages will be prepared in manuscript.

Place	Date	Hour	Summary of Events and Information	Remarks and references to Appendices
	20th DECEMBER 1915		Still in the Arabian Sea. Practised Emergency parade issuing returning life Belts. Weather quite fine. Cavallo	NIL
	21st DECEMBER 1915		At sea in the Gulf of Oman. Arabian and Persian Coast can be seen on each side. Quite warm with a cool land wind towards evening. Cavallo	NIL
	22nd DECEMBER 1915		Passed through the Straits of ORMUZ and entered the PERSIAN GULF. Land guarding on each side. Passed a British Gunboat about 5.10 P.M. Cavallo	NIL
	23rd DECEMBER 1915		In PERSIAN GULF. Sandy & mountainous and desert quite close on Starboard side. Commanding Officer inspected B. & C. Companies in marching order without packs. Cavallo	NIL

T2134. Wt. W708—776. 500000. 4/15. Sir J. C. & S.

Army Form C. 2118.

WAR DIARY
or
INTELLIGENCE SUMMARY.
(Erase heading not required.)

Instructions regarding War Diaries and Intelligence Summaries are contained in F. S. Regs., Part II. and the Staff Manual respectively. Title pages will be prepared in manuscript.

Place	Date	Hour	Summary of Events and Information	Remarks and references to Appendices
	23rd December 1915		Entered the Persian Gulf. Coast quite clear all starboard side. Nine root beige. C.O. expected to send troops in with Buoies hoisting orders received.	Nil
	24th December		In the Persian Gulf. Very rough weather throughout. At 4 P.M. we stopped outside of the mouth of the Shatt-al-Arab, remembered orders were received to proceed to KOWAIT awaiting transhipment to another boat for BASRAH.	Nil
	25th December 1915		Anchored in the Roads at KOWAIT at 10.30 A.M. where we remained at anchor all day awaiting the arrival of the boat to take us up to BASRAH.	Nil
	26th December 1915		H.E.M.S.S. NIZAM arrived and company changed aboard. Being of the same bent on board. Transhipped the BENBOW at 4.30 P.M. and convoy sailed for BASRAH	Nil

T2134. Wt. W708—776. 500000. 4/15. Sir J. C. & S.

Army Form C. 2118.

WAR DIARY
or
INTELLIGENCE SUMMARY.
(Erase heading not required.)

Instructions regarding War Diaries and Intelligence Summaries are contained in F. S. Regs., Part II and the Staff Manual respectively. Title pages will be prepared in manuscript.

Place	Date	Hour	Summary of Events and Information	Remarks and references to Appendices
	27th December 1915		At 9 A.M. passed ABBADAN, and a little later MUANIMRAH both on the left Bank of the SHATTEL ARAB. Sailing up the river we anchored in midstream at 10 A.M. Remained on board all day. Officers were allowed on shore to make some purchases. Casualties Nil	
	28th December 1915		At 10 A.M. commenced to travel up on River steamers and barges and at 12.30 P.M. left BASRAH and sailed up the SHATTELARAB enroute for ALI GARBI, men were crowded in lighters and made arrangements for not at all good. In addition to the troops the Barges were also laden with Stores, Rations, Eng¹ Equipments etc for shipment to ALI GARBI. Casualties 1 Sick	
	29th December 1915		Proceeding up the river under the River Tigris at QURNAH at which place 2000 the fresh meat was taken on board for the troops. Fair weather with a fresh cool breeze, but cold for night. Casualties Nil	

Army Form C. 2118.

WAR DIARY
or
INTELLIGENCE SUMMARY
(Erase heading not required.)

Instructions regarding War Diaries and Intelligence Summaries are contained in F. S. Regs., Part II. and the Staff Manual respectively. Title pages will be prepared in manuscript.

Place	Date	Hour	Summary of Events and Information	Remarks and references to Appendices
	30th December 1915		Still on the TIGRES. Passed QALAT SALAH about 9 a.m. and at 7.10 p.m. entered in midstream at AMARAH remaining there during the night.	Casualties NIL
	31st December 1915		Still at AMARAH. Disembarked at 11.35 a.m. and marched off for AH GARBI at 2 p.m. Cases a long column on the left bank marching N.E. and another ones column on the right bank marching about to miles from Amarah and working parallel with it. In checking the casualty returns of the Bn from its arrival in France on 11th October 1915 until the 31st December 1915 the following total was arrived at. Officers wounded 28, Officers wounded & Officers killed 8, Officers returned to duty with the Bn of the wounded and sick 8 returned to duty with the Bn. Non commissioned Officers and men killed 409, wounded 938, Sick 861, Of the wounded and sick 637 returned to duty with the Bn.	Casualties

Lt. Col. Thomas
Cmdg.
1/Newport I.R.

www.ingramcontent.com/pod-product-compliance
Lightning Source LLC
Chambersburg PA
CBHW080843010526
44114CB00017B/2364